78-399/685

TRAFALGAR

TRAFALGAR

❖

John Terraine
Eye-witness accounts compiled by
John Westwood

WORDSWORTH EDITIONS

First published in 1976
by Sidgewick and Jackson Limited,London
Copyright © 1976 John Terraine and
Sidgewick and Jackson Limited

This edition published 1998
by Wordsworth Editions Limited
Cumberland House, Crib Street, Ware,
Hertfordshire SG12 9ET

ISBN 1 85326 686 8

Printed and bound in Great Britain
by Mackays of Chatham plc, Chatham, Kent.

CONTENTS

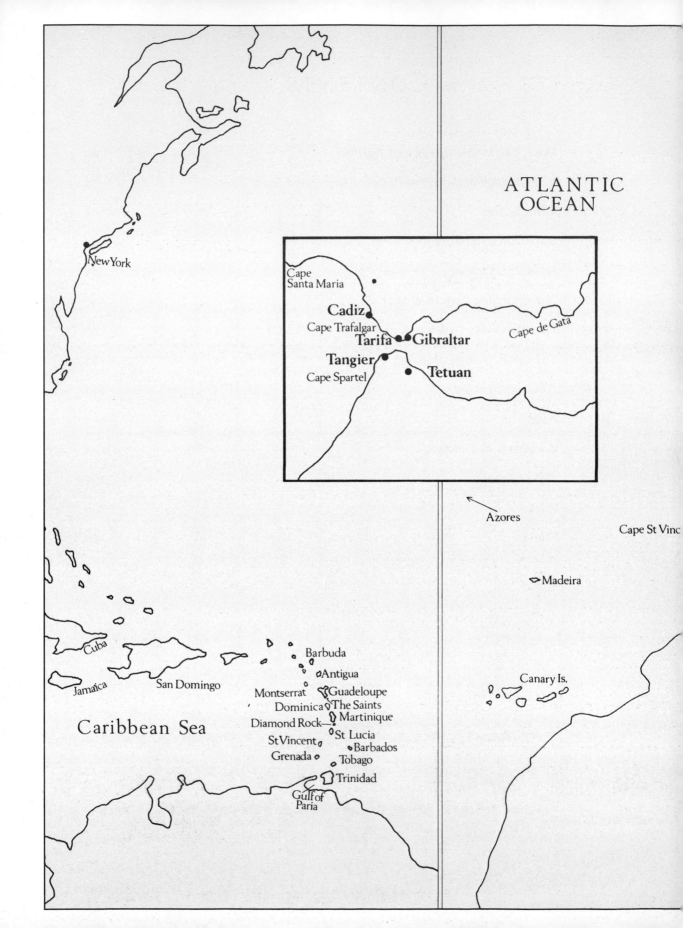

ATLANTIC
OCEAN

Cape
Santa Maria

Cadiz
Cape Trafalgar
Tarifa **Gibraltar** Cape de Gata

Tangier
Cape Spartel **Tetuan**

New York

Azores

Cape St Vinc

Madeira

Cuba

Barbuda

Antigua

Jamaica San Domingo Montserrat Guadeloupe
Dominica The Saints
Diamond Rock Martinique
Caribbean Sea St Lucia
St Vincent Barbados
Grenada Tobago

Canary Is.

Trinidad

Gulf of
Paria

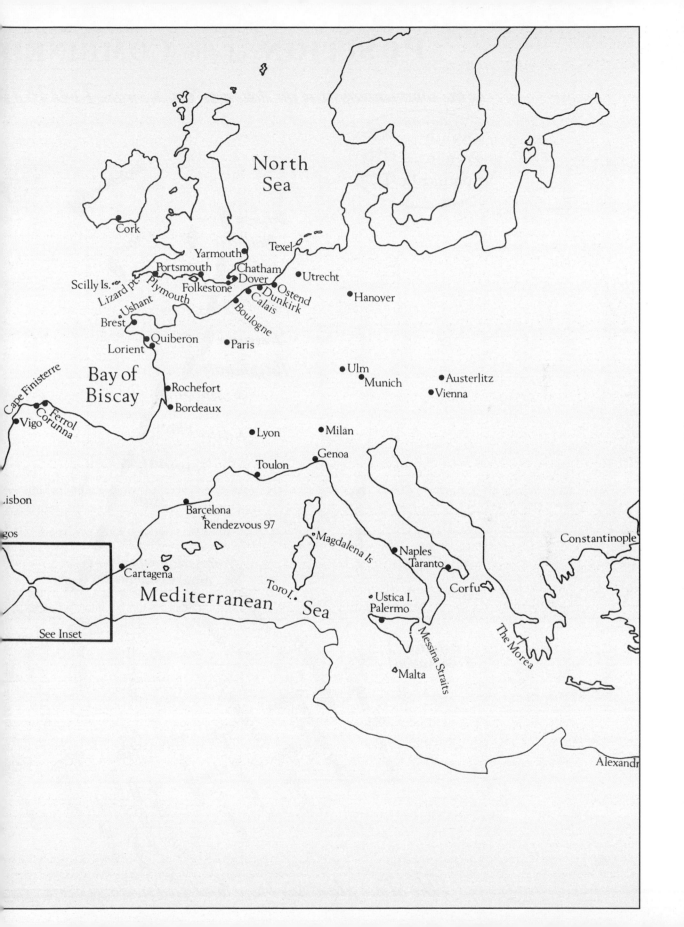

North
Sea

Cork

Texel

Yarmouth

Portsmouth
Chatham
Dover
Utrecht

Scilly Is.
Lizard pt.
Plymouth
Folkestone
Ostend
Dunkirk
Calais
Hanover

Ushant
Boulogne

Brest

Lorient
Quiberon
Paris

Ulm
Austerlitz
Munich
Vienna

Cape Finisterre

Bay of
Biscay

Rochefort

Bordeaux

Lyon
Milan

Ferrol
Corunna

Vigo

Genoa

Toulon

Lisbon

Barcelona

Rendezvous 97

Constantinople

gos

Magdalena Is

Cartagena

Naples
Taranto

Toro I.

Corfu

Mediterranean

Sea

Ustica I.
Palermo

Messina Straits

The Morea

See Inset

Malta

Alexandr

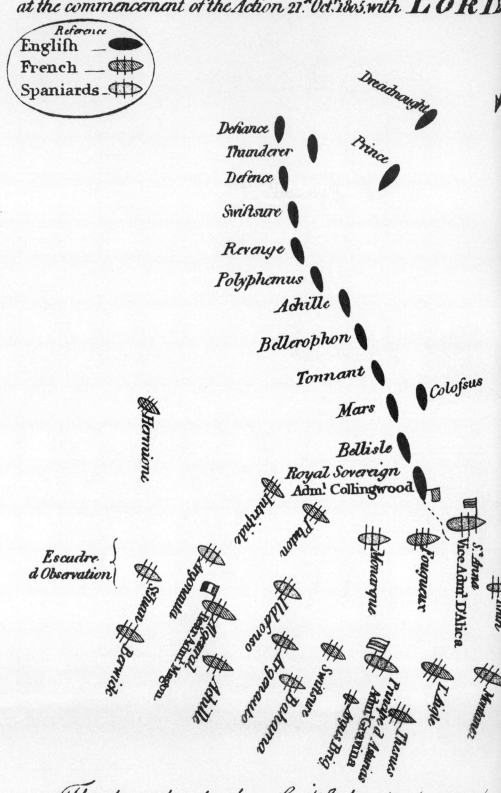

POSITION of the COMBINED

at the commencement of the Action 21.ᵗ Oct.ᵗ 1805, with LORD

Reference
English ___
French ___
Spaniards ___

Dreadnought

Defiance
Thunderer
Defence
Swiftsure
Revenge
Polyphemus
Achille
Bellerophon
Tonnant
Mars
Bellisle
Royal Sovereign
Adm.ᵗ Collingwood

Prince

Colossus

Hermione

Intrepide

Pluton

Escudre.
d Observation

Argonaute

Monarque

Fougueux

S.ᵗ Anna
Vice Adm.ᵗ D'Alica

Swan Berwick

Algesiras
Rear Adm.ᵗ Megon

Ildefonso

San Bohama

Swiftsure

Argonauta

Principe d'Asturia
Adm.ᵗ Gravina

L'Aigle

Theseus

Montanes

The above plan has been Certified as to its correctness

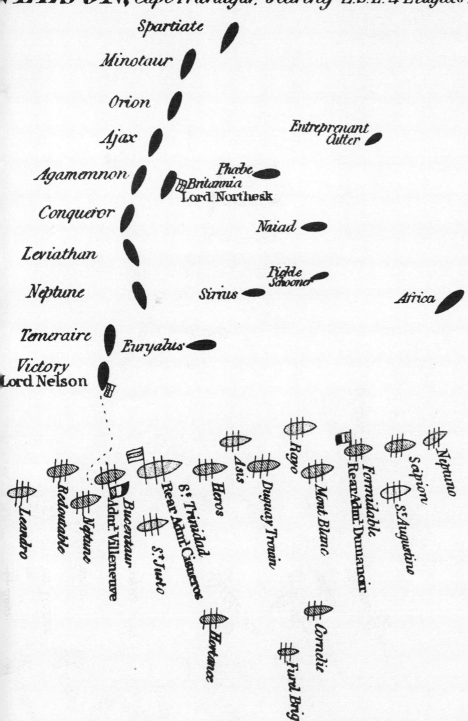

ORCES of FRANCE & SPAIN,

NELSON, *Cape Trafalgar, bearing E.S.E. 4 Leagues.*

Spartiate

Minotaur

Orion

Ajax

Entreprenant
Cutter

Agamemnon

Phœbe

Britannia
Lord Northesk

Conqueror

Naiad

Leviathan

Pickle
Schooner

Neptune

Sirius

Africa

Temeraire

Euryalus

Victory
Lord Nelson

Neptuno

Rayo

Sapion

Formidable
Rear Adm.¹ Dumanoir

S.ᵗ Augustino

Leandro

Redoutable

Neptune

Bucentaur
Adm.ˡ Villeneuve

6.ᵗ Trinidad
Rear Adm.ˡ Cisneros

Heros

Asis

Duguay Trouin

Mont Blanc

S.ᵗ Justo

Hortence

Cornelie

Furet Brig

The Flag Officers of the Euryalus, & Adm.ˡ Villeneuve.

TRAFALGAR

INTRODUCTION

THE BATTLE OF TRAFALGAR was fought on 21 October 1805, and has gone down in British history as the very epitome of victorious British sea power. This is scarcely surprising: Lord Nelson's victory over the combined French and Spanish fleet had a devastating completeness which would have captured the public imagination in any case, even without the rich additional ingredients of Nelson's strange, romantic yet ruthless character, and his tragic death at the very moment of his triumph.

Trafalgar was followed by a century of apparently unchallenged British naval supremacy, and so loudly does the great victory seem to call for every laurel that it is easy to attribute that supremacy simply to the battle, forgetting the arduous continuing effort of the Royal Navy between 1805 and 1815, and forgetting also the two technical revolutions which soon compelled a complete fresh start in naval reckonings: the changes from sail to steam and from oak to steel.

On reflection, then, Trafalgar emerges as the spectacular finale of a particular style of war: the style evolved by an island power to counter a major naval threat. Looked at in that light, the battle is only the last act of a long drama. The Trafalgar campaign itself began the moment that war was declared in 1803; the style of war goes back much further: the first clear enunciation of its basic principle was in 1745.

What I shall try to display in this book, then, is a situation in which a powerful Continental enemy – Napoleon – held the strategic initiative against Britain, and used a battle fleet as a factor in that initiative; in which a school of British naval officers, educated by the experience of the American Revolutionary and French Revolutionary Wars, checked him by the remorseless application of a system which bears the hallmark of true professional certainty; and in which William Pitt struggled to regain the initiative for Britain. This was the framework within which Nelson's work was done. If we are really to understand what happened on that October day in 1805, we must appreciate it not as an act of individual magic, however breathtaking, but as the fruit of a great collective endeavour.

JOHN TERRAINE

1. NAPOLEON'S INITIATIVE

'The peace that was no peace': an optimistic
contemporary French cartoon showing Napoleon
bringing the blessings of peace to Europe

The peace that was no peace ended on 18 May
1803; it had lasted barely fourteen months.
When the Peace of Amiens was signed in
March 1802 it came gratefully to the British.
During the last twenty-seven years they had had
their fill of war; they had fought the American
War of Independence from 1775 to 1783, and in
the course of it had also been at war with France,
Spain and Holland, with disastrous consequences:
not merely the loss of the American colonies, West
Indian islands, East India merchant convoys and
much other valuable trade, but also the penalty of
fierce political faction at home and isolation
abroad. The financial cost was, for those days,
frightening: £114 million added to the national
debt. Yet ten years of peace, backed by the
muscularity of the Industrial Revolution, had so
far repaired the damage that, 'By 1793 England
was already a generation in advance of the
Continent in the science, machinery, and processes
of production, and of the distribution and
organisation of industry'.[a] But 1793 was the year
in which Britain went to war with Revolutionary
France, and war with the successive governments
of the Revolution and the Consulate continued
until peace preliminaries began at the end of 1801.

This long and bitter war had taken Britain by
surprise, and proved to be full of surprises, few of
them pleasant. In February 1792 the Prime
Minister, William Pitt, had confidently told the
House of Commons: 'There never was a time in
the history of this country when, from the
situation in Europe, we might more reasonably
expect fifteen years of peace than at the present
moment.' When, ten years later, peace briefly
returned, Pitt and his countrymen had seen two
coalitions against France collapse, despite the
pouring out of British money in subsidies; they
had seen the Royal Navy forced to abandon the
Mediterranean; they had seen the very foundations
of British power stagger when the navy itself
mutinied at Spithead and the Nore in 1797; they
had endured French threats to Ireland and an
Irish rebellion;[1] a French army had invaded
Egypt, and a direct threat to England herself had
been mounted across the Channel. High prices,
food shortages and severe taxation had undermined
the popularity of the Prime Minister, while
successive crises and setbacks had undermined his

health. In February 1801 Pitt resigned; he had
held office since 1783, and it seemed like a reversal
of the natural order of things.

For Britain and her future security and
prosperity there was a greater menace, during
these years, even than the whole sum of the
misfortunes which I have listed above. This was
the rise of Napoleon Bonaparte, who was to become
one of the most implacable foes of England in her
entire history. It was in action against an English
expedition supporting French royalists at Toulon
that Napoleon made his first mark, directing the
besieging artillery although still only a captain.
That was in 1793; the peril of the guillotine hung
over every ambitious and rising man in
Revolutionary France in those days, but in 1795
Napoleon himself did much to dispel it. Once
more his tool was artillery, turned this time against
the Paris mob; the result was the setting up of the
less bloodthirsty Directory. Napoleon's reward
for this service was the command of the Army of
Italy which he led to a succession of brilliant
victories against Austria in 1796 – the foundation
of his reputation as a genius for war. In 1797 he
was commanding the forces arrayed for the invasion
of England, but he was quick to see that the right
conditions did not yet exist. Instead, the next year
he was conquering under the shadow of the
pyramids. His Egyptian expedition came to
nothing, frustrated by the Royal Navy, and
Napoleon abandoned his army to return to France.
In the strange climate of those times, he was not
forthwith court-martialled and shot, as one might
suppose, but very shortly conducting a coup d'état
against the very Directory which he had helped to
create.[2] In December 1799 a new constitution was
promulgated – the Consulate – and Napoleon
became First Consul with office for ten years. The
next year he won the Battle of Marengo which
brought Austria to her knees, and in the year after
that all his enemies, one by one, were glad to make
peace with him. Peace, however, did not always
mean to Napoleon what it meant to other men.

All this constituted the debit side of England's
balance in the French Revolutionary Wars – and a
formidable debit it was. Fortunately, there was a
credit side also. During these years, despite the
abuses which caused the mutinies of 1797 –
profiting, indeed, by that alarming experience

'Conquering under the shadow of the Pyramids';
a panoramic view of Napoleon's famous victory
outside Cairo in 1798: painting by General Lejeune

– the Royal Navy had evolved a degree of professionalism rare in any institution. These, after all, were the years of 'The Glorious First of June' (1794), Cape St Vincent and Camperdown (1797), The Nile (1798) and Copenhagen (1801).

The string of victories was accompanied by a string of illustrious names to which we shall be returning; and what made them illustrious was a corporate expertise evolved out of long years of hard experience, and a loyalty to each other, and understanding, which was usually in sharp contrast with the jealousies and bickerings of Napoleon's lieutenants. The British, however, have always had a strange capacity for throwing away their advantages, and the fourteen months of

the Peace of Amiens did much to diminish this splendid asset.

It was a bad peace for England, because Napoleon never intended it to be anything else. British manufacturers found that the European ports remained closed to their goods. British trade in the Levant and the Black Sea was threatened. Holland (now called the Batavian Republic) remained, with its fleet, firmly under French control. Napoleon himself[3] became President of a Cisalpine Republic containing Milan, Modena, Ferrara, Bologna and Romagna. A Ligurian Republic containing the port of Genoa was controlled by France, as was the Helvetic Republic (the new name for Switzerland). French influence was powerful in Germany, and increasing in the

eastern Mediterranean. Even India seemed to be once more threatened by French power. Most serious of all, though less immediately obvious, was a gigantic programme for the rebuilding and expansion of the French navy, at the very moment that the misguided zeal of Lord St Vincent, First Lord of the Admiralty, was reducing the Royal Navy and depleting its dockyards in the name of administrative reform and economy.

To all this Britain could only find one, not very satisfactory, answer: by the terms of the peace treaty she was pledged to give up Malta, which the French had captured from the Knights of St John on their way to Egypt in 1798, and the British had taken from them in turn in 1800. Now, faced by Napoleon's mounting threats in the Mediterranean, threats pointing sometimes at Egypt again, sometimes at Greece (then part of the feeble Ottoman Empire), sometimes at Naples and Sicily, the British government concluded that it would be madness to give up Malta. This tiny trespass upon his own predatory rôle infuriated Napoleon, but the more he blustered the more adamant the government, which under the Hon. Henry Addington rarely displayed adamantine qualities, became. Malta would not be given up. By May 1803 the breaking point was reached. On the 12th the British ambassador left Paris; on the 18th Britain declared war. For the next twelve years, with only one brief intermission, there was to be a struggle to the death between Napoleon and his island enemy.

In February 1798 Napoleon, as commander of the French forces deployed for the invasion of England, visited Dunkirk and the Flanders coast. On the 23rd of the month he drew up a report on his tour for the government:

'Whatever efforts we make, we shall not for some years gain the naval supremacy. To invade England without that supremacy is the most daring and difficult task ever undertaken . . . If, having regard to the present organization of our navy, it seems impossible to gain the necessary promptness of execution, *then we must give up the expedition against England, be satisfied with keeping up the pretence of it* [my italics], and concentrate all our attention on the Rhine, in order to try to deprive England of Hanover and Hamburg: . . . or else undertake an eastern expedition which would menace her trade with the Indies.'

Yet, despite this insight, when war broke out again in 1803 Napoleon at once pointed a new threat of invasion at England. How seriously then did he mean it?

There is a deal of evidence that he meant it very seriously indeed, and certainly that is the way the threat was taken in England – above all, south-eastern England – at the time. On the French side we learn:

'Thiers, the great French historian, who was probably the first writer to thoroughly peruse the State papers and other documents having reference to the invasion, dismisses the question of whether the First Consul really meant to descend upon England in a single sentence. He says: ". . . If the credulous who have questioned the reality of his (Napoleon's) project could read his private correspondence with the Minister of Marine, the infinite number of his orders, and the secret communication of his hopes to the Arch-Chancellor Cambacérès, they would no longer entertain any doubt as to the reality of that extraordinary resolution." '[b]

Coming from such a source, this is a statement that carries conviction; but most convincing of all is the actual force assembled by Napoleon for his purpose. Some 160,000 troops were arrayed in a wide arc from Hanover to Brest, collectively known by different names at different times: 'The Army of the Coasts of the Ocean', somewhat prematurely 'The Army of England', and, finally, when the dream faded, the name by which they marched into history 'La Grande Armée' – 'The

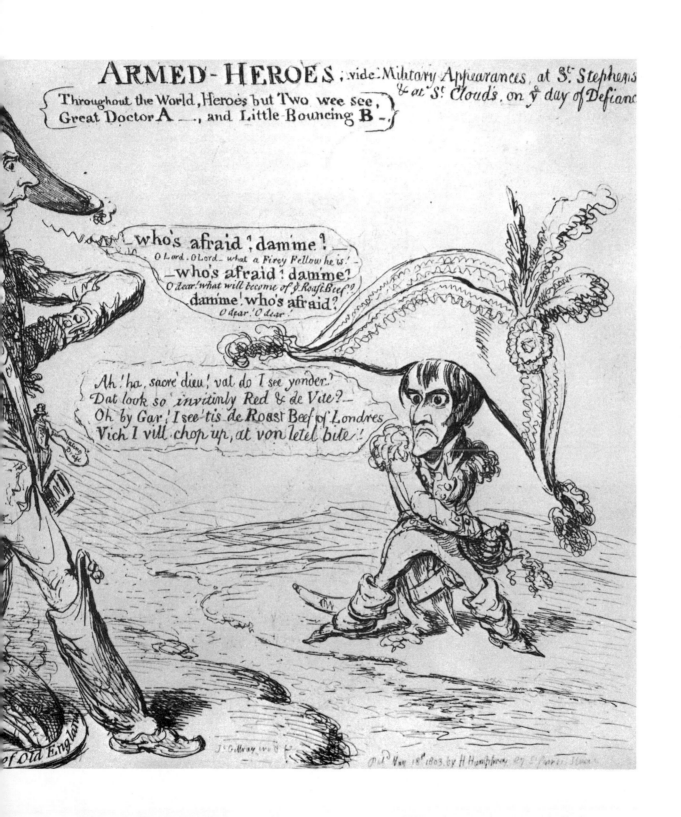

French Order of Battle, March 1803

(Ships of the line)

Locality	Ordered	Building	Afloat
Flushing	5		
Ostend	1		
St Malo	1		
Brest		3	18
Nantes	2		
Lorient	2	3	
Rochefort	3	3	
Bordeaux	1		
Marseilles	1		
Toulon		4	8
Genoa	1		
			10
At sea Total	17	13	36
Grand Total			**66**

Grand Army'. Clothed in some of the most sumptuous military finery ever seen, still unspattered by the mud of exhausting marches, not ripped or slashed in rough-and-tumble skirmishes, not yet stained by the blood of battle, this army was at its most parade-ground magnificent, but it was very far from a parade-ground army. At least half of the men in it were the veterans of Italy and Egypt, the survivors of the famous Army of the Sambre-et-Meuse, men who had fought for the Republic under Moreau and Masséna, assembled now, some gladly, some sullenly, under a new leader who would soon captivate them all.

The war was one year old precisely when the First Consul ceased to exist; on 18 May 1804 the Senate proclaimed him Emperor of the French, with the title of Napoleon I. On 2 December he crowned himself in Notre Dame Cathedral, gently

pushing aside Pope Pius VII, as though to say that God's blessing was sufficient, God's sanction was not required. Each of these occasions was promptly followed by a dramatic gesture towards the army. On 19 May fourteen distinguished generals were designated Marshals of the Empire, and four retired veterans became honorary marshals. So the higher echelons of the officer corps were won over to the imperial idea. Then, three days after the coronation in December, all the regiments of the army received their eagle standards from Napoleon himself at a spectacular ceremony on the Champ-de-Mars. 'Soldiers, here are your colours!' cried the Emperor. 'These eagles will always be your rallying point. They will fly wherever your Emperor deems necessary for the defence of the throne and his people. Do you swear to lay down your lives in their defence, and by your courage to keep them ever on the road to victory?' The

answer came back in a mighty shout: 'We swear!' The march of the eagles had begun. But could they fly to England?

If talent could take them there, there was little doubt of it. The Army of England was commanded by the cream of the new marshals; the average age of the fourteen on the active list was only forty. These were men in the prime of their energies and abilities, some with resounding names already, all soon to be heard of in all the corners of Europe. Six of them, in 1804, commanded army corps, a new element of military organization devised by Napoleon for speed of manoeuvre and flexibility. The corps varied in size, but each was in fact a miniature army, complete in all respects and capable of conducting independent operations.

At the very outbreak of war, one of Napoleon's first acts had been to occupy Hanover, then a domain of King George III in his capacity of Elector. Now Hanover was held by the French I Corps, 18,000 men commanded by Marshal Bernadotte,[4] who had first met Napoleon in Italy in 1796, and was now the brother-in-law of his elder brother, Joseph Bonaparte- a member of the family, if sometimes an uneasy one. At Utrecht was the headquarters of the II Corps, under General Marmont, an old friend of Napoleon and the reorganizer of the French artillery; Marmont was aggrieved at not receiving a baton,[5] but nevertheless drilled his 20,000 men to a high pitch of efficiency. Marshal Davout's III Corps, of 28,000 men, was distributed between Flushing and Dunkirk, with headquarters at Bruges. The IV Corps, under Marshal Soult, 32,000 strong, was at Boulogne, its camp marked by a bronze monument which stands on the cliffs to this day. Also close to Boulogne was the V Corps, 27,000 men under the fire-eating Marshal Lannes. At Montreuil (where British G.H.Q. would reside in the next great Continental war) was another fire-eater, Marshal Ney, commanding the VI Corps, with 25,000 men. At Brest, the naval base in Brittany, was Marshal Augereau, a lapsed republican; his VII Corps numbered 15,000. Marshal Bessières commanded the Imperial Guard, the strategic reserve, and Marshal Murat, Napoleon's brother-in-law, had the Reserve Cavalry. The chief of staff was Marshal Berthier.

All in all, this was an impressive array:

impressive in efficiency, in equipment and in reputation. A moment's reflection, however, shows that although it is normal to refer to the whole mass as 'The Army of England', only a part of it could really fulfil that rôle. Bernadotte's corps in Hanover could only come to England as a reserve; there was no question of launching an actual invasion from Hamburg or Bremen. The same was true of Augereau; his corps really pointed not at England, but at Ireland, an area of great sensitivity to the English government. And the same, strangely enough, was also true of Marmont's II Corps. The nearest he ever came to playing an active part in the invasion proceedings was in making a show of activity, embarking troops and stores to suggest to the British that he might sail for Ireland by the north-about route, round the top of Scotland. Nevertheless, even deducting these three formations, the potential invading force was not less than 112,000 men, not counting the Guard and the Reserve Cavalry. The question was, how to get them across that narrow strip of water, where the cliffs of Folkestone and Dover can look so deceptively close on a clear day.

Napoleon was born in a sea port on an island – Ajaccio in Corsica – yet he never understood the sea; it was always his enemy. To him and his army leaders standing at Boulogne, on a bad day the prospect of crossing the turbulent Channel must have seemed appalling, but on a fine day it could look like nothing more serious than passing over an unusually wide river. Even so, Napoleon recognized that specialized equipment would be required, and the scale of his preparation of this equipment – to say nothing of its cost – is another convincing argument for the complete sincerity of his determination to invade England. Fore-runners of the diverse assault and landing craft which made the crossing in the opposite direction 140 years later, Napoleon's invasion flotilla was no random collection of likely-looking vessels from the French and Dutch harbours. It consisted mainly of craft specifically designed for their purpose.

They fell into four categories. The largest of them were the *prames*, over 100 feet long, and 25 feet in the beam; they were fitted with three keels to give them some stability, but nothing could have made them stable in anything like a heavy sea. They carried no less than twelve 24-pounder guns, a large armament whose purpose it is not easy to perceive; more important was their man-carrying capacity: a crew of 38 and 120 soldiers. Somewhat more practical (at least from this distance in time) were the *chaloupes canonnières*, 70–80 feet long and 17 feet wide, with a draught of 5–6 feet. Their armament was three 24-pounders and a howitzer, and one can see that this could have been very useful for the close support of a landing. The crew numbered 22 men, and the *chaloupe* could carry 130 soldiers without crowding. *Bateaux canonniers*, looking rather like fishing smacks, were built with the special purpose of transporting horses and artillery. There was a stable in the hold, with stalls for two horses, a loaded artillery waggon on deck, one naval 24-pounder and either a field artillery gun or a howitzer. The crew was no more than 6 men, and the boat could carry 100 soldiers and officers with artillery gunners and drivers in addition. Finally there were the *péniches*, by far the most numerous class of all, and intended to carry the bulk of the Army of England. These were 60 feet long and 10 feet wide; they carried two small howitzers, a crew of 5 and 55 soldiers. At its peak the flotilla attained – on paper – formidable dimensions; its distribution was as follows:

Port	Units	Capacity			
Étaples	365	27,000	men	1,390	horses
Boulogne	1,153	73,000	,,	3,380	,,
Wimereux	237	16,000	,,	769	,,
Ambleteuse	173	15,000	,,	673	,,
Total	1,928	131,000		6,212	

It was, as I have said, on paper a formidable force, and for a time Napoleon deluded himself that 'Only ten hours would be needed for landing 150,000 disciplined and victorious soldiers upon a coast destitute of fortifications and undefended by a regular army'. The combined influences of tides and weather, the pleas of his own seamen, and a daily view of the Royal Navy in its element,

slowly won him with deep reluctance away from this opinion. At first he believed that he would be able to take advantage of periods of dead calm, or fog, or after a great gale, when the British ships of the line would be held motionless or at a far distance, in order to push his flotilla across the Channel; he had no doubt that he could brush aside any defending force on land, strike swiftly at London and bring the British government to its knees before its fleet could do anything to save it. Napoleon did not like people to argue with him, and his deeply dismayed sailors found it hard to persuade him that such ideas were utterly unrealistic. Fortunately, they had powerful advocates on their side.

What Napoleon had at first failed to take into account – though his seamen had not – was a British flotilla, operating out of the harbours of Kent and Sussex, which, quite apart from any intervention by ships of the line, would make a massacre of his own crowded, unseaworthy vessels in any weather. The presence of the Royal Navy, however, was constantly thrust before his attention: frigates, sloops and gun-brigs insolently put their noses almost inside the French harbours, attacked the invasion craft while building, captured or sank them when they moved, and generally played havoc with the invasion preparations. The cool authority with which the Royal Navy ruled the Channel is nicely echoed in the staccato phrasing of this typical narrative of an episode in 1803:

'On the 14th of September, at 8 a.m., the *Immortalité* frigate, in company with the bomb-vessels, *Perseus*, Captain John Methuist, and *Explosion*, Captain Robert Paul, commenced an attack upon the batteries that protect the town of Dieppe, also on 17 gun-vessels building in the port. The firing was continued on both sides until 11h. 30m. a.m.; when, the lee-tide making strong, and the town having taken fire badly in one place, and slightly in two others, the frigate and bomb-vessels weighed, and proceeded off St.-Valéry en Caux, where six gun-boats were constructing. At 3 p.m. the British opened a fire upon that place, and continued it for an hour, apparently with some effect: Captain Owen then retired, with the loss of one man missing and five men wounded.'[c]

The Royal Navy's almost daily teaching rubbed in one lesson; wind and water taught another. There was an appalling scene at Boulogne in July

'Specialized equipment would be required': models in the Musée de la Marine in Paris of (left) a *chaloupe canonnière* and (right) a *péniche*, the most numerous class of Napoleon's invasion craft

1804. On the 20th of that month, Napoleon ordered an imperial review of the Boulogne flotilla. His admirals pointed out the clear signs of a coming gale, but Napoleon refused to make any postponement; Admiral Bruix, commanding at Boulogne, was dismissed from the service for remonstrating with him, and the review went forward. So did the gale: 'More than 20 gun sloops filled with soldiers and sailors were flung ashore, the unfortunate occupants crying out for aid which none could afford them as they battled against the furious waves.'[d] Some 2,000 men were drowned under Napoleon's eyes to ram home the lesson that the Channel is not to be trifled with.

Already he had recognized that far more than ten hours would be needed to put his army ashore; his estimates mounted at such speed as his reluctance permitted: three days, a fortnight, three weeks. To cover the flotilla for any such length of time, and to fend off the British small craft which so annoyed him, Napoleon sadly accepted that he would need the intervention of a fleet. And the lamentable fact was that the French navy, in May 1803 and for a long time afterwards, was by no means ready for war. Not only was it widely dispersed – a fact made inevitable by France's coastline – but it was also caught in the midst of a building programme which might

Chief French/Dutch/Spanish Squadrons, 1803–5

Locality	Ships of Line	Frigates	Authority
Texel (Dutch)	6		Fuller
Brest (French)	21	6	Howarth
	21	9/10 cruisers	Corbett
	20		Mahan
	22	5 named	James (iii)
	21		Fuller
Rochefort (French)	5	5 cruisers	Corbett
	5		Mahan
	6	4	James (iii)
	5		Fuller
Ferrol	5 Fr. ⎫ 5 Span. ⎬	8/9 cruisers	Corbett
	5		Mahan
	5 Fr. ⎫ 7 8 Span. ⎬		James (iii)
	9	2	Fuller
Cadiz	12/15 Span. ⎫ 1 Fr. ⎬		James (iii)
	10		Fuller
Cartagena	6		James (iii)
	5		Fuller

Authorities :
David Howarth: *Trafalgar : The Nelson Touch*; Collins, 1969
Sir Julian Corbett: *The Campaign of Trafalgar*; Longmans, Green & Co., 1910
A. T. Mahan: *The Life of Nelson*; Sampson Low, Marston & Co., 1897
William James: *The Naval History of Great Britain*; Richard Bentley, 1847
Major-General J. F. C. Fuller: *The Decisive Battles of the Western World*; Eyre & Spottiswoode, vol. ii pub. 1955

'The cool authority with which the Navy ruled the Channel'; the cutter *Admiral Mitchell* engaging a French brig and invasion craft near Boulogne

certainly one day make it a force to reckon with, but which in May 1803 had still a very long way to go. The French naval ports, between which their ships in home waters were divided, were Brest, Lorient and Rochefort on the Atlantic side, and Toulon on the Mediterranean. The two chief of these were Brest and Toulon, and it is normal to say that the Brest squadron consisted of twenty-one ships of the line, and the Toulon squadron of twelve. These totals are correct, but it is important to note that in May 1803 the twenty-one at Brest were made up as follows: four actually afloat; nine in dock, being repaired and nearly ready; three still on the stocks, but nearly finished; and five waiting to go into dock for repairs. The Toulon squadron was in rather better shape: eight ships afloat; two on the stocks, nearly finished; and two more about to be begun. It would be a long time before these unseasoned

ships with their inexperienced crews could put to sea – if, indeed, they ever did so. For in front of every French port there stood a British squadron, defying the French to come out. Very truly has it been said by a famous American historian:[e]

'Those far distant, storm-beaten ships, upon which the Grand Army never looked, stood between it and the dominion of the world'.

Nevertheless, in the very fact of the main strength of the Royal Navy being tied to these French ports on ceaseless watch, in the fact of the energetic counter-invasion preparations which Britain undertook – a rapid expansion of the military forces in the country, the building of Martello towers along the coast, the construction of the Royal Military Canal, and so forth – absorbing most of her energies and attention, we can see that Napoleon's initiative at this stage was very real, and none the less so because it was

exercised in seeming inactivity. Furthermore, it was a double initiative: he called a tune not merely by his own occasional presence and constant threat in the sector of the English Channel; there was also the army corps under General Gouvion St Cyr[6] which he had despatched into the kingdom of Naples immediately on the outbreak of war. St Cyr crouched at Taranto, apparently waiting to spring out into the Mediterranean, either eastwards towards the Ionian Islands or Greece, or to Egypt, or westwards towards Sicily. We shall see how menacing he appeared; indeed, he and his 17,000 men exercised an influence not much less than that of the whole Army of England. But for the time being the war was in a deadlock; either Napoleon would have to exercise his initiative in a great action, or Britain would have to take it from him. That was the question for 1804.

Footnotes

Ch I

1 In reaction, the first Orange Lodge was founded in 1795.

2 The coup d'état of 19 Brumaire (9 November).

3 He became First Consul of France for life in August 1802.

4 In 1810 Bernadotte was invited by the Swedes to become their crown prince, and in 1818 he ascended the throne as King Charles XIV; the Swedish dynasty thus preserves the last flicker of the fame of Napoleon's marshals.

5 Marmont received his baton in 1809.

6 He became a marshal in 1812.

Note Lettered references will be found on p. 209 under Sources.

BRITONS TO ARMS!!!

Cheerly my hearts of courage true, the hour's at hand to try your worth; a glorious peril waits for you, and valour pants to lead you forth. The Gallic fleet approaches nigh boys, now some must conquer some must die boys, but that appals not you nor me, for our watch word, it shall be Britons strike home, revenge your country's wrongs. Britons strike home, revenge your country's wrongs.

2
Undaunted Britons now shall prove
The Frenchman's folly to invade
Our dearest rights, our country's love,
Our laws, our freedom, and our trade;
On our white cliffs, our colours fly boys,
Which we'll defend, or bravely die boys,
For we are Britons bold and free,
And our watch word it shall be
Britons strike home &c.

3
The Tyrant Consul then too late
Dismayed shall mourn th' avenging blow,
Yet vanquishd, meet the milder fate
Which mercy grants a fallen foe;
Thus shall the British banners fly boys,
On Albions cliffs still raisd on high boys,
And while the gallant flag ye see,
We'll swear our watch word still shall be
Britons strike home &c.

Published July 30. 1803 by John Wallis N.º 16 Ludgate Street London.

'The sense of Napoleon's initiative lay heavily on people in the coastal regions'. Centre: A Martello Tower in Pevensey Bay. Left: Rowlandson's drawing of a volunteer in a Home Defence corps. Right: some British counter-propaganda

2. BRITAIN'S INITIATIVE

The sense of Napoleon's initiative lay heavily upon people living in Britain's coastal regions between 1803 and 1805; for those of nervous disposition it seemed that at any time there might be a French incursion somewhere between Penzance and the Humber. Naval men might scoff at the possibility – and we ourselves have the advantage of hindsight – but there were many who were not sure. Like a later generation, facing invasion again in 1940, they found it hard to grasp that '. . . Britain and the English Channel looked vastly different from Paris, that Britain which seemed so vulnerable from within, and so puny from across the Atlantic, bore a formidable aspect when observed from the vantage point of, say, the Eiffel Tower. It was seen to be a kind of inner core within the convex curve of European coast, *a land on interior lines* [my italics] capable of threatening a very wide area.'[f] The British naval system, against which Napoleon struggled in vain, and over which he could only have prevailed by extraordinary chance (a freak gale, perhaps, or another, more successful mutiny), was firmly based on the use of these 'interior lines'.

To contain the French fleet, to check at base any attempt at invasion by the flotilla, and to protect the continuous flow of trade on which British prosperity depended, the Navy, taught by twenty-seven years of war, had evolved a system which came as near as any human instrument could, particularly in those days of difficult communication, to being fool-proof. Apart from overseas squadrons (in the East Indies or West Indies or on special duties) there were four elements in the system. There was a cruiser squadron (frigates and smaller vessels) based on Cork, whose chief function was to protect homing merchant convoys from enemy cruisers and privateers. There was a squadron (under Admiral Lord Keith) with its headquarters in the Downs, watching the coastline from Dunkirk to Texel, where the Dutch fleet lay. It consisted chiefly of frigates and other light craft, backed by some smaller ships of the line. There was an important squadron in the Mediterranean, commanded by Vice-Admiral Lord Nelson, whose duties will be described more fully later, but may be briefly summarized as 'containing' the French squadron in Toulon.

The core, the centrepiece, of British naval power, however, was what was then called 'The Western Squadron', or sometimes 'The Channel Fleet', and what a later generation would have called 'The Home Fleet' or 'The Grand Fleet'.

Its position was Ushant, that stretch of storm-prone water where the mouth of the English Channel joins the Bay of Biscay – two notorious names for sea and weather. Ushant lies off the tip of the Brittany peninsula, which adds its own contribution of rocky reefs and shoals on a lee shore, treacherous tides among the isles and inlets, and fogs to blind a sailor and draw him to destruction. And near the tip of the peninsula stands the great port of Brest, where twenty-one ships of the line and attendant cruisers under Vice-Admiral Honoré Ganteaume were being made seaworthy as fast as the French shipwrights could perform.

The officer commanding the Western Squadron on this exacting station was Admiral William Cornwallis. He was fifty-nine years old in 1803, and forty-eight of those years had been spent in the Royal Navy. During the fifty odd years that Cornwallis was on the active list, twenty-five were occupied with fighting against the French; it could be said that by 1803 he had learned to know them, as he had learned to know the Ushant station, which had been his command in 1801. It was the prime command in the navy, because this was the main fleet of Britain. Cornwallis was entrusted with the task of blockading the French in Brest and defeating them if they came out, also of containing the detachments in Lorient and Rochefort and later Ferrol – sufficient duties, one might suppose; but this was only a part, not necessarily the most important, of the function of the Western Squadron.

'Napoleon regarded it, as many do to this day, as a squadron blockading Brest, whereas it was in reality a squadron holding the approaches to the Channel for all purposes of home and trade defence. The blockade of Brest was incidental, as were the blockades of Rochefort and Ferrol, and in no circumstances of reasonable war risk could a serious hostile squadron enter or even approach the Channel until the Western Squadron had been brought to action and defeated.'[g]

25

'The hazards of sea and wind'. An unknown artist's
impression of ships on a lee shore, in the Royal
Naval Museum, Portsmouth

Long experience had taught the British
Admiralty, Cornwallis himself, and his brother
admirals, and not least the French admirals also,
that Britain could come to little harm as long as
the Royal Navy held firmly to the mouth of the
English Channel. This, says Sir Julian Corbett,
'was the kernel of our traditional defensive
strategy, as it stood firmly based on the Western
Squadron. No fleet could hope to reach Dover
without being brought to action, and the further
it got the greater were the advantages of the home
fleet and the more crushing the results of failure.'
At the same time, Cornwallis and the others all
knew full well what the hazards of sea and wind
might do; at any moment a gale might spring up
which would blow the British squadron off
station, and it was not always certain that the same
gale would hold the French in port. 'Nothing ever
kept the French Fleet in at Toulon or Brest,
whenever they had a mind to come out,' wrote
Nelson in 1803.[1] Generally, if his precious line of
battleships were placed in too much danger,
Cornwallis would retire with them to Plymouth
and other harbours in Devon and Cornwall,
leaving some frigates to hang on in the teeth of
the gale by sheer seamanship and determination
outside Brest. On Christmas Day 1803, however,
a tempest arose of such violence that the whole
squadron had to retire to England. Eight French
ships of the line and eight cruisers came down to
the outer road of Brest harbour, but they thought
better of coming out; Ganteaume was not
prepared to risk his untried vessels in seas like
that. Meanwhile Cornwallis was earning his
nickname, 'Billy Blue'; whatever the weather,
when forced back into harbour he kept the Blue
Peter, the signal for immediate sailing, always at
the masthead, warning his ships that at the first
favourable change of the weather they would be
making back to Ushant. It was a hard service,
requiring hard ships and hard men; Cornwallis
possessed the confidence of the government and
the country, and despite the rigours of the station
he also possessed the affection of the fleet.

This, then, was the British naval system which
held Napoleon's initiative constantly in check.
The essential feature is that it was firmly grasped
by admirals and captains, who instinctively
applied the system, instinctively kept each other

informed and supported each other, and never doubted that all would do so – hence the outcries at any falling short. 'At the end of our long series of maritime wars with France,' wrote Corbett,

'the faculty of interpretation had reached in the sea service its fullest powers. So wide was the theatre, so slow the means of communication and so precious every rare item of news, that sharp necessity had developed an acuteness of sense that gives at times an impression of second sight. The whole service was as it were irradiated with an alert sympathy, a mutual understanding between the War Staff and the fighting lines, by which admirals afloat seemed always to see into the mind of the Admiralty and the Admiralty to rest assured of what the admirals would do. It was a factor in the struggle which Napoleon failed to take into account, or even to appreciate.'

It was, as we shall see, a decisive factor in the Trafalgar campaign.

We talk of fleets, squadrons, ships of the line, frigates and cruisers; all these words have continued in use into our own times, but their meanings have changed so much that we need to remind ourselves of what they meant at the beginning of the nineteenth century. Ever since the placing of broadside batteries of guns on the decks of warships (impossible for a galley, or any other oar-propelled vessel, as it was again in the brief days of paddle-steamers) the favoured fighting formation was in line ahead, so as to bring into action the largest possible number of guns simultaneously. Consequently, what we would call 'battleships' were then called 'ships of the line (of battle)'. There were three ratings of these: the heaviest, all three-deckers, carried 100 guns or more. H.M.S. *Victory*, Nelson's flagship in the Mediterranean, was a first-rate (100 guns); H.M.S. *Ville de Paris*, Admiral Cornwallis's flagship, was another (112 guns); so was H.M.S. *Royal Sovereign*, Vice-Admiral Collingwood's flagship (100 guns). Second-rates carried 90–98 guns, and were also three-deckers; among them were the *Prince of Wales* (98), Vice-Admiral Sir Robert Calder's flagship, the 'Fighting' *Téméraire* (98), and the *Dreadnought* (98). The commonest class, the hardest-working because they were called on for all sorts of duties at

different times, were the third-rates, 64–80 guns, of which the most numerous were 74s. Ships with fewer guns than this were going out of fashion; they tended to be assigned to quieter stations, like Lord Keith's command, facing the weak Dutch navy, or to convoy duty. Some of the best third-rates, the 80-gun ships, were as powerful as the older second-rates, very fine ships indeed, of which an example is the *Malta*, which as the *Guillaume Tell* fought as part of the French fleet at the Battle of the Nile, and was captured in 1800 by the *Foudroyant* (80), herself also named after a capture. [2] One of the most famous 74s was the *Superb*, celebrated in song, commanded by one of Nelson's favourite captains, Richard Keats. [3] A famous 64 was the *Agamemnon*, Nelson's first ship of the line, to which he was appointed in 1793.

Such were the components of the battle squadrons, the final sanction of naval power. In 1801 the Royal Navy had had no less than 127 ships of the line in commission; in May 1803, thanks to inevitable peacetime retrenchment and to St Vincent's economies, the number was fifty-two; by the end of the Napoleonic Wars there were 214 of them, an astounding array of strength. Supporting them, and performing a multitude of services, were the 'ships under the line': an intermediate class of fourth-rates, with 50–60 guns, and two classes of frigates, fifth-rates with 32–40 guns, and sixth-rates carrying 20–28. There were sloops, with 16 or 18 guns, and gun-brigs, cutters and other small craft whose armament varied from 6 to 14 guns, or even none at all; these were the eyes, ears and messengers of the battle squadrons. The admirals constantly complained that they never had enough of these maids-of-all-work, yet by 1815 the navy possessed 792 of them – far more than it would ever be able to man for active service.

It is customary, for convenience, to count simply the numbers of opposing fleets – at the Battle of Trafalgar itself Nelson's twenty-seven of the line against Villeneuve's thirty-three, or at a crucial moment of the campaign Cornwallis with eighteen facing Ganteaume in Brest with twenty-one. These comparisons, however, are misleading; they fail to take into account the special qualities of the three-deckers, the class in which the British almost always held the numerical advantage. It was not simply that the three-deckers obviously carried a heavier weight of metal, there was also the fact that their superior height enabled their top tier of guns to use plunging fire; the same factor was also an advantage in boarding. In addition, their greater size and weight made them more stable as gun platforms in heavy seas, while the solidity of their build gave them superior resistance to the enemy's shot. It is hard to be exact about the relative values of two- and three-deckers, but Corbett says this:

'. . . if we analyse the opposing squadrons of the campaign, we find again and again, that by counting three-deckers as two units, and seventy-fours as one unit, we get something like equality between the two squadrons. So constant and so nearly exact is this relation, at least for the more vital positions, that it is just possible this was actually the rough basis on which our Admiralty made their distribution. The idea indicated is that, having thus secured nominal equality, they trusted to the superior efficiency of our service as a whole for the necessary margin of strength. A similar basis of calculation appears to have prevailed in France.'

Thus Ganteaume, estimating at one stage that Cornwallis might have thirty ships, including twelve three-deckers, against his own twenty-one, described this to Napoleon as 'a force which would be almost double ours'. Cornwallis's eighteen ships referred to above, facing Ganteaume's twenty-one, included ten three-deckers as compared with Ganteaume's three, which by Corbett's reckoning would have given Cornwallis twenty-eight units against Ganteaume's twenty-four. From almost all points of view, the Trafalgar campaign shows the French admirals faced with daunting problems.

By contrast, the Royal Navy has never surpassed the proficiency and mastery which it displayed at that period. The serious deficiencies in armament and armour revealed at Jutland in 1916, or the great difficulties encountered by a whole fleet in sinking the *Bismarck* in 1941, are all seen in reverse in the war against Napoleon. He himself, the great artilleryman, confessed that France was 'ten years behind' the Admiralty in the adoption of a most important type of naval artillery: the carronade. Carronades are short, stubby cannon, looking rather like howitzers without elevation, of very heavy calibre indeed, 24-, 32- and 68-pounders, carried on the open decks, and used at very short range with pulverizing effect. 'In this war,' wrote Napoleon to his Minister of Marine, Decrès, in 1805, 'the English have been the first to use carronades, and everywhere they have done us great harm. We must hasten to perfect their system, for the argument is all on one side for sea service in favour of the system of large calibres.'

As with three-deckers and carronades, so with signals. In 1803 the Navy was bringing into universal use a new flag-signalling code devised by Commodore Sir Home Popham which, in all reasonable conditions of visibility, went a long way towards speeding up communication and dispelling the darkness of uncertainty in which admirals were used to operating. Popham's first version, which he brought into use in 1800, contained about 1,000 words which were numbered and could be signalled by simple groups of flags; this became Part I of the 1803 version, with a Part II containing about another 1,000 words, and a Part III containing a number of sentences and phrases. The command 'Engage the enemy more closely' was No. 16 in the book, consisting of two flags only, No. 1 above No. 6. 'The enemy's ships are coming out of port' was No. 370. This signal, made by an inshore frigate in a murky light, and passed from ship to ship as the light improved, reached Nelson, fifty miles away, in two and a half hours to announce the last act of the great drama. But no less important was the constant flutter of flags at mastheads by which cruiser spoke to cruiser, squadron to squadron, across the Bay of Biscay, up and down the Channel, or across the blue waters of the Mediterranean during the hard years of watching and waiting.

If Napoleon's plumed marshals, striding across Europe, provided a galaxy of remarkable military talent, the admirals and captains of the Royal Navy of that period, their weather eyes rarely closed in all the seas they sailed, supplied at the very least a matching picture. At the head of the profession, First Lord of the Admiralty from the outbreak of war until Pitt formed his second

H.M.S. VICTORY

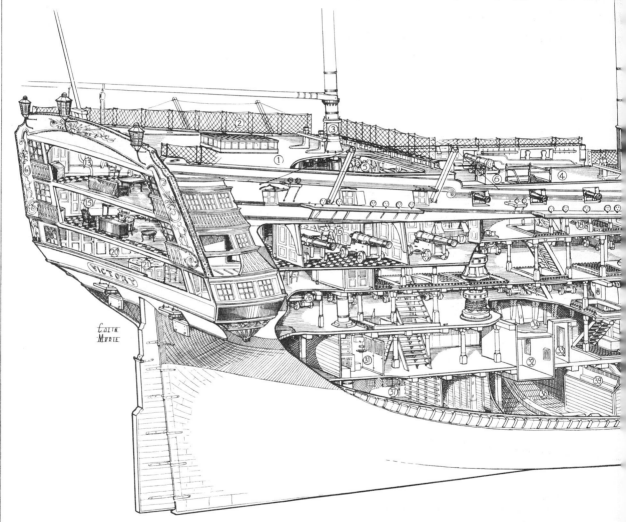

Drawing of the *Victory* by Colin Mudie.

Armament—1805

Lower Deck	30 32-pounders and 2 12-pounders
Middle Deck	28 24-pounders
Upper Deck	30 12-pounders
Quarter Deck	12 12-pounders
Forecastle	2 68-pounders (Carronades)

Particulars

Length on Gun Deck	186′ 0
Length of Keel	151′ 0
Moulded Breadth	50′ 6
Extreme Breadth	51′ 1
Depth in Hold	21′ 6″
Displacement (Approx.)	3,500
Burthen	2,162

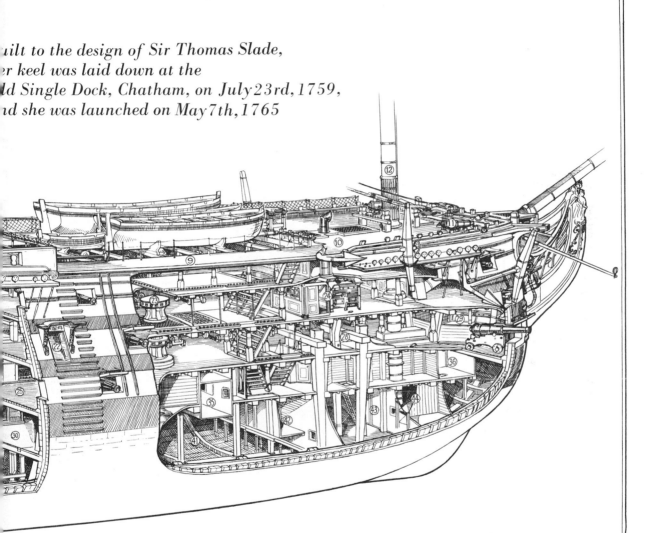

uilt to the design of Sir Thomas Slade,
er keel was laid down at the
ld Single Dock, Chatham, on July 23rd, 1759,
nd she was launched on May 7th, 1765

Key to Drawing

1	Poop	12	Foremast	23	Capstan Head	34 Midshipman's Berth—here Nelson died
2	Hammock Nettings	13	Captain Hardy's Cabin	24	Galley and Stove	35 Forward Hanging Magazine
3	Mizzenmast	14	Upper Deck	25	Lower Deck	36 Powder Store
4	Quarter Deck	15	Nelson's Day Cabin	26	Tiller	37 Powder Room
5	Steering Wheels	16	Nelson's Dining Cabin	27	Chain & Elm Tree Pumps	38 Aft Hold
6	Here Nelson Fell	17	Nelson's Sleeping Cabin with cot	28	Mooring Bitts	39 Shot Locker
7	Pikes	18	Shot Garlands	29	Manger	40 Well
8	Mainmast	19	Middle Deck	30	Orlop	41 Main Hold
9	Gangway	20	Wardroom	31	Sick Bay	42 Cabin Store
10	Fo'c'sle	21	Tiller Head	32	Aft Hanging Magazine	43 Main Magazine
11	Carronades	22	Entry Port	33	Lamp Room	44 Filling Room

'The same spirit actuates the whole profession'.
Left: Lord Barham, who gathered in his fingers
the threads of the British naval system; centre:
Lord St Vincent, an inspiring leader at sea; right:
Lord Collingwood, Nelson's friend and successor
as C-in-C Mediterranean

ministry in May 1804, stood Admiral Earl St
Vincent. At sea he had been an inspiring leader,
his title deriving from the famous victory which
he had won, as Sir John Jervis, in 1797, when
the young Commodore Nelson had also greatly
distinguished himself. At his Admiralty desk, St
Vincent's reforming zeal outstripped his discretion,
but when war came again it found his grasp of
operations still firm. He refused to serve under
Pitt, who had said hard things about him, and
was replaced by Lord Melville, a friend of Pitt.
Almost exactly a year later Melville was brought
down by his political opponents, and once more
a sailor came to the head of the Navy.

Admiral Sir Charles Middleton was over eighty
years old when he became First Lord, with the
title of Lord Barham. No great victory was
associated with his name; he had not even
commanded a fleet. But his whole professional
life had been dedicated to improving the efficiency
of the service, and making the naval art as close to
an exact science as its nature would permit. In
advisory capacities he had already done much,
and now, despite opposition from several quarters,
Barham would do more than advise, he would
rule; 'and thus,' says Corbett, 'at the crying
moment the country, by Pitt's firmness and
sagacity, secured for her councils the man who,
for ripe experience in the direction of naval war
in all its breadth and detail, had not a rival in
the service or in Europe.' Even one of Barham's
disappointed rivals for the post said, on hearing
the news; '. . . he is indisputably the fittest man
that could be chosen to occupy it at the time. His
abilities were always considered great, his
experience is consummate, and he has few equals
in application and method of business.'

It is common, and quite understandable, to see
the Trafalgar campaign as a sort of duel between
Napoleon and Nelson; the drama surrounding
Nelson's actions lends itself to that interpretation.
But that is to compare a vice-admiral with an
emperor, the commander of one fleet among
several with a supreme warlord, and to do an
injustice to Nelson's contemporaries which he
himself would have resented. Sir Julian Corbett,
the most distinguished historian of these events,
sees the 'duel' in very different terms:

'A hundred years of rivalry for the lordship of the sea was drawing to a culmination, and the protagonists, as in some old drama of destiny, were fairly face to face upon the imposing stage. On the cliffs of Boulogne, at the zenith of his powers, was the greatest master of war the long struggle had produced, alert and straining for the catastrophe amidst the sound and pomp of the Grand Army. Over against him, unknown to fame and bent with his eighty years, a sailor sat alone in the silence of his room at Whitehall. Unseen and almost unnoticed he was gathering in his fingers the threads of the tradition which the recurring wars had spun, and handling them with a deft mastery to which the distant fleets gave sensitive response. The splendour of quick success and an unrivalled genius for war was arrayed against hard-won experience and the instinct it had bred, and it was arrayed in vain.'

The 'threads of tradition' linked the whole navy. We have already noted the key rôle of Cornwallis; he and Barham were so much embodiments of the tradition that at a vital moment Barham would write to him: 'you have entered completely into my views.' Despite their difference in rank, Nelson habitually addressed Cornwallis as 'My Dear Friend'. He would not have used that form of address to Admiral Lord Keith, who had found him a difficult subordinate in the Mediterranean in 1799. Other reputations also suffered from having Nelson as a subordinate. We should not be blinded by this; Keith also was part of the tradition, applying it coolly and correctly on his own station. The names of Admiral Sir Charles Cotton and Admiral Lord Gardner should not be forgotten; both bore the high responsibility of commanding the Western Squadron during Cornwallis's unavoidable absence.

The tradition was a hard one, its code of conduct difficult for outsiders to interpret. Nothing illustrates this better than the case of Vice-Admiral Sir Robert Calder, who held the Ferrol station in 1805; having engaged twenty enemy ships with fifteen of his own, and taken two of them, he was officially reprimanded by a court of enquiry for not having done much better. The tradition pressed hard on Vice-Admiral Collingwood also; in forty-four years' service in the navy, he only spent six ashore; after the summer of 1803 he never saw his home or his family again; he became

commander-in-chief of the Mediterranean Fleet after Nelson's death, and from 1805 to 1810 he bore the heavy responsibilities of that appointment. And, 'though a strong man, [he] was killed by them, through general debility resulting from confinement, and through organic injury produced by bending over his desk'.[h] The list of names goes on: Cochrane, Saumarez, Bickerton, Pellew, Ball. All part of the tradition, all acting by the tradition according to their lights, the British admirals almost unfailingly lent each other loyal support. So we find Cochrane handing over to Admiral Dacres at Jamaica five out of his six ships, because he thought Dacres might need them more. We see Collingwood, entrusted with a squadron of ten, sending two to Nelson in case he needed them, and giving three to Bickerton who was in an awkward situation. Admiral Graves, sent to watch Rochefort, unhesitatingly sent on two of his ships to help Calder – and so it goes on.

As with the admirals, so with the captains. Captain Sir Richard Strachan of the *Renown*, by quick wits and strenuous exertion, saved Sir John Orde's squadron from certain destruction.[4] Captain Lord Mark Kerr of the frigate *Fisgard* was refitting at Gibraltar, with half his gear ashore, in April 1805 when Villeneuve escaped from Nelson and passed through the Straits. Kerr sent off a lieutenant in a hired brig to warn Nelson, abandoned his gear and cut short his refit, and fighting foul winds proceeded to carry his news first to Admiral Calder at Ferrol, then to Lord Gardner with the Western Squadron, then to Plymouth for the Admiralty and finally to Cork – a splendid, spontaneous, comprehensive act of illumination. Captain Thomas Baker of the frigate *Phoenix* (36) was so anxious to come up with the French *Didon* (40) that he disguised his ship as a 20-gun sloop, in order to be sure of a fight, with what results we shall see on a later page.[5] And finally, because it would be ridiculous not to mention him, there was Henry Blackwood of *Euryalus*, 'the king of cruiser captains', with an extraordinary instinct for being in the right place at the right time, and an unrivalled audacity in the plying of his dangerous trade right in the jaws of enemy harbours and under the noses of hostile fleets. It was Nelson himself who

VOLUNTEERS.

G.   R. III.

God Save the King.

LET us, who are Englifhmen, protect and defend our good KING and COUNTRY againft the Attempts of all *Republicans* and *Levellers*, and againft the Defigns of our NATURAL ENEMIES, who intend in this Year to invade OLD ENGLAND, *our happy Country*, to murder our gracious KING as they have done *their own*; to make WHORES of our *Wives* and *Daughters*; to rob us of our Property, and teach us nothing but the *damn'd Art of murdering one another.*

ROYAL TARS
Of OLD ENGLAND,

If you love your COUNTRY, and your LIBERTY, now is the Time to fhew your Love.
REPAIR,

All who have good Hearts, who love their KING, their COUNTRY, and RELIGION, who hate the FRENCH, and damn the POPE,
TO

Lieut. W. J. Stephens,

At his Rendezvous, SHOREHAM,

Where they will be allowed to Enter for any SHIP of WAR,
AND THE FOLLOWING
BOUNTIES will be given by his MAJESTY.
in Addition to Two Months Advance.

To Able Seamen,	*Five Pounds.*
To Ordinary Seamen,	*Two Pounds Ten Shillings.*
To Landmen,	*Thirty Shillings.*

Conduct-Money paid to go by Land, and their Chefts and Bedding fent Carriage free.
Thofe Men who have ferved as PETTY-OFFICERS, and thofe who are otherwife qualified, will be recommended accordingly.

LEWES: PRINTED BY W. AND A. LEE.

pronounced the ultimate tribute to his fellow officers. As he was preparing his last campaign, Barham invited him to select his own officers, and he replied: 'Choose yourself, my lord, the same spirit actuates the whole profession; you cannot choose wrong.'[i]

For nearly two years the blockade of the French ports was, to all intents and purposes, the war. The bulk of the French fleet, Ganteaume's twenty-one ships of the line in Brest, five more under Rear-Admiral Missiessy in Rochefort, one in Lorient and (at the opening of 1805) another five in Ferrol, faced Cornwallis's Western Squadron. The constant possibility was that these different groups of French ships would unite, and this imposed on Cornwallis and his subordinates the need for a close blockade of all the Atlantic ports in almost all weathers. At Brest it was usual for the main body of the British fleet to be over the horizon, with an inshore squadron on constant watch. The smaller squadrons would use cruisers for close work, while the ships of the line sheltered from storms in the lee of friendly capes, or held sea stations on preselected rendezvous. As we shall see in a moment, the Mediterranean method was somewhat different, but there were certain factors in common to all.

The undertone, sometimes loud and menacing, sometimes barely perceptible, to all naval transactions at that time was the system of recruitment. It was quite impossible for the Royal Navy to man its ships with volunteers; in 1805 the number of ships of the line in commission was 105 – they alone required some 70,000–75,000 seamen at a modest estimate, to say nothing of the frigates and smaller craft. The only way of obtaining such numbers was by the press gang, a method which bore with hard injustice upon the inhabitants of the coastal towns and districts, especially in the south-east. It bore roughly on the merchant seamen also; in 1805, when the crisis of the naval war required every possible ship to be commissioned, the only resource for some of them was to wait for the return of the West and East Indies convoys and press their crews – a poor reward for much toil and hardship.

Every other method of obtaining men was tried: tempting posters were published by enterprising captains, holding out glittering prospects of prize money (frigates, of course, had the advantage here); bounties were offered to qualified men; and, at the other end of the scale, debtors, rogues and vagrants, even foreigners, were thrust, willy-nilly, into His Majesty's ships. The ship's company of H.M.S. *Victory* in 1805 may be taken as reasonably typical: 30 per cent are described as 'volunteers', of whom 22 per cent were 'prime seamen', many attracted by the bounty money; 8 per cent were boys, orphans, waifs or strays, some of whom may well have liked the idea of life on the ocean wave, but in general it takes some imagination to think of them as volunteers; 50 per cent of the crew were pressed men; 12 per cent were rogues and debtors; no less than 8 per cent (nearly seventy men out of a full complement of 850) were foreigners. One obvious consequence of this state of affairs was that it was impossible to allow the sailors any shore leave during the period of a ship's commission. Many of them would never have been seen again. Working parties for victualling, watering and refitting or other tasks there had to be – with a Royal Marine guard watching them closely. Otherwise, the crews remained aboard, month after month, and as the months dragged into years. Devon or Cornwall men, driven to harbour by storms, might even be in sight of their own homes, but they could never reach them. And if a Royal Navy ship found itself sharing a harbour with an American, the Royal Marines had to exercise exceptional vigilance. In 1804 the United States were at war with the Barbary Corsairs of Tripoli, and, according to the historian William James, 'the complements of their ships in the Tripolitan war consisted chiefly of British seamen'. He adds: 'To such as know, the facility with which, either in the ships or on the shores of the United States, a deserter, or an emigrant, can obtain his naturalization, the term "American" requires an epithet to render it intelligible.'

What could be done to counteract the worst miseries of this existence was done or attempted by the more humane admirals and captains – and at this period there was a general swing away from the brutal punishments of the eighteenth

'The undertone ... was the system of recruitment':
Rowlandson's drawing shows the Press Gang hard
at work

century, which had played their evil part in provoking the mutinies of 1797. One is conscious of a certain high-mindedness in the upper ranks of the navy which seems to anticipate the characteristics of the coming Victorian age, and sometimes contrasts sharply with the profaner redcoats. Certainly the disposition to be concerned with the well-being and health of the lower deck was increasing, and it is as well that it did so, because otherwise it is hard to see how the wearing grind of the blockades could have been maintained without serious trouble. For the unfortunate Western Squadron, at the mercy of Channel weather, there was not much that could be done. In the Mediterranean, Nelson tried to relieve the monotony of the blockade routine by constant cruising – now looking close into Toulon, now inspecting the Ligurian ports, dropping away when the fierce north-westers blew in the Gulf of Lions to his 'rendezvous 97' off Cape San Sebastian on the coast of Spain near Palamos, or calling in at the Madalena Islands, at the northern tip of Sardinia, for refits and supplies. For twenty-two months the Mediterranean Fleet never put into port as a whole (though individual ships might be compelled to do so), and for twenty-two months Nelson treated himself as he treated the ordinary seamen: he never went ashore. It says something for the condition of morale which he was able to produce by example and command that, in December 1804, he could report to the Admiralty: 'The Fleet is in perfect good health and good humour, unequalled by anything which has ever come within my knowledge, and equal to the most active service which the times may call for.' And this was confirmed by his physician, Dr Gillespie ,who joined the fleet in H.M.S. *Victory* the following month, and found with some astonishment that she had only one man confined to bed by sickness out of 840, and that the rest of the fleet could make a similar return. 'The great thing in all military service is health,' wrote Nelson, and when one considers the terrible ravages of disease in the expeditions of the period – 40,000 dead and another 40,000 permanently disabled by malaria, yellow fever and dysentery in the West Indies between 1793 and 1796, a third of the Walcheren expedition of 1809 brought down by fever, and so on – these amazing medical returns in the

Mediterranean Fleet must be acknowledged to display yet another, and by no means the least, aspect of the Royal Navy's deep professionalism.

———————————

It is now time for us to consider the rôle of the Mediterranean Fleet, and the special circumstances which guided Nelson in his command of it during the twenty-two months of blockade, and the high drama of 1805. To control the Mediterranean, or at any rate to maintain an important presence there, had been a principle of British strategy since the seventeenth century. The capture of Gibraltar in 1704 gave Britain a firm hold of the gateway to that sea, but inside it matters did not always go well. In 1796, indeed, the navy withdrew from the Mediterranean – with inevitable serious consequences, such as the capture of Malta from the Knights of St John by the French less than two years later, and the invasion of Egypt. These were recent and bad memories, and, as we have seen, the determination not to risk Malta falling into French hands again had been the direct cause of war in 1803.

Two days before the new war broke out, Nelson was appointed commander-in-chief in the Mediterranean;[6] it is interesting to see what his instructions from the Admiralty were – they throw much light on his subsequent actions. Malta was now the headquarters of the British Mediterranean Fleet, and Nelson's first instructions were:

'On your Lordship's arrival at Malta, you are to lose no time in concerting with Sir Alexander Ball, his Majesty's commissioner at that island, such arrangements as may be necessary with a view to the protection and security of that island; you are then to proceed off Toulon, with such part of the squadron under your command as you may judge to be adequate to the service, and take such a position as may, in your Lordship's opinion, be most proper for enabling you to take, sink, burn or otherwise destroy, any ships or vessels belonging to France, or the citizens of that Republic . . .'

So, first the security of Malta, then the French fleet in Toulon; what next was Nelson to attend to?

'Your Lordship is to be very attentive to the proceedings of the French at Genoa, Leghorn, and other ports on that side of Italy . . .' The reason for this 'attention' was spelt out; it was the

The Toulon Squadron, July 1803

Vice-Admiral René-Madeleine Latouche Tréville, succeeded by Vice-Admiral Pierre de Villeneuve

Afloat	*In dock*	*Building*
*Formidable (80)	†Annibal (74)	*Bucentaure (80)
*Indomptable (80)	*†Swiftsure (74)	*Neptune (80)
Atlas (74)		Borée (74)
*†Berwick (74)		Phaeton (74)
*Intrépide (74)		*Pluton (74)
*Mont-Blanc (74)		
*Scipion (74)		

*Present at Trafalgar
†Once British. *Annibal* is the British *Hannibal*, captured in 1801; *Swiftsure* was taken in the same year, and retaken at Trafalgar.

The Toulon Blockade 1803

Kent (74) *Rear-Admiral Sir Richard Bickerton*
Gibraltar (80)
*Donegal (74)
*Superb (74)
†*Belleisle (74)
Renown (74)
Monmouth (64)
Agincourt (64)
Frigates : Active, Phoebe

Arrived 8 July
Frigate : Amphion *Vice-Admiral Lord Nelson*

Arrived 30 July
†*Victory (100)

Arrived August
*Canopus (80) *Rear-Admiral George Campbell*
Triumph (74)
Frigates : Seahorse, Narcissus

Arrived November
Excellent (74)

*Went to West Indies with Nelson
†Present at Trafalgar

Admiralty's (and, of course, the government's) deep concern about French operations directed against Egypt again, or against other parts of the Turkish empire (the Morea, in southern Greece, in particular), the Ionian Islands or Sicily. Nelson's fourth instruction was 'to afford to the Sublime Porte and his Sicilian Majesty and their subjects, any protection or assistance which may be in your power . . .' It is most important to notice this strong direction of Nelson's attention to the eastern Mediterranean; it naturally influenced him profoundly, while as regards the kingdom of Naples and Sicily he would need little prompting, because he already had warm friendship and sympathy with both the king and the queen (it was at their court that he had first met Lady Hamilton, his mistress, in 1793). It should be noticed that only fifthly was he ordered to watch any naval preparations in the ports of England's old enemy, Spain, and sixthly to prevent any junction of French and Spanish warships, the combination of which had twice given Britain serious trouble since 1779. The remainder of his instructions were routine.

It is clear from this that there are profound differences between commanding in the Mediterranean, and commanding at Ushant or other stations nearer home. It is easy to overstate them:

'If the command in the English Channel was the most critical when invasion threatened, the responsibilities in the Mediterranean were the more complex. . . . The admiral was not, like the commander in the Channel, primarily the commander of a blockading fleet under the close supervision of the Admiralty. He performed alone in the Mediterranean the functions of co-ordination which the Admiralty itself shared with the commanders in home waters; corresponded with the allied and neutral governments in the theatre; and arranged with the military commanders and diplomatists the measures in which British policy was embodied.'[j]

The same writer says of Nelson's appointment in 1803: 'Now at last he entered upon his inheritance – the most important sea-going appointment in the Royal Navy.' This is, as we have seen,[7] to fall into the same error as Napoleon, the error of regarding the Western Squadron simply as a blockading force, whereas it was, in fact, the main fleet of Britain, the ultimate strategic naval reserve. In the words of Major-General J. F. C. Fuller, 'Ushant . . . was the centre of gravity of British naval defence, and, in consequence, Cornwallis's fleet excelled all others in importance.'[k] It is clearly true, however, that there was a political factor governing the commander-in-chief in the Mediterranean – indeed, a welter of political factors – which did not apply at Ushant, and which explain Nelson's actions when purely military considerations do not. It is easy to see, for example, how he would be affected by General Gouvion St Cyr's invasion of Naples and occupation of Taranto, to which we referred on page 21. In fact, there was never a moment when Nelson did not have, as it were, half an eye cocked in that direction, in case St Cyr should begin any of those movements which he was expressly ordered to prevent. And, as we shall further see, it was precisely in the eastern Mediterranean that the first beginnings of the counter-offensive against Napoleon took place.

Nelson arrived at Malta on 15 June 1803, and left two days later to join his fleet, then cruising off Toulon under Rear-Admiral Sir Thomas Bickerton. Just three weeks later, fighting foul winds all the way, Nelson reached the fleet; this impossibly long passage convinced him that Malta was a hopeless base for the blockade of Toulon. Furthermore, as long as he held command of the Mediterranean, Malta (and all else) would be safe from French attacks, and, as Piers Mackesy says, 'The command of the seas between Spain and Italy was the command of the Mediterranean.' This was what dictated Nelson's choice of rendezvous, especially No. 97 and the Madalena Islands. It was in this area that he concentrated the bulk of his ships of the line (eight of them under Bickerton when Nelson arrived, afterwards a fluctuating number, ten, eleven or twelve) with an always too small number of cruisers, while the remainder of his fleet (totalling thirty-two vessels of all descriptions in 1803, forty-six in 1805) was scattered upon its various exacting duties up and down the 2,000 miles of the Mediterranean Sea.

Nelson did not favour the close blockade which Cornwallis adopted to prevent the junction of neighbouring French squadrons. The French in Toulon had no close neighbours. In any case, Nelson was above all a fighting admiral, and his constant hope was that he could lure them out to their destruction.[8] The condition of many of his ships, having had no chance to refit after long service, was lamentable, but never for one moment did Nelson doubt that they could at all times out-weather, out-manoeuvre and out-fight their enemies. The French, first under Admiral Latouche Tréville and then under Vice-Admiral Villeneuve, were of the same opinion, and refused to oblige him. So the weary months of watching passed by, with Nelson's nerves constantly at full stretch with waiting and expectation, to the great damage of his health. And then, just as he feared that his health would finally break down, the events began to unroll which would transform Napoleon's initiative, and set Britain herself on a new course.

Footnotes
Ch II
1 Nelson to Sir Alexander Ball, 12 August 1803.
2 One could almost say that the French were the shipbuilders of the Royal Navy – and very good shipbuilders they were! Nelson, off Toulon, acknowledging a consignment of shells, says that he does not mean to use them at sea, 'for that I hope to consider burning *our own ships*'. On the other hand, three of the fourteen ships of the Toulon squadron were captures from the British, and two of them fought in the French fleet at Trafalgar under their old names, *Berwick* and *Swiftsure*.
3 'I esteem his *person* alone as equal to *one* French 74, and the *Superb* and her Captain equal to two 74-gun Ships.' Nelson to Hugh Elliot, 11 July 1803.
4 See p. 70.
5 See p. 118.
6 Nelson's appointment was on 16 May; war was declared on 18 May; he sailed on 20 May.
7 See p. 25.
8 'I beg to inform your Lordship that the Port of Toulon has never been blockaded by me: quite the reverse – every opportunity has been offered to the Enemy to put to sea, for it is there that we hope to realize the hopes and expectations of our Country, and I trust that they will not be disappointed.' Nelson to the Lord Mayor of London, 1 August 1804.

3. THE CHANGING PATTERN OF WAR

When William Pitt became Prime Minister for the second time in May 1804, he faced a situation not dissimilar, in some important respects, to that which Churchill faced in 1940–41. An invasion was threatened on each occasion, and on each occasion it was blocked; recovery from a serious shortage of war materials, due to various causes, was taking place in each case (in 1804, eighty-seven new British warships were launched; in 1940 fighter aircraft production just matched the demands of the Battle of Britain); but in each case Britain had to face the fact of being alone against a triumphant and seemingly invincible enemy, and, despite a lot of boastful talk to keep up spirits, in each case thoughtful men knew that Britain alone could never defeat that enemy. There had to be allies; the war would have to become a coalition war; and it was to that end that Pitt bent all his endeavours.

The problem was to find the allies. Austria, twice defeated, bankrupted and humiliated in wars with France during the last eleven years, would require all the goading of Napoleon's provocations, as well as English subsidies, to make her fight again. Prussia was disgusted at the French presence in Hanover because she coveted that territory herself – which made her a very unlikely ally of England at this juncture. Sweden was happy to accept a large subsidy, but could offer very little in return for it. Naples and Sicily hated Napoleon deeply, but with St Cyr's army already on their soil they hardly dared even to supply Nelson's fleet. That only left Russia.

The penetration of the Soviet navy into the Mediterranean in the 1970s has startled many people; 170 years ago it would not have done so. Russian influence, when the Peace of Amiens collapsed, reached to the centre of the inland sea. Since the days of Peter the Great there had been increasingly close relations between the tsars and the Order of St John in Malta. The Tsar Paul took the title of Protector of the Order, and when his inability to protect it was clearly displayed by the French capture of Malta in 1798 and the dispersion of the knights, the order gratefully awarded the tsar the title of Grand Master. His successor, Alexander I, was one of the guarantors of the order's independence by the terms of the Treaty of Amiens, and Britain's refusal to evacuate the island led to ill-feeling and distrust in Russia which were only beginning to be dispelled in 1804.

The Mediterranean was Britain's most important point of contact with Russia at that time. Not only did the tsar consider Malta as coming under his protection, but the same was true of Naples and Sicily, despite the fact that, like Malta, only British sea power could make them accessible. There was obviously a case for combining Russian military strength with Britain's naval strength for the real protection of the central Mediterranean, and this was precisely the project that Pitt tried to push forward. There were also other areas of possible cooperation, but unfortunately more likely to involve discord.

Both Russia and Britain were deeply interested in the Turkish empire, already the 'sick man of Europe'. Russia was naturally much concerned with who controlled the Bosphorus, the Sea of Marmora and the Dardanelles Straits; she was also concerned with Turkey's Greek subjects who, as Orthodox Christians, looked to the tsar for defence against the worst severities of Turkish rule. A Russian force occupied the Ionian Islands, protecting them from the attentions of the Turkish pasha in Albania, while a Russian naval squadron gathered in the fortified harbour of Corfu. Britain, too, had her strong interests in Turkey, especially the province of Egypt, control of which meant control of the Isthmus of Suez and access to the Indian Ocean – in unfriendly hands it became a direct threat to India.

Both Britain and Russia desired to keep the tottering Turkish empire intact; what they dreaded above all was any extension of French influence in that unsettled area. Their own activities often conflicted, however; the British feared that Russian support for the Greeks would give Napoleon an opening in the Balkans; the Russians warned that British support of the Mamelukes in Egypt against the Turkish viceroy would have the same effect. With much mutual meddling taking place, there were obstacles enough to understanding; they did not need the addition of Nelson's own personal distrust of Russia. 'If Russia goes to war with France,' he wrote in July 1804,

'The march of the eagles had begun'; Napoleon
receiving the allegiance of the army at Boulogne,
August 1804

'I hope it will be her own War, and not joined with us.
Such Alliances have never benefited our Country . . .
Russia's going to war in the way I am sure she will,
will cause the loss of Naples and Sardinia; for that
Court will not send 100,000 men into Italy, and less
are useless for any grand purpose. *No*; Russia will
take care of the Ionian Republic, the Morea, and, in
the end, Constantinople. The views of Russia are
perfectly clear.'[1]

Nevertheless, despite all conflicts of interest and
mistakes of intention, it was on Anglo-Russian
collaboration, and nothing else, that Pitt's
coalition depended, and it was his good fortune
that, just as he came to power, the Russians themselves were offering to make a large force available
in the Mediterranean if Britain would also
contribute an effective expeditionary force. 'It is
here,' says Corbett, 'we pick up the thread that
led directly to the decision at Trafalgar. Slender

as it proved to be, it is the only sure guide through
the labyrinth of the campaign.'

Negotiations continued; Britain's mounting
military strength – the regular army at home,
numbering only about 50,000 in May 1803, had
risen to 87,000 by the summer of 1804 – made it
possible at last to contemplate the sending of
expeditions; difficulties seemed to be being
slowly ironed out. An expedition to the
Mediterranean, under General Sir James Craig,
was agreed upon; if required to join the Russians
for the defence of Naples and Sicily, or to drive
the French out, it was accepted that the British
force might put themselves under a Russian
general of superior rank. Even so, old suspicions
and prejudices revived at the very last moment,
with a treaty of alliance actually signed in St
Petersburg;[2] the tsar determined to make one
more attempt to come to terms with Napoleon,

and once more demanded that Britain should give up Malta. So determined was Pitt not to abandon the alliance that he was even prepared to accept this condition, and remove the Mediterranean Fleet base to Minorca, but fortunately it did not come to that.

'The times are big with great events,' wrote Nelson to his old friend, Sir Alexander Ball, governor of Malta, on 4 October 1804. It is not surprising if, in his sensitive Mediterranean station, he was aware of a tensing of the atmosphere, as Pitt's policy developed and new ideas stirred in Napoleon's mind. Yet Nelson had no means of knowing the complexity of the pattern into which he and his fleet were being woven. He did not know how Pitt's plans for a coalition were forming (and would not have approved if he had); he did not even know that the government was contemplating an act of war against Spain; still less did he know the alteration that was taking place in Napoleon's naval strategy.

By the summer of 1804, his squadrons locked in apparently permanent immobility by the British blockading forces, Napoleon was beginning to have doubts about his invasion of England. In June, Vice-Admiral Latouche Tréville made a brief sortie from Toulon; in Nelson's words, 'Mons. La Touche came out with eight Sail of the Line and six Frigates, cut a caper off Sepet, and went in again. I was off with five Ships of the Line, and brought to for his attack, although I did not believe that anything was meant serious, but merely a gasconade.'[3] Latouche reported the occasion to Napoleon in somewhat different terms; Nelson, he said, 'sheered off' at the appearance of the French squadron. 'I pursued him until nightfall: he ran to the south-east. The next day, at dawn, I had lost touch with him.' Misled by this little piece of bombast (which also infuriated Nelson) Napoleon produced one more plan for seizing control of the Channel: on 2 July he ordered Latouche to come out again, pick up a French ship of the line that was in Cadiz, release the Rochefort squadron and come into the Channel.

As usual, the presence of the Royal Navy at its several stations was disregarded. But the scheme came to nothing, frustrated by the death of Latouche, the best of the French admirals, in August. Not long afterwards, Napoleon completely changed his ideas: according to his new plan, the Brest fleet, with Augereau's army corps aboard, or in transports, was to attack Ireland, while the Toulon and Rochefort squadrons were to sail independently to the West Indies, where they would recapture the Dutch islands taken by the British and strengthen the French islands, doing all the damage to Britain that they could, and then return via Ferrol, where they would pick up the squadron locked in there, and make for a French port. The British government and Admiralty, Napoleon appears to have assumed once more, would be so dazed and bewildered by these brilliant manoeuvres, their fleets so dispersed in wild-goose-chases, that 'the war is ours'. Whatever else this plan may have portended, it had a profound effect on the invasion preparations in the Pas de Calais: Corbett says:

'For the winter at least the whole project was abandoned. Large sections of the flotilla were dismantled, the ports of departure were neglected, and the Channel sands began rapidly to devour the millions they had cost to make. After eighteen months of undisturbed effort, with a century of experience behind him, [Napoleon] had failed to solve even the initial problem of the operation; and to save his face before his disappointed country and demoralised army he faced about against Austria.'

This somewhat exaggerates the situation; there are no indications that the Army of England was at all 'demoralised' in the autumn of 1804 – on the contrary, it was having rather a good time. And although peace with Austria was always uneasy, it was not until the following year that Napoleon embarked on the deliberate policy of provocation that led to war. It was in a quite different direction that Napoleon began to apply his new pressures, and the results were as complex as any other part of the political proceedings of this year.

Spain's neutrality had already stretched the word to the very limits of its meaning: French warships were permitted to remain in the sanctuary of Spanish harbours (so that Ferrol had to be watched by a British squadron as though it was an enemy port), French crews were permitted to pass through Spain to reach their ships, while Spain also paid to Napoleon a secret tribute of 72 million francs a year. Towards Britain, on the other hand, Spanish neutrality showed a changing face. At the end of July 1803, Nelson reported that one of his officers, buying bullocks in Spain, 'found the Spaniards very much inclined to be civil',[4] and a little later he told the Prime Minister, Henry Addington: 'I am making what use I can of Spain, to get water and refreshments, and shall do so as long as they will allow us; but I suppose the French will not suffer it very long.'[5] For over a year, despite increasing unfriendliness, Nelson and his officers trod a delicate course in all their dealings with Spain. As late as 13 October 1804 we find him writing: 'I am clearly of opinion that Spain has no wish to go to War with England, nor can I think that England has any wish to go to war unnecessarily with Spain.'[6] What he did not know until later that same day was that already an act had been sanctioned that would inevitably bring the two countries to war.

It was characteristic of Pitt's firmer and bolder direction of the war that the British government had by now determined no longer to permit the treasure of the Spanish empire to flow into Europe for Napoleon's benefit. In September a squadron of four Spanish frigates from Montevideo was approaching Cadiz with cargo of a total value of about £1,300,000 or more. Suffering, perhaps, from a touch of understandable, but regrettable, over-confidence, the British Admiralty sent out a squadron also of only four frigates to intercept and detain the Spanish treasure ships. The British frigates, led by the 44-gun *Indefatigable*, were stronger and more heavily armed than their opponents; indeed, Mr James says that the *Indefatigable* and any two of her three consorts would have been a match for the four Spaniards. But the Admiralty reckoned without Spanish pride, the *pundonor*. The two squadrons met on 5 October; faced with an equal number of opponents, Rear-Admiral Don Joseph Bustamente could not bring himself to lower his country's flag without at least making a gesture of resistance. It was a brave decision, but it led to tragedy. After only nine minutes' action, the ship next in line to his own, the *Mercedes*, blew up, 240 of her

crew and passengers out of 280 being killed. One by one the other Spanish frigates surrendered, with a further loss of twenty killed and eighty wounded; the total British loss was two killed and seven wounded. All in all, it was a distressing affair; one unfortunate Spanish officer, returning home, lost his wife, four daughters and four sons in the explosion of the *Mercedes*, as well as a fortune of £30,000, the savings of thirty years' industry. The money was reimbursed by the

British government; nothing could bring the family back to life. Mr James remarks: 'Many persons, who concurred in the expediency, doubted the right, of detaining these ships; and many, again, to whom the legality of the act appeared clear, were of opinion, that a more formidable force should have been sent to execute the service, in order to have justified the Spanish admiral in surrendering without an appeal to arms.' It is not to be wondered at that Spain declared war on England; what is strange, in our less leisurely age, is that she did not do so until over two months later, on 12 December 1804. So a big new factor entered the calculations of the war.

On paper, Spain's entry into the war spelt a marked tilting of the naval balance in Napoleon's favour. The Spanish fleet nominally contained thirty-two ships of the line; added to all the French and Dutch ships existing or building, these would bring Napoleon's strength up to ninety-eight,

while out of the Royal Navy's 105 in commission
only eighty-three were seagoing. But even
Napoleon, with his habitual disregard of maritime
facts, knew that for the time being these were
only paper fleets. The Spanish navy was
unprepared for war in December 1804; the most
that could be realistically expected from it was
between twenty-five and twenty-nine ships of the
line by the end of March 1805. Like the French,
the Spanish squadrons were widely separated:
Ferrol was to supply Napoleon with a reinforcement of seven or eight (added to the five French
already in that port); Cadiz would contribute
twelve to fifteen (with one French seventy-four,
the *Aigle*), and Cartagena would provide another
six. It was fortunate indeed for the British that the
Spanish ships were mostly unfit to go to sea (the
Cartagena squadron being in particularly poor
shape); even so, their very existence added to the
strain on the Royal Navy. When the condition of
the Spaniards improved, and they became an
effective force, it was clear that this strain would
be much increased, and that a transformation, or
at least a shift of emphasis, of the war would take
place. Meanwhile Napoleon's plan for raiding
the West Indies still held sway, and this by itself
was to bring a sudden change to the scene which
had been static for so long.

'Sir,' wrote Nelson to Mr William Marsden,
Secretary to the Admiralty, on 15 August 1804,

'It is with much uneasiness of mind that I feel it my
duty to state to you, for the information of their
Lordships, that I consider my state of health to be
such as to make it absolutely necessary that I should
return to England to re-establish it. Another winter,
such as the last, I feel myself unable to stand against.
A few months of quiet may enable me to serve again
next spring; and I believe that no Officer is more
anxious to serve than myself...'

Just over a month later, on 29 September,
Nelson entered his forty-seventh year, which was
to bring him both to the pinnacle and to the end
of his career.[7] His genius, acknowledged by his
country and his profession (including the French
who had to meet him), was about to be put to its
severest test. In his own words: 'to be burnt in

effigy or Westminster Abbey is my alternative.'
It is hard, sometimes, considering the brilliant
flashes that illuminated his career, to avoid the
impression that from the moment he went to sea
at the age of twelve Westminster Abbey was his
objective.[8] At seventeen he was an acting
lieutenant, the rank being confirmed the following
year; when still under twenty-one he was a
post-captain. Ten years of peace and the inevitable
naval retrenchment saw him for some years on
half-pay, but when war broke out with
Revolutionary France in 1793 he was given a ship
of the line, the *Agamemnon*, at the age of
thirty-five. Three years later he hoisted the broad
pennant of a commodore. In 1797, aged thirty-
nine, he captured two Spanish ships at the Battle
of Cape St Vincent, and was promoted to rear-
admiral. In 1798 he won the overwhelming
victory of the Nile, and 1801 saw him promoted
to vice-admiral; in April of that year he won
another crushing victory at Copenhagen, and in
May became commander-in-chief in the Baltic,
receiving the title of Viscount Nelson of the Nile
and Burnham Thorpe. As we have seen, 1803
was the year in which he 'entered upon his
inheritance'[9] – the command-in-chief in the
Mediterranean.

At every stage a halo of ardour seems to shine
around him. He was, says General Fuller, 'the
greatest fighting admiral England has ever had' –
and he wore on his body, like decorations, the
scars that proved it. Always eager for battle, and
always in the front of it, he inspired officers and
men by his example – and paid the price. In 1794,
commanding an exposed battery at the siege of
Calvi in Corsica, he lost the sight of his right eye;
in 1797, once more leading a landing party in the
attack on Santa Cruz in Tenerife, he lost his
right arm; at the Battle of the Nile, in the following
year, he received a wound on the forehead from
which he thought he would die. All these injuries,
sustained by a frame that had never been robust,
which had barely survived the terrible sicknesses
of the West Indies, and which was constantly
racked by the seasickness which he never over-
came, played havoc with his constitution, but
never, in any degree, daunted his spirit.

The spiritual side of Nelson, that ineluctable
quality which adds love to respect – the quality,

for example, which distinguishes him from that admirable sailor, kindly commander and good friend of his, Collingwood – a quality without which leadership can rarely inspire, has always appealed to the popular imagination. Generation after generation, not only in Britain, has taken fire at the tale of Nelson's exploits; long after his death, he is still a leader of men. Women too, intrigued by the passion of his affair with Emma, Lady Hamilton, and by the curious mixture of flamboyance and pathos, deep affection on the one hand, and clear unkindness (towards Lady Nelson) on the other, which are its ingredients, have always responded to the idea of Nelson, expressed in poetry, fiction, plays or films, as to no other admiral. Fortunately, there have been a number of writers, naval and others, who have made it their business to penetrate the clouds of satisfying sentiment to the cool professional sailor at the centre.

It comes to the average British reader as something of a shock to encounter the reverse image of Nelson. A recent French writer on the Battle of Trafalgar calls him 'un Anglais, froid, dur, cruel et résolu'.[1] 'Un Anglais'? Certainly, in the sense that he was born in the parish of Burnham Thorpe in Norfolk, of parents whose respectable but not exalted stock was unquestionably English; but this was an Englishman far removed from the hearty, extrovert, stiff-upper-lip traditions of the shires, soon to be enshrined in the nineteenth-century public schools; an Englishman whose marital and emotional life revealed attitudes also very far distant from those of the middle class which was soon to place its stamp on succeeding generations. The 'unEnglishness' of Horatio Nelson is nowhere better displayed than in his dying request, 'Kiss me, Hardy', and the efforts of so many of his embarrassed fellow countrymen to explain it away, even to the point of pretending that what he actually said was 'Kismet, Hardy'! No; the fact is that Nelson was most unlike the majority of the Englishmen who came after him. Bravery aside, he was decidedly not what they would mostly have wished their sons to be. But Englishmen of the age of Shakespeare and Marlowe would have recognized him as one of themselves easily enough.

'Froid, dur, cruel'; again, it jolts the English

reader, even the informed student of Nelson, to see him described as 'cold', 'hard' or 'cruel'. Yet consideration shows that these epithets have their truth. We think of the Nelson fretted to illness by inactivity, burning for action, pouring out his heart to Emma: 'I love you most dearly; and hate the French most damnably.' Cold? We think of the great affection with which he habitually spoke of his colleagues, his subordinates, his sailors. In his first command, the frigate *Albemarle*, he writes: 'I have an exceeding good ship's company. Not a man or officer in her I would wish to change.' And in the *Agamemnon*: 'We are all well; indeed, nobody can be ill with my ship's company, they are so fine a set.' We remember the most famous saying of all, after the Battle of the Nile: 'I had the happiness to command a band of brothers . . . *My friends* readily conceived my plan.' Hard? Cruel?

But the other side of this character, of which the French were mostly aware, and which they could best appreciate, is expressed in sayings of a quite different order. When all the glamour that surrounds so many of his actions is stripped away, we find a single principle. As Mahan says, '. . . the only sure guide to a man's feet is principle; and Nelson's principle was the destruction of the French fleet.' 'The destruction of the French fleet': the French would have known well how cold and iron-hard that determination was within him. Mahan continues: 'No other interest, his own least of all, could divert him from it. For it he was willing not only to sacrifice fortune, but to risk renown; and so, amid troubles manifold, he walked steadfastly in the light of the single eye.'

It was not a Nelson filled with loving kindness that the French perceived waiting for them outside Toulon, or in the last act of all outside Cadiz. It was the man who could frame the words: 'It is, as Mr. Pitt knows, annihilation that the country wants, and not merely a splendid victory of twenty-three to thirty-six. Numbers only can annihilate.' This is no Shakespearean Henry V,[10] crying 'wish not a man from England . . . do not wish one more!' This is a professional, an admiral who describes himself as '*very, very, very* anxious for the arrival of the force which is intended' because he means to annihilate, and only numbers will do it. This was the commander who, sending off two of his frigates to cruise together in October 1804, gave the captains special instructions,

'. . . in case they should get an opportunity of attacking two of the French frigates, which now got under weigh more frequently. The principal one was, that they should not each single out and attack an opponent, but "that both should endeavour together to take *one frigate*; if successful, chase the other; but if you do not take the second, still you have won a victory, and your country will gain a frigate." Then, half laughing, and half snappishly, said kindly to them as he wished them good-bye, "I daresay you consider yourselves a couple of fine fellows, and when you get away from me you will do nothing of the sort, but think yourselves wiser than I am!" 'm

How Nelson himself would have behaved in such circumstances is not open to any doubt. At the Battle of the Nile, in 1798, he faced a French fleet of thirteen ships of the line (which included a first-rate of 120 guns and three eighties) with thirteen seventy-fours. His tactic, as tersely described by him to Lord Howe, was simple: 'By attacking the Enemy's van and centre, the wind blowing directly along their Line, I was enabled to throw what fire I pleased on a few ships.' The French were crushed by superior force at every stage, with the result that only two of their thirteen ships of the line escaped, and only two of the four frigates which accompanied them. Thirteen ships were sunk or taken out of seventeen; no British ship was lost; 5,225 Frenchmen were captured, killed or missing, compared with a total British loss of 218 killed and 677 wounded: that was what Nelson meant by 'annihilation'. And that was the medicine he intended to dispense again, from the moment he took up station outside Toulon in July 1803 until he made his last signal, 'Engage the enemy more closely', on 21 October 1805. Small wonder that he seems 'cruel' in French eyes.

There remains 'résolu', and on the subject of Nelson's resoluteness there is no quarrel between French and British. This quality in him was perhaps best illustrated by a phrase first uttered in June 1798, amid all the frustrations of his search for the fleet that he was going to smash at the Nile. He wrote to Lord Spencer, First Lord of the Admiralty: '. . . be they bound for the Antipodes your Lordship may rely that I will not lose a moment in bringing them to action . . .'

The phrase recurs. In August 1803 there is a report that the French are about to sail from Toulon for an unknown destination. Nelson tells the Prime Minister: 'I shall follow them to the Antipodes.' He issues orders to his captains accordingly, and tells one of them: '. . . I am determined to follow them, go where they may . . .' A year later, in September 1804, we find his resolution still unfaltering: 'Whatever may be their destination, I shall certainly follow, be it even to the East Indies.' Admiral Mahan, in his biography, comments on this last: 'The splendid decision, formulated so long before the case arose, to follow wherever they went, held in its womb the germ of the great campaign of Trafalgar . . .' But clearly it held much more than that: the fact that Nelson's mind was working in that manner as far back as a previous war shows that in this resoluteness of purpose we may find the germ of his genius itself, the essence of the 'Nelson touch'. By making the enemy's fleet his permanent objective, Nelson places himself in the ranks of the great offensive commanders. By resoluteness he imposed his will upon his foes, beginning their physical annihilation by defeating them in spirit long before a gun was fired. 'Résolu': agreed.

All the resolution, all the cold, hard, cruel determination to annihilate, all the ardour for battle and passion in combat, might yet have come to nothing. Chance might have nullified it all, as Nelson knew only too well – 'nothing is sure in a Sea Fight beyond all others'. In 1798 the chance of a great storm had robbed him of all his frigates just when he needed them to find the enemy; the chance of bad visibility permitted him to cross the track of a fleet and convoy of 400 sail without knowing they were there; chance brought him to Alexandria before the French, so that he had to go all the way back to Sicily to look for them and then back again to Alexandria. Chances like that leave their mark on a man's very soul.[11] As the action develops in 1805, we shall see Nelson, haunted by the memory of so much mischance, operating not by the 'inspired daring' that is generally thought to be his chief characteristic, but by a 'sober calculation' whose object was to remove the element of chance from the whole campaign as far as that could ever be possible.

No man is perfect; Nelson certainly had his defects. A hasty temper was often noted in him, a liability to flare up, and an impatience at contradiction. At times we find him giving way to spasms of self-pity and each winter drew from him protests at his failing health: 'My heart . . . is warm, my head is firm, but my body is unequal to my wishes. I am visibly shook; but as long as I can hold out, I shall never abandon my truly honourable post.' We have already noted the extraordinary degree of his dislike of foreigners, summed up in one of the most sweeping denunciations ever penned: 'The Powers on the Continent are a dirty set of fellows . . .'[12] In the case of the French this dislike turned into a hatred which, in this respect at any rate, shows a mind definitely unbalanced: 'I never trust a Corsican or a Frenchman. I would give the devil ALL the good ones to take the remainder.' 'God knows I only serve to fight those scoundrels . . .' And the reason for all this ferocity? 'Forgive me, but my mother hated the French.'

That Nelson's tense, nervous, highly strung dispostion did unbalance him in more ways than one is certain; there was a decided element of schizophrenia in him. Many people noted, with dislike, his vanity and egotism, and the most luminous reference to these attributes comes from no less a man than his most distinguished contemporary, the Duke of Wellington. The one occasion on which the two great commanders actually met was in September 1805, shortly before Nelson sailed on his last campaign; the scene was a little waiting room at the Colonial Office (then in Downing Street) where both had business with the Secretary of State. Nelson was famous, and Wellington – then Major-General Sir Arthur Wellesley – had no difficulty in recognizing him. Wellington's own fame was only just beginning to resound, and his face was not yet familiar to many of his fellow countrymen. He told Mr Croker, an indefatigable diarist and collector of anecdotes, in 1834:

'He could not know who I was, but he entered at once into conversation with me, if I can call it conversation, for it was almost all on his side, and all about himself, and in, really, a style so vain and silly as to surprise and almost disgust me. I suppose something that I happened to say may have made him guess that I was

somebody, and he went out of the room for a moment, I have no doubt to ask the office-keeper who I was, for when he came back he was altogether a different man, both in manner and matter. All that I had thought a charlatan style had vanished, and he talked of the state of this country and the aspect and probabilities of affairs on the Continent with a good sense, and a knowledge of subjects both at home and abroad, that surprised me equally and more agreeably than the first part of our interview had done; in fact he talked like an officer and a statesman.'

Wellington remarked that it was fortunate that the Secretary of State had not been punctual, since if he had been, 'I should have had the same impression of a light and trivial character that other people have had, but luckily I saw enough to be satisfied that he was really a very superior man; but certainly a more sudden and complete metamorphosis I never saw.'[n]

So it is by a study of contrasts and opposites, not by following a single consistent thread, that we approach an understanding of Nelson. There is great warmth – and icy determination; there is great love – and fierce hatred; there is great affection – and great prejudice; there is unquestioned vanity – and unsparing dedication to duty and to his country (reflected even in the last words to pass his lips[13]). On Nelson as a professional sea warrior, we may leave the final statement to Mahan: 'No man ever was served better than Nelson by the inspiration of the moment; no man ever counted on it less.'

December 1804 found Nelson, if not in a low state of morale, at any rate in a high state of disgust. His application for leave, coinciding with the virtual certainty of war with Spain, had posed a problem for the Admiralty; of the Spanish complication, Nelson, of course, was unaware; but he did know that he was causing some difficulty. What he hoped was that his post would be held open for him while he was taking his leave, with his able second-in-command, Sir Richard Bickerton, as acting commander-in-chief. But Nelson knew that it would not be easy for the Admiralty to adopt this course. One of his captains tried to reassure him, but 'I do not think so, for they are so beset by Admirals. Sir John

'An ominous name'; Sir John Orde, Nelson's 'bête-noire', appointed to command the 'Spanish Squadron' in October 1804

Orde, I am told, is likely . . .'[14] This was an ominous name; Vice-Admiral Sir John Orde was senior to Nelson; he had hoped to command the squadron that fought the Nile in 1798; Nelson firmly believed that Orde still held a grudge against him on that account, though in fact the opposite was probably the case. Now, in December, he learned that Orde had been appointed to command a new squadron, and that his own sphere of command was accordingly diminished.

Until the end of 1804 the Mediterranean command stretched up to Cape Finisterre, where it met the Western Squadron area. There was clear logic in including the great Spanish arsenal and port of Cadiz, and above all Gibraltar, the most important British base, in the responsibilities of the Mediterranean admiral. It is not at once easy to see why, in October 1804, the Admiralty decided to create a new 'Spanish Squadron' working between Gibraltar and Ferrol, and it is equally puzzling that they should have appointed Sir John Orde to command it, in view of the previous difficulty between him and Nelson. In fact, however, the latter puzzle is probably the easier to solve: Orde was now professing great admiration for Nelson – he was a pall-bearer at Nelson's funeral – and at such a distance Lord Melville and his colleagues may be forgiven for not realizing that Nelson's feelings had not softened in the same way. In any case, Nelson had asked for leave, which had been granted, so any friction there might be would soon be over. As regards the setting up of the new command itself, that too can probably be best explained by reference to Nelson's leave. The likelihood is that as soon as Nelson had come home Orde would have been appointed commander-in-chief, and the Mediterranean station restored to its original scope.

For the time being, however, nothing but mischief could come from the division of responsibility and the clash of personalities. What particularly galled Nelson, and brought out one of the less pleasing sides of his character (while at the same time illustrating the evils of a bad naval practice), was that, in Mahan's words, 'Orde thus got the station for prize-money, and Nelson that for honour . . .'[15] As Nelson put it: 'He is sent off Cadiz to reap the golden harvest, as Campbell

The Rochefort squadron got away first'; a view of
Rochefort by the painter Joseph Vernet

was to reap my sugar harvest. It's very odd, two
Admiralties to treat me so: surely I have dreamt
that I have "done the State some service." But
never mind; I am superior to those who would
treat me so.'[16] And a little later: 'I have learnt
not to be surprised at anything; but the sending
an officer to such a point, to take, if it is a Spanish
war, the whole harvest, after all my trials (God
knows unprofitable enough! for I am a much
poorer man than when we started in the *Amphion*,)
seems a little hard; but patienza.'[17]

Disgusted by the arrival of Orde, sick and
depressed ('I am but very, very so-so. My cough,
if not removed, will stay by me for ever'), waiting
only to go home, Nelson also suffered particularly
at this time from the inevitable sense of isolation
that afflicted officers on distant stations. He wrote
to Hugh Elliot, British Minister at Naples, on
19 December: 'It is now ninety days since I have
heard from England; it is rather long at these
critical times.' Such were the communication
difficulties of the days of sail. By the same token,

it was not until Christmas Day that Nelson received the Admiralty letter of 6 October, granting him the leave he had requested on 15 August. He replied on 30 December: 'I am much obliged by their Lordships' kind compliance with my request, which is absolutely necessary from the present state of my health, and I shall avail myself of their Lordships' permission, the moment another Admiral, in the room of Admiral Campbell,[18] joins the Fleet, unless the Enemy's Fleet should be at sea, when I should not think

of quitting my Command until after the Battle.'

He never took the long awaited, much desired leave, because the enemy's fleet was at last about to put to sea, and the action which he had also so much desired was about to commence.

Action, pending the refitting of the Spanish ships, would develop along the lines of Napoleon's latest plan[19] – the attack on the West Indies. With a propaganda sense that anticipates a later age, and also, no doubt, with a view to testing out the diplomatic ground, he made an offer of peace directly to King George III. The British answer, signed not by the king but by the Secretary of State, and carefully refraining from addressing Napoleon by his new imperial title, was a curt refusal to negotiate except in conjunction with associated powers, especially Russia. It gave Napoleon an opportunity for public bluster, but the hypocrisy of this is apparent when we note that his orders for the attack on the West Indies went out a week *before* the peace offer.

It was the Rochefort squadron, under Rear-Admiral Missiessy, that got away first, and the story of its escape from Rochefort is a miniature of the tribulations of the various blockades throughout the winters of their discontent. Missiessy's squadron (the 120-gun three-decker *Majestueux*, four 74s, three 40-gun frigates and two brig-corvettes) came out on 11 January 1805. The wind (easterly) was at first favourable, but the weather thick, with snow, and the wind shifting to south-westerly and rising to gale force. Rear-Admiral Sir Thomas Graves, with a detachment of the Western Squadron, was watching Rochefort and the coast as far down as the mouth of the Gironde. It was almost impossible, at this time of the year, to take in supplies at sea, and Graves had had to take his squadron to Quiberon Bay, on the south side of the Brittany peninsula, for water, leaving the frigate *Doris* (Captain Patrick Campbell) to watch Missiessy. On 8 January Campbell had looked into Rochefort and seen Missiessy embarking troops. At once he set out to inform Graves, fortunately meeting the schooner *Felix*, which was able to give him the admiral's position, and herself continue the watch on Rochefort.

The *Doris* sped towards Quiberon on the swelling wind, with damage to her rigging which simply had to be endured – only to find that Graves had gone. Trying to beat out of the treacherous waters of Quiberon Bay to find him, she ran onto a rock. By tremendous efforts at the pumps, the leaks were brought under control, and then in came the *Felix*, with more news of the French squadron. She had seen them flying northwards in front of the gale, also badly battered by it. Now the urgent matter was to try to stop Graves coming back into the bay as he would normally do for refuge, because once in he would never get out while this wind held. But the *Doris* was too badly damaged, despite all Campbell's efforts, to fight the gale; he had to anchor, and two days later the *Doris* foundered, all hands being saved by the *Felix*. Now it was the schooner's turn to try to head Graves off; as soon as he appeared, on the 16th, she signalled that Missiessy was at sea. It was still the wind that prevailed: Graves saw the signal and tried to turn back, but the force of the gale was too much for him. He too had to anchor. Further north, Cornwallis also had been driven off the Ushant station by this storm, and was sheltering in Plymouth. And so Missiessy, damaged but determined, got clean away on his run to Martinique, and the intricate drama of 1805 began.

Nelson, as the year opened, was at his rendezvous 97, off Cape San Sebastian; on 3 January he sailed for his victualling place, the Madalena Islands. He had with him two 100-gun first-rates, the *Victory* and the *Royal Sovereign*, one 80 and eight 74s. The two 38-gun frigates, *Active* and *Seahorse* – all that he could muster in this part of the Mediterranean – kept a close watch on Toulon. Inside that port, Vice-Admiral Villeneuve, who had succeeded Latouche Tréville, was awaiting his chance to carry out Napoleon's orders. His squadron contained no first- or second-rates, but included four 80s and seven 74s, giving him numerical equality to Nelson in ships of the line, with no less than seven frigates. For a fortnight the wind veered between north-east and south-east, good quarters for a run to Gibraltar, but not sufficiently strong, in Villeneuve's opinion, to offer a good chance of escape. On 17 January the wind shifted towards the north-west, the

prevailing quarter at that season for the Gulf of Lions, and began to freshen for a gale. Villeneuve decided that the time had come to make a dash; and so at last, after twenty weary months, the French emerged from Toulon.

It was late afternoon by the time the whole French squadron was out, and at 6.30 p.m. its leading division was sighted by the *Active* and the *Seahorse*. All through the 18th the British frigates kept their enemy in sight, and at 1.50 p.m. on the 19th they were sufficiently close to Nelson at 'Agincourt Sound'[20] in the Madalena Islands to make a distant signal that the French were at sea. This was the moment that Nelson had been waiting for, at such cost to health and nerves, for such an unconscionable time, and now that it had come it found him more than ready. Though in the midst of victualling, in just over two and a half hours the whole British fleet was in motion, the *Victory* leading through the narrow channel that led to the eastern side of Sardinia. Everything – the course the French were steering when last seen, and the direction and strength of the wind – pointed in only one direction: '. . . from all I have heard from the Captains of the Frigates, the Enemy must be bound round the South end of Sardinia, but whether to Cagliari, Sicily, the Morea, or Egypt, I am most completely in ignorance. I believe they have six or seven thousand Troops on board . . .'[21] Nelson accordingly set a course for Cape Carbonara, at the southern tip of Sardinia. The British ships were at first sheltered by the island on their starboard beam, but as they pressed southwards they began to encounter hard gales from the south-west. The *Seahorse*, sent ahead to look for the enemy, was chased by a French 40-gun frigate in the Gulf of Cagliari, but in any case the weather was by now so thick that she could see nothing until she was on top of it. On the 22nd she rejoined Nelson to report that contact with the enemy was effectively lost; the first of the periods of terrible uncertainty which 1805 was to supply in brimming measure had begun.

'What would I give to know where they are bound to, or to see them!' wrote Nelson on 22 January. But the next three days were full of frustration, as his two frigates searched in vain for the vanished enemy. 'God knows their intentions! perhaps it may be Egypt again,' he

'Action would develop along the lines of
Napoleon's latest plan'. Left: Napoleon's Minister
of Marine, Decrès. Right: Vice-Admiral Pierre
Villeneuve, commanding at Toulon

wrote on the 25th, and on the same day, 'I am in
a fever. God send I may find them!' The next day
he received encouraging but not enlightening
news: the frigate *Phoebe* rejoined and reported
that she had seen a French 80-gun ship dismasted
and crippled at Ajaccio in Corsica. But where
were the rest of them? Nelson's quandary was
certainly increased (and his solution to it partly
dictated) by misinformation about the number of
soldiers aboard Villeneuve's ships. Six or seven
thousand men indicated 'a destination of
importance'; had he known that Villeneuve was
only carrying half as many, he would almost

certainly have behaved differently. As it was,
Nelson could only consult the three prompters of
all commanders in times of serious doubt: their
experience, their common sense – and their
instructions. With the French at sea, and all winds
foul for a westward passage, the key instruction
was: '. . . to afford to the Sublime Porte . . . any
protection or assistance which may be in your
power . . .'[22] By 29 January his mind was made
up; he wrote to the Admiralty:

'One of two things must have happened, that either
the French Fleet must have put back crippled, or that
they are gone to the Eastward, probably to Egypt,
therefore, I find no difficulty in pursuing the line of
conduct which I have adopted. If the Enemy have put
back crippled, I could never overtake them, and
therefore I can do no harm in going to the Eastward;
and if the Enemy are gone to the Eastward, I am
right.'

The next day the whole squadron passed through the Straits of Messina, heading east.

The action that now followed constitutes one of the most controversial episodes in Nelson's career, one about which he himself was certainly extremely sensitive. Very briefly, what happened was this: on 30 January Nelson passed Messina; on 2 February he was off Koroni in southern Greece, learning that the Morea was safe; on the 7th he was approaching Alexandria, and heard that the French were not there (just as well, since he also learned that Egypt was virtually defenceless); he at once turned back, and, after a twelve-day struggle with contrary winds, on the 19th found himself off Malta, where he learned that Villeneuve was back in Toulon after all.

The fact was that the French had only stayed out three days. It was the great gale of 20 January that brought their sortie to an end. Villeneuve described what happened in graphic terms to Decrès, Minister of Marine:

'My fleet looked well at Toulon, but when the storm came on, things changed at once. The sailors were not used to storms: they were lost among the mass of soldiers: these from sea-sickness lay in heaps about the decks: it was impossible to work the ships: hence yard-arms were broken and sails were carried away: our losses resulted as much from clumsiness and inexperience as from defects in the materials delivered by the arsenals.'

Villeneuve, whatever his faults (and we shall see them in full operation before long), was a professional sailor; he added: 'I had a presentiment of this before I sailed; I have now only too painfully experienced it.' His master, Napoleon, chose to believe that the British squadrons would be worn out by the rigours of their blockade stations, while his own would steadily improve in port. He could not understand why it was not so, and was furious when he heard that Villeneuve had returned. 'What is to be done,' he asked, 'with admirals who allow their spirits to sink, and determine to hasten home at the first damage they receive? All the captains ought to have had sealed orders to meet off the Canary Islands. The damages should have been repaired en route. A few topmasts carried away, some casualties in a gale of wind, are every-day occurrences. But the great evil of our Navy is, that the men who command it are unused to all the risks of command.'o The 'great evil' of the French navy, had he but realized it, lay not in his commanders, but in the contrast of professionalism that enabled Nelson to report to the Admiralty, having endured the same weather not for three days, but for over thirty: 'The Fleet under my command is in excellent good health, and the Ships, although we have experienced a great deal of bad weather, have received no damage, and not a yard or mast sprung or crippled, or scarcely a sail split.'23

The fact nevertheless remains that Nelson had spent practically three weeks pursuing the French in a direction opposite to that in which they had intended to go, and almost equally divergent from the direction in which they were forced to go. There is no doubt that when he heard that they were not in Alexandria he was badly shaken; 1798 was repeating itself all too dismally. He became very defensive about his movements; on 11 February he wrote to Ball at Malta:

'Although I have not yet heard of the French Fleet, and remain in total ignorance where they are got to, yet to this moment I am more confirmed in my opinion, from communicating with Alexandria, that Egypt was the destination of the French Armament from Toulon; and when I call all the circumstances I know at this moment, I approve (if nobody else does) of my own conduct, in acting as I have done.'

The following day he wrote to the Admiralty Secretary: '. . . I have not the smallest doubt but that the destination of the French Armament which left Toulon the 17th, and the Coast of France the 18th January was Alexandria . . .' Two days later, on 14 February, he felt constrained to explain to Lord Melville himself the reasons for his reaching that conclusion:

'Feeling, as I do, that I am entirely responsible to my King and Country for the whole of my conduct, I find no difficulty at this moment, when I am so unhappy at not finding the French Fleet, nor having obtained the smallest information where they are, to lay before you the whole of the reasons which induced me to pursue the line of conduct I have done. I have consulted no man, therefore the whole blame of ignorance in forming my judgment must rest with me. I would allow no man to take from me an atom of my glory, had I fallen in with the French Fleet, nor do I desire any man to partake of the responsibility – all is mine, right or wrong.'

And then he gives his reasoning in detail.[24]

Nelson never knew how completely wrong he had been; it was bad enough for him that he had not perceived the return to Toulon. Frankly, it never occurred to him that so great an opponent as Napoleon would fritter away his resources in expeditions against colonial islands; and we shall see that Napoleon did not long hold that intention. Nelson was definitely misled by the wrong information he had received about the size of the French military expedition. Undoubtedly the memories of 1798 were actively revived within him with unfortunate effect. Yet, when all is said and done, he had nothing to reproach himself with; his defence was sure. Against the gale then blowing it was literally impossible for the French to make Gibraltar. What else could they have done? They could have tried Sardinia; he was there to meet them. They could have tried Sicily; he was very close, and bound to find them. They could have gone back to Toulon – crippled. Or they could have gone east; it would have been a dereliction of his duty not to find out if they had done so. It was a job for frigates – but he had none. So we may sum it all up by saying that it was only their lack of seamanship and their damage that saved the French; as Nelson said: 'Had they not been crippled, nothing could have hindered our meeting them on January 21st, off the South end of Sardinia. Ever since, we have been prepared for Battle: not a bulk-head up in the Fleet. Night or day, it is my determination not to lose one moment in attacking them.'[25] To Lady Hamilton Nelson confessed 'that nothing can be more miserable, or unhappy, than your poor Nelson'. But his offensive spirit was undiminished – whetted, rather; and their whole wretched experience went some distance towards establishing in his opponents that sense of inferiority which haunted them for the rest of the campaign.

Footnotes
Ch III
1 Nelson to Hugh Elliot, 8 July 1804.
2 11 April 1805.
3 Nelson to Hugh Elliot, 18 June 1804.
4 Nelson to Sir Evan Nepean, Admiralty, 30 July 1803.
5 Nelson to Rt Hon. Henry Addington, 10 August 1803.
6 Nelson to Captain John Gore, H.M.S. *Medusa*, 13 October 1804.
7 At Waterloo, in 1815, Wellington was also in his forty-seventh year, while Napoleon was reaching the end of his forty-sixth.
8 One is reminded of the French First World War flying 'ace', Georges Guynemer, of whom it was said that it was 'his vocation to become one of the illustrious dead' – at twenty-three. Nelson is, in fact, in Westminster Abbey, in wax effigy, but his tomb is in St Paul's Cathedral.
9 See pp. 39–40.
10 Though *Henry V* was Nelson's favourite play, and gave him the phrase 'band of brothers'.
11 Nelson to the Duke of Clarence (later William IV), 15 October 1803: 'I am actually only now recovering the shock of missing them in 1798.'
12 24 August 1804.
13 See p. 159.
14 Nelson to Sir Alexander Ball, 22 October 1804.
15 Orde, as admiral commanding the station, was beneficiary of the capture of the Spanish treasure ships.
16 To Ball, 5 December 1804.
17 To Elliot, 19 December 1804.
18 Rear-Admiral George Campbell, Nelson's third-in-command, who had gone home on sick leave.
19 See p. 45.
20 Named after H.M.S. *Agincourt*, which discovered the anchorage.
21 Nelson to Sir John Acton, 22 January 1805.
22 See p. 40.
23 To William Marsden, 22 February 1805.
24 See Appendix A, p. 204.
25 Nelson to Alexander Davison, 11 March 1805. Bulkheads are the partitions of the gun-decks which formed cabins, offices, etc.; they were taken down when battle was imminent, to allow freer communication, and to lessen fire risks.

4. THE OFFENSIVES DEVELOP

North Sea

Cork

Yarmouth
Texel
Portsmouth
Chatham
Dover
Utrecht
Scilly Is.
Lizard pt.
Plymouth
Folkestone
Ostend
Hanover
Ushant
Dunkirk
Calais
Brest
Boulogne
Quiberon
Lorient
Paris

Cape Finisterre
Bay of Biscay
Rochefort
Bordeaux
Ferrol
Corunna
Vigo

Ulm
Munich
Austerlitz
Vienna

Lyon
Milan
Toulon
Genoa

Lisbon

Barcelona
Rendezvous 97
Cape St Vincent
Lagos

Cartagena
Mediterranean Sea
Magdalena Is.
Toro I.
Ustica I.
Palermo
Naples
Taranto
Corfu
Constantinople

Messina Straits
The Morea
Malta
Alexandria

See Inset

Inset:
Cape Santa Maria
Cadiz
Cape Trafalgar
Tarifa **Gibraltar**
Cape de Gata
Tangier **Tetuan**
Cape Spartel

Villeneuve, with the larger part of Napoleon's raiding force – for that is really all that it amounted to – was back in Toulon; and Missiessy reached Martinique on 20 February, but for all the good he was to do in the West Indies he might as well have stayed at home. Even with a strong force of soldiers aboard and with the advantage of surprise, French admirals ventured into the Caribbean like mice into a kitchen occupied by a ferocious cat. Missiessy's particular orders were to capture the British islands of Dominica and St Lucia, and to levy tributes on the smaller islands. In the event all that he managed to achieve was the taking of some £40,000 in prize and ransom money and the reinforcement of the French garrison of San Domingo, pressed to extremity by a revolt of the negroes of that island. In all, he spent less than six weeks in the West Indies occupied with these futilities, and seized the first chance he could to return to France: a despatch telling him of Villeneuve's failure, and ordering him to come home. He could not have known that this order had been countermanded, but there is nevertheless something almost indecent in the haste with which he left the West Indies after all the trouble of getting there. The ironies that beset Napoleon's maritime adventures are nowhere better illustrated than by Missiessy's reappearance in Rochefort, just one week *after* Villeneuve arrived in Martinique on his second attempt!

When we seek the reasons why Napoleon changed his plans yet again, they seem to be two: one negative, one positive. The negative reason is simply the inadequacy of mere colonial raiding after the grandiose preparations and boastful declarations with which the war had begun. Capturing Dominica and St Lucia was hardly to be compared with entering London and forcing the British government to sue for peace! The positive reason was the approaching readiness of the Spanish fleet – approaching faster than previous experience of Spanish lethargy had allowed it to seem possible. By the end of February Napoleon felt so far encouraged as to send to Missiessy the order to remain in the West Indies that the admiral did not wait to receive. On 2 March he issued his new set of orders to all squadrons for the next phase of the campaign.

Once more Napoleon determined upon an invasion of England, and although he had learned little about naval warfare during the last two years, one thing at least had become clear to him: that he would have to control the Channel, at least for a time.[1] The accession of strength from Spain at last offered a chance of achieving that, and the new plan was framed accordingly. In one sentence, it was this: to unite all the French squadrons, together with as many Spanish ships as were ready, in the West Indies, and return to the Channel in overwhelming strength. One sentence, however, does not encompass the complexities contained in this idea.

At the centre of it was Ganteaume's fleet in Brest; his twenty-one ships of the line were the main fleet of France, and although he was junior to Villeneuve it was Ganteaume who was intended to take the united command. Ganteaume was ordered to go first to Ferrol, where he would collect the five French ships of the line blockaded there (plus Spaniards) and if possible destroy the British squadron. Then he was to go to Martinique to meet Missiessy with five more ships of the line and Villeneuve with eleven from Toulon and one more from Cadiz, again with an unspecified number of Spaniards. This would give him no less than forty-three French battleships alone, and with luck a combined fleet of over fifty – enough, Napoleon considered, to thrust aside the British at Ushant, and establish complete superiority in the Boulogne area some time between 10 June and 10 July. Even if for some reason the Toulon squadron failed to appear, Ganteaume was still to make the attempt on the Channel, unless his squadron should, by some adversity, be reduced to less than twenty-five in which case he was to go to Ferrol, where every available French and Spanish ship would concentrate to reinforce him. Villeneuve, for his part, was ordered to wait forty days for Ganteaume in the West Indies; if he did not arrive the Toulon-Cadiz-Rochefort fleet would go to the Canaries, wait there another twenty days, then return to Cadiz to receive further orders.

It requires no strategic genius to see that this 'grand combination' was riddled with dubious quantities. Above all, once more, it ignored the existence of the Royal Navy, as though Napoleon's mind balked at that subject, as though he could not bring himself to think clearly about this enemy. He never, for a moment, understood the strategic function of the Western Squadron or its place in the British naval system; nevertheless, he must have appreciated that Cornwallis would be doing *something* if Ganteaume came out of Brest. He must have known, also, that if Ganteaume did meet a British squadron and bring it to battle off Ferrol, even if he destroyed it, the damage to his own squadron would be considerable. He knew there were also British ships off Cadiz; what would *they* be doing? And Nelson? Villeneuve's last performance against him had been the reverse of impressive; even if he did escape this time, would Nelson just tamely let him go? Some French writers have been so struck by all these weaknesses that they refuse to believe in the whole thing: 'Such a plan would be unworthy both of Napoleon and his genius, if we could discover nothing deeper in it.'ᴾ The proposition is put forward that the entire scheme was simply a gigantic demonstration of the impossibility of invading Britain (now secretly recognized by Napoleon), framed in such a way that when disaster came it would 'merely' involve the loss 'in distant seas of mediocre squadrons', and the blame would fall on other heads than his, while he won himself new fame with dazzling victories on land. It is a theory in which hero-worship and hindsight mingle to produce their worst effects; it ignores Napoleon's vast vanity, so great that he could not recognize his invincible ignorance of the sea.

It was on the same day that he despatched his 'stand fast' order that Missiessy never received that Napoleon also ordered Rear-Admiral Gourdon, at Ferrol, to be ready to come out at short notice. This was now the station of Vice-Admiral Sir Robert Calder, with a detachment of six ships from the Western Squadron.² Calder soon became aware of the galvanizing of enemy naval activity which was the fruit of Napoleon's brainwave, and learned that Gourdon's squadron would be ready to sail on 22 March. Ganteaume and Villeneuve were also busy, as Napoleon's instructions reached them. On 26 March the first act of the revised drama began.

It was the fortune of war – an ill fortune – that

Admiral Cornwallis, worn out by the winter gales, was taking sick leave ashore. In his absence the Western Squadron was to be commanded by Admiral Lord Gardner, commander-in-chief at Cork. But Gardner had not yet arrived, and until he did so the squadron was in the hands of Admiral Sir Charles Cotton, Cornwallis's second-in-command. It is an invidious position, to be the locum tenens between two commanders-in-chief, and in the action that now followed Admiral Cotton was probably oppressed by a sense of obligation to hand over the fleet in sound condition. At any rate, an opportunity – albeit a slender one – of doing the French important damage was missed.

What happened was this. On 24 March Ganteaume had told Napoleon that he considered it impossible to come out of Brest without a battle, but that with twenty-one of the line (including three three-deckers) against Cotton's seventeen he also considered that 'Success is not doubtful. I await your Majesty's orders.' Unimpressed by the swagger, and with his mind fixed on his grand combination, Napoleon replied: 'A naval victory in existing circumstances can lead to nothing. Keep but one end in view – to fulfil your mission. Get to sea without an action.' The only way of doing this was to escape in darkness or bad weather when the British would not see him go. Ganteaume moved his fleet down to the Bertheaume anchorage at the mouth of Brest harbour to be ready for the dash on 26 March, and when the next morning dawned with fog and poor visibility he thought his chance had come. But just as the French fleet began to move, the fog lifted, and a brilliant March day showed the French lookouts the British squadron standing in at full strength.

Ganteaume was in a dilemma. The northerly wind which was bringing the British down upon him prevented him from returning to Brest; yet he was forbidden to fight. He ordered his fleet to anchor where it was, hoping that the British would be content to stand off and watch; but Cotton held his course. Time passed, and Ganteaume's anxieties grew; the British were not much more than five miles off, and if they caught him at anchor, as Nelson had caught the unfortunate Brueys in 1798, there could be another Battle of the Nile. He decided that he must disregard Napoleon's orders and form line of battle – although a closer view of the British fleet raised doubts about the issue which three days earlier he had airily dismissed. But the light was beginning to fade, and just as Ganteaume made his signal Cotton tacked and stood out to sea again, leaving Rear-Admiral Graves with a detachment to watch the French. Cotton's decision is understandable; these were dangerous waters for a fleet action in uncertain light, and by taking up a position further out he was quite confident that he would be able to intercept any French forward movement, while safeguarding his own ships. But the next morning the wind veered round, forcing Ganteaume to run back into Brest, where he remained – impotent, but undamaged.

So the first and largest part of Napoleon's new offensive soon ended, once more, in frustration. And precisely as it did so, the first part of the British counter-offensive began to receive animation. General Sir James Craig had been collecting a force near Portsmouth since the beginning of the year, for service in the Mediterranean. In March the cabinet began to consider its precise purposes, and by the 28th – the day Ganteaume retired into Brest – they were reaching their decisions. Craig's destination would be Malta; his main purpose would be to prevent Sicily from falling into French hands (one of Nelson's long-standing anxieties); he was also to have in mind the defence of Sardinia and Alexandria, if they should be attacked; finally,

'. . . if it should appear to you . . . that by co-operating with the force under your command, upon the continent of Italy, you can materially contribute to the safety of the dominions of the King of Naples, and forward the objects of the campaign, which may there be opened, his Majesty authorises you to concert with the Generals of his Allies, as to the most effectual manner of effecting that important end.'

Craig's expedition numbered only some 4,000 soldiers; added to those already in the Mediterranean, his force would amount to about 7,000. It was a very small army, compared with the vast hosts that Napoleon could deploy, but its significance was out of proportion to its size. Piers Mackesy says: 'The arrival of Craig's force would create a strategic reserve in the Mediter-

ranean, not primarily for continental operations, for which it was too small to be effective, but as one arm of our maritime strategy.' This expresses about half of the truth; Craig's force was, indeed, a strategic reserve, a welcome addition to Britain's maritime strategy for which Nelson had been pleading for nearly two years, but which had only now become possible. But it was much more than that, because the strategy itself had changed. Corbett says: 'The British fleet was no longer to be used merely for maritime operations. England bound herself to use it in furthering a vast continental war.' And Craig's expedition, to the extent that it contributed to that end, meant that Napoleon would face, not 7,000 enemy soldiers, but perhaps as many as half a million. In its implications, if not in its present might, Sir James Craig's force was something that Napoleon would have to take into account, and in the end we shall see how it contributed powerfully to the destruction of his fleet.

It was on the day that Ganteaume came down to the Bertheaume anchorage that Villeneuve also received peremptory orders to sail. Napoleon always had difficulty in accepting that, though he might command admirals, he could not command the wind, and it was not until four days later that Villeneuve actually emerged from Toulon, sailing south-south-west on a moderate north-east breeze.[3] The last he had heard of Nelson was that he was off Barcelona, which was daunting; 'If he maintains this position, I shall have great difficulty in reaching the Straits.' Yet he could not disobey Napoleon, so he set a course which, he hoped, would carry him well clear of Barcelona, round the southern side of the Balearic Islands. But the next day the wind shifted to north-north-west, and dropped, slowing the French fleet considerably,[4] and in the afternoon they were found by the frigates *Active* and *Phoebe*.

Where was Nelson, at this crisis of his life? What were his thoughts? His letters show him still deeply shaken by the deceptions and disappointments of January and February. His physical health had undoubtedly suffered. On 13 March he wrote to the Admiralty to say that as long as the possibility of the French coming out

of Toulon remained, he would defer his leave, but
if they seemed to be locked in for the summer,[5]
'I shall embrace their Lordships' permission and
return to England for a few months for the
re-establishment of a very shattered constitution.'
This was obviously a bad day for him; for he tells
Collingwood that 'my constitution is much shook'.
Another letter, to Alexander Davison, goes
further: 'I am useless if I die; and for what should
I?' England was much in his desires; the next day
he writes: 'My health is but so-so; and the
moment after the Battle, I shall go home for a
few months.' On the 16th: 'My wretched state of
health ought, long since, to have induced me to
go to England for its re-establishment: but I
could never bring myself to quit my post when
the Enemy was coming to sea.' And so he
continues, right up to 1 April: 'My health does
not improve; but, because I am not confined to
my bed, people will not believe my state of health.'

The question is, were his mind and judgment
equally affected? It is hard to resist the conclusion
that, to some extent, they were. The dash to
Egypt, and the long, hard haul back (and losses
inflicted on a merchant convoy in his absence) had
definitely left their mark. And while, as we have
seen, the decision to go to Egypt in January can
be easily justified, the defence of that decision
seems, by March, to have produced in him a
curious and dangerous rigidity. On 9 March he
wrote to Lord Melville: 'Everybody has an
opinion respecting the destination of the Enemy,
mine is more fully confirmed that it was Egypt:
to what other Country could they want to carry
saddles and arms?' So once again we see the baleful
influence of Nelson's false information about the
soldiers aboard Villeneuve's ships; they loomed
larger in his thoughts than the ships themselves.
The information itself, as falsehoods often are, was
horribly exact; on 27 March Nelson wrote to

Hugh Elliot at Naples: 'The original destination of the French Fleet, I am every day more and more confirmed, was Egypt. To what other Country should they carry 5,000 saddles, &c. &c., and flying artillery?'

And so it was with Egypt firmly lodged in his mind that he framed his new plans. The kernel of them is contained in a 'Most Secret Memoranda' (sic) of 11 March: 'I shall, if possible, make my appearance off Barcelona, in order to induce the Enemy to believe that I am fixed upon the Coast of Spain, when I have every reason to believe they will put to sea, as I am told the Troops are still embarked . . . I think Egypt is still their object.'

The ironies abound: Nelson believed that by letting himself be seen off Barcelona he would tempt Villeneuve out; in fact, had Napoleon's orders not been so peremptory, this would have been the very thing to hold Villeneuve in port. And Nelson's real point of concentration, as we shall see, was one which, Villeneuve once out and on his way to the West Indies, placed the British squadron at a severe disadvantage in bringing him to battle. So it is not difficult to criticize Nelson's strategy at this stage; it is necessary also to understand the reasons for his mistakes. His health provides one important clue, the precision of his information about Villeneuve's soldiers[6] another. There is also a third.

On 29 January Nelson was at Messina, just about to begin his ill-fated journey to Alexandria. On that same day, in a furious gale blowing off Cadiz, the sloop *Raven* was wrecked and sank; she was carrying mail and despatches for Sir John Orde, Nelson and Malta. We do not know what was in those despatches, but we do know what the loss meant to Nelson. It was not until 7 March that he heard of it: 'It is now from November 2nd that I have had a line from England.' Over four months! It is almost impossible for anyone in

'I have not the smallest doubt but that the
destination of the French . . . was Alexandria . . .'
Alexandria Harbour, more or less as Nelson knew it

modern times to imagine that degree of non-communication. Did the *Raven* carry the news that Missiessy had left Rochefort – a matter of immediate concern to Sir John Orde, and scarcely less to Nelson? If she did, the winds being what they were, it would have been no more than a week before the information reached Malta, in which case Nelson would have learned that Missiessy had come out at the same time that he learned that Villeneuve was back in Toulon – 19 February.[7] What would he have made of it? Would this knowledge have helped him towards a better idea of French intentions? It is hard to tell. The Admiralty itself did not even know whether Missiessy was still at sea or not, let alone his destination, until the end of the first week in February, so it could not have helped Nelson with specific information. He himself, when at last he did hear of Missiessy's escape, seems not to have been able to fit it into any comprehensive picture. His first reference to it is in his letter to Colling-wood on 13 March: 'I am told the Rochfort Squadron sailed the same day as that from Toulon.' Just that: his only comment is to the effect that Napoleon would now be knowing what

difficulties his fleet could meet at sea. And Nelson's only other reference to Missiessy is equally unhelpful; it is in a letter to Captain Sutton, of the frigate *Amphion*, one of those which had taken the Spanish treasure ships, and belonging to Sir John Orde's squadron: 'I think you will soon be drove off your Cruizing ground; the Rochfort Squadron will be with you before long, therefore make hay whilst the sun shines.'

For what purpose did Nelson suppose that Missiessy would be interfering with Sir John Orde? Did he really imagine that the French admiral would take all the risks and undergo all the hardships involved in his escape just to drive Orde off the Cadiz station? Unfortunately, Nelson's thinking on this subject is impenetrable. And, equally unfortunately, his plans were made before he even heard about Missiessy, let alone weighed him properly in the balance of factors affecting the campaign. He clung to the idea that Villeneuve's objective was Egypt; he offered the 'bait' of pretending to be at Barcelona; in reality he made for his rendezvous 98, the Gulf of Palmas at the south end of Sardinia, where he arrived by 26 March. Whatever the despatches

in the *Raven* may or may not have contained
one has the inescapable feeling that Nelson at this
time badly needed closer touch with the central
direction of the war, and if the loss of the sloop
did nothing else, it did much damage by depriving
him of that.

At eight o'clock in the evening of 31 March the
Phoebe set her course to bring Nelson the news
that the French were out. It took her four days to
reach him, on the morning of 4 April, and at three
o'clock that afternoon the *Active* also came in – to
say that she had lost the French fleet in the night.
Once more Nelson entered the shadowy world of
uncertainty and speculation, which is also a world
of icy loneliness.

Villeneuve had had a wonderful stroke of luck –
or rather, two strokes. He certainly must be
counted lucky to have thrown off an old campaigner
like the *Active* on the night of the 31st. Mahan
suggests that he had used the fresh night breeze
to make a long circuit in the dark before resuming
his course, and this is probably correct, though it
implies that he took the risk of scattering the
French squadron. At all events, it was with his
squadron well in hand and a happy absence of
British watchers that Villeneuve went on to enjoy
his second and larger piece of good fortune. On
the morning of 1 April he encountered a neutral
merchantman who informed him that she had
sighted the British fleet in the Gulf of Palmas. So
Nelson was not at Barcelona after all; there was
now no need to pass outside the Balearic Islands,
and Villeneuve accordingly set course round the
north of the islands, making first for Cartagena,
where there were six Spanish ships of the line. If
every one of his ships had instantly foundered, he
could not have vanished more effectively from
Nelson's view, and this disappearance lasted no
less than fifteen days.

Confident that the French would be bound for
the eastern Mediterranean, Nelson hastened to
place himself in their way. The channel between
Sardinia and North Africa is 140 miles wide, and
it was from a midway point in this channel that
Nelson addressed Lord Melville on 5 April:

'My dear Lord,
Although I feel so far comfortable that the French
Fleet is at sea, yet I must have a natural, and I hope a
laudable anxiety of mind, until I have the happiness
of seeing them. However, I have covered the Channel
from Barbary to Toro,[8] with Frigates and the Fleet.
The French could not pass before today, if this be
their route. *I must leave as little as possible to chance,*[9]
and I shall make sure they are to the Eastward of me,
before I risk either Sardinia, Sicily, or Naples; for they
may delay their time of coming even this distance,
from an expectation that I shall push for Egypt, and
thus leave them at liberty to act against Sardinia,
Sicily, or Naples. I have taken everything into my
most serious consideration; and although I may err
in my judgment, yet your Lordship may rely, that I
will do what I think is best for the honour of my King
and Country, and for the protection of his Majesty's
Allies. I will not say more. I am, &c.
Nelson and Brontë.'

This letter gives the clearest explanation of all
that followed. All Nelson's eagerness to meet the
French is there: the 'happiness' that was to be
denied him for over six months! But no eagerness
is allowed to overrule his responsibilities: hence,
'I must leave as little as possible to chance.' So he
places himself firmly at the centre of the
Mediterranean, and there he remains until his
doubts are one by one eliminated. 'I have taken
everything into my most serious consideration,'
he says – everything but one. It simply did not
occur to him that Villeneuve would leave the
Mediterranean; it was, as Corbett says, 'of all
dangers the least that could befall'.

The following days must have held, for Nelson,
a nightmarish quality. He wrote to Ball on 6 April:
'I am, in truth, half dead . . .' and in the same
letter: 'I am very uneasy and unwell; therefore,
I cannot write more.' And to Alexander Davison
on the same day he adds: 'I can neither eat, drink,
or sleep. It cannot last long what I feel . . .' It
must, at times, have seemed to him that everything was happening in slow motion. He had a
frigate at the island of Galita, off the African
coast; another on that coast itself, with a small
cruiser looking into Tunis; two more vessels at
Toro, a frigate inspecting the Straits of Bonifaccio,
in case the French had gone north-about round
Sardinia after all; another frigate on the way to
Naples. He himself was preparing to move to the
island of Ustica in the Tyrrhenian, north of
Palermo, a central point amidst all this activity.

'It must have seemed that everything was
happening in slow motion'; Nelson searches for
Villeneuve, April 1805

As each ship parted company, his hopes would go with it; as each returned, his heart would sink again: '*Ambuscade* is now in sight, but not having any signal flying, of course has seen nothing . . .' Always the same story: one disappointment after another. Yet always one thought firmly held; as he said to Ball: '. . . what man can do to find them out, shall be done; but I must not make more haste than good speed . . .'

The days passed. 'I am uneasy enough,' Nelson wrote to Hugh Elliot on 7 April, 'but I must bear it as well as I can. You must forgive a short letter; for I have nothing worth relating.' On the 10th, with every frigate searching, there was still no news of the French. There was news of something else, however – a fresh source of anxiety in the midst of so much. In a letter to Ball, Nelson wrote: 'I can hardly suppose that any Expedition would be sent to this Country, without my having some intimation, and I have not the most distant idea of such a thing. If they are sent, they will be taken, for the French know everything that passes in England. However, I can do no more than I have done, for I am sorely vexed at the ignorance in which I am kept.' This was Nelson's first expression of awareness that Sir James Craig's expedition even existed, let alone that it was already at sea. Almost at once the rumour was confirmed, and the implications swiftly presented themselves: '7 A.M. – Hallowell[10] is just arrived from Palermo. He brings accounts that the great Expedition is sailed, and that seven Russian Sail of the Line are expected in the Mediterranean; therefore I may suppose the French Fleet are bound to the Westward. I must do my best. God bless you. I am very, very miserable . . .'

Now the bad news began to come in fast; 16 April:

'We have a report from the Vessel spoke by the *Leviathan*, that the French Fleet (at least a Fleet) was seen on Sunday, the 7th April, off Cape de Gatte,[11] with the wind Easterly, steering to the Westward; therefore you must tell any Ships in search of me, that I am going to ascertain that the French Fleet is not in Toulon, and then proceed to the Westward, and this is all I can tell at present.'[12]

The decision to take one last look at Toulon, just in case, is probably the best example out of many

at this time of what Nelson meant by leaving 'as little as possible to chance'. It shows him, in spite of all his fevers and his miseries, firmly in control of himself. He needed certainty; for the time being there was only the dreadful possibility that, all unwittingly, he was permitting Craig's expedition to sail right into a powerful French fleet. 'If this account is true, much mischief may be apprehended. It kills me, the very thought.'[13] Two days later all doubts were at an end; a neutral reported having seen the French pass through the Straits of Gibraltar on 8 April. Nelson knew that once again he had been out-manoeuvred. There was only one thing to be done; he wrote to Hugh Elliot: 'I am going out of the Mediterranean after the French Fleet.' Sadly he felt constrained to add: 'It may be thought that I have protected too well Sardinia, Naples, Sicily, the Morea, and Egypt, from the French; but I feel I have done right, and am therefore easy about any fate which may await me for having missed the French Fleet.'

Once again, not surprisingly, he was on the defensive, and the effort to justify himself led him to strange conclusions. To the Admiralty he even suggested that it was because of him that the French had sailed westward: 'by my vigilance the Enemy found it was impossible to undertake any Expedition in the Mediterranean.' He was a long way yet from fathoming Villeneuve's movements or Napoleon's orders, but at least he was heading physically in the right direction – with difficulty. On 19 April he complained to Ball: 'My good fortune seems flown away. I cannot get a fair wind, or even a side wind. Dead foul! – dead foul! But my mind is fully made up what to do when I leave the Straits, supposing there is no certain information of the Enemy's destination . . .' In his lonely perplexity, it was the well-tried naval system itself that came to his help. He explained his intentions to the Admiralty on that same day, as the *Victory* and her consorts struggled against a north-west wind to win a little ground to westward:

'The circumstance of their having taken the Spanish Ships which were for sea, from Cadiz, satisfies my mind that they are not bound to the West Indies, (nor probably the Brazils;) but intend forming a junction with the Squadron at Ferrol, and pushing direct for Ireland or Brest, as I believe the French have Troops on board; therefore, if I receive no intelligence to do away my present belief, I shall proceed from Cape St. Vincent, and take my position fifty leagues from Scilly . . . My reason for this position is, that it is equally easy to get to either the Fleet off Brest, or to go to Ireland, should the Fleet be wanted at either station. I trust this plan will meet their Lordships' approbation . . .'

So, for the wrong reasons, he was going to do the right thing: he was going to close on the Western Squadron in the area of greatest danger, the very area that Napoleon had selected for the objective of his grand combination. Such was the strength of the naval system that even when the best of its servants went awry, it was there to bring them back on course – for, as we shall see, Nelson was not the only one in perplexity or peril.

As we leave him now, chafing against the foul winds that held him back, still mistaken about the destination of his enemies, but over the worst of his troubles nevertheless, we may note that none of these shocks and tribulations had in the slightest degree diminished his courtesy and generosity towards respected brother officers whom he believed to be more fortunate than himself, nor the offensive spirit which was always the mainspring of his actions. To Lord Gardner, now commanding the Western Squadron, he wrote, also on the 19th:

'My dear Lord,
If the Toulon Fleet, with that of Cadiz, is gone your road, the Ships under my command may be no unacceptable sight. If you do not want our help, tell us to go back again. I feel vexed at their slipping out of the Mediterranean, as I had marked them for my own game. However, I hope, my dear Lord, that now you will annihilate them, instead of, my dear Lord, your most faithful, humble servant,
Nelson and Brontë.'

As always with Nelson, what mattered was the annihilation.

In a campaign full of ironies, none is more striking than the frame of mind of Villeneuve at this stage. It is easy to understand why Nelson, deceived and delayed, should have been half distracted by anxiety. It is important to realize that Villeneuve, despite the fact of having made a successful escape, and enjoying favourable winds for its continuation, was in no less a state of agitation. On 6 March he was at Cartagena, where the six Spanish ships of the line under Rear-Admiral Salcedo were practically ready to sail. Villeneuve invited them to join him; he says they refused, having different orders. The Spanish version is that they would have been only too glad to have his company to Cadiz, but needed to get their powder on board. Villeneuve refused to wait; he was becalmed at Cartagena on the 7th, but evening brought an easterly breeze and he set sail at once for Gibraltar, leaving the Spaniards behind. Ever since the Battle of the Nile, says General Fuller, Villeneuve had been 'haunted by the spectre of Nelson'. Certainly, at every stage of the campaign, he seems to have been a man looking over his shoulder, fretting that Nelson was on his tail at the very times that Nelson himself was fretting at being so far away.

On 8 April Villeneuve passed through the Straits of Gibraltar, and at 4 p.m. he stood into the Bay of Cadiz. Here an opportunity awaited him. Sir John Orde's squadron – the *Glory* (98), one 74 and three 64s, was taking in stores from transports in the bay when in came Sir Richard Strachan in the *Renown* under full sail to say that Villeneuve was close behind him. It was a bad moment; Orde cast off his transports, sent them away, and formed his squadron as best he could for battle, in case he had to cover them. The French duly appeared, and the extraordinary spectacle followed of Orde's squadron slowly making its way out of the bay, while Villeneuve's eleven of the line and six frigates entered it, making no attempt to interfere with Orde's retreat. No doubt Villeneuve wanted to avoid damage and delay, but this cannot have been an inspiring moment for his crews.

For two days Orde was in doubt as to what he should do. But he had the advantage of more up-to-date information than Nelson possessed. He knew, not only that Missiessy was at sea, but also that Ganteaume had just made his attempt to break out of Brest. Now here was Villeneuve joining up with Admiral Gravina's fleet in Cadiz. Everything pointed to a great and dangerous French combination, and Orde, in his turn, took guidance from the tried tradition. He wrote to the

Admiralty: 'I shall make the best of my way to join Lord Gardner, as an immediate accession of force may be of importance at this critical juncture.' Two days later, having given matters more thought, Orde reached a further conclusion, for which he deserves full credit, since no one else had yet reached it: 'I am persuaded the enemy will not remain long in Cadiz, and I think the chances are great in favour of their destination being westward where by a sudden concentration of several detachments, Bonaparte may hope to gain a temporary superiority in the Channel, and availing himself of it to strike his enemy a mortal blow.' It is not a very grammatical sentence, but Orde was the first to penetrate Napoleon's plan.

Orde was correct in another matter, too: Villeneuve certainly did not 'remain long in Cadiz' – indeed it was almost Cartagena all over again. He anchored in the mouth of the bay at eight o'clock in the evening of 8 April, sending in a frigate to inform Gravina and the captain of the French 74 *Aigle*. At ten o'clock they began to emerge from Cadiz. The Spanish contingent consisted of two eighties (one of which promptly ran aground), two 74s and two 64s. At 2 a.m. on the 9th the Combined Fleet began its run to the West Indies, the Spanish ships trailing behind. Orde has been blamed for not pursuing them, and cutting off their stragglers, but it is hard to blame him for not foreseeing that Villeneuve's stay at Cadiz would only last six hours! Once more we seem to feel the hot breath of Nelson on his neck. It was a significant moment, because the addition of the Spanish squadron, taken in conjunction with Ganteaume's failure to escape from Brest, made Villeneuve's fleet the main fleet of France. And both the fleet and its commander were overawed by Nelson; it was not an auspicious change. For the moment, however, what mattered most was that once more Villeneuve had vanished in the night, and the great guessing game had begun all over again.

─────────────────

The war was now at a point of transformation; April was the month of decision. On the 11th, after many delays and many cross-purposes, the treaty of alliance between England and Russia was signed in St Petersburg. Eight days later Sir James Craig's expedition set sail from Portsmouth – a timing which, as we have seen, added significantly to the hazards of the war. The treaty and the expedition meant that from now on it would be a Continental, not merely a naval war. The next problem would be to expand it from an alliance to a coalition, and here Napoleon himself now took a hand. On 20 April, the day after Craig sailed, he set out for Milan to embark on a series of policies in Italy which would infallibly antagonize Austria and draw her towards the Anglo-Russian camp. Meanwhile party politics in England brought about the fall of Pitt's friend Melville (and nearly produced a breakdown in Pitt himself); yet good came out of this evil, for its final outcome was the appointment of Barham as First Lord of the Admiralty. And so, as the great crisis of 1805 approached, the hour would be matched by the man.[14]

Footnotes
Ch IV
1 As late as 9 June 1805 we find Napoleon writing to Decrès: 'il ne faut être maître de la mer que six heures pour que l'Angleterre cesse d'exister.' On 1 September, with hindsight already at work, he spoke of '15 days'; he never did resolve this question. See William James, *The Naval History of Great Britain*, R. Bentley & Son, London, 1886, Vol. iii, pp. 316 and 318.
2 Sir Alexander Cochrane, previously commanding on this station, had been sent off with a similar force to find Missiessy – another factor missing from Napoleon's calculations.
3 It is James who supplies the wind direction and the French course, but he says they came out on the evening of 29 March; every other authority I have consulted says the 30th. James probably refers to a preparatory move to the mouth of Toulon harbour.
4 It consisted of eleven ships of the line, six frigates and two brigs.
5 In the Mediterranean the summer months, with their short nights and brilliant days, were the easiest for the blockading force, the most difficult for escape.
6 How fatal a simple word like 'saddles' can be! The French would not want saddles in the West Indies.
7 Perhaps even earlier, if Sir Alexander Ball sent the news on.
8 A small island off the south-west tip of Sardinia.
9 My italics.
10 Captain Benjamin Hallowell, H.M.S. *Tigre*.
11 Cape de Gata, on the eastern side of the Gulf of Almeria.
12 To Captain Thomas, H.M. Bomb *Aetna*.
13 To Hugh Elliot, 16 April.
14 See pp. 32–4.

5.THE CRISIS OF THE CAMPAIGN

At the centre of all military transactions is Intelligence; without it there can be no ordered action. Enjoying the historian's advantage of panoramic hindsight, we have seen the opening moves of a great strategic combination unfold and the counter-moves, good or bad, begin. We have seen how lack of Intelligence, or false Intelligence, have already produced serious results. Now it is time to see how Intelligence reached the brain of the Royal Navy, and with what further results. It is important to bear in mind that the development of the ensuing naval crisis all took place against the background of a diplomatic crisis as the tsar's hesitations endangered the Treaty of St Petersburg even after it was signed, and a party-political crisis which, at its very least, ensured the distraction of Pitt and his colleagues at the precise time when their full energies were required to be spent in the national interest.

All too often, in the matter of obtaining and transmitting Intelligence, it is accident that plays a large part; in April 1805 it was a mixture of accident and discretion. It was the accident of being in the midst of a refit that placed Captain Lord Mark Kerr and the frigate *Fisgard* in Gibraltar on 8 April, as Villeneuve passed by on his way to Cadiz. We have already noted[1] how Kerr reacted; it is necessary to go a little deeper into his story. We have seen that his first action was to try to warn his chief, Nelson. He cleared Gibraltar on the 11th, and on the 15th he spoke to the frigate *Melampus*, belonging to Sir Robert Calder's squadron off Cape Finisterre. The *Melampus* carried Kerr's news to Calder, who sent her on at once to warn Lord Gardner at Ushant, leaving Kerr to take the news to Ireland, always a sensitive area when the French were on the move. On the way, he made contact with one of Gardner's cruisers on 23 April, and Gardner (informed twice over) at once sent the news on to the Admiralty, who had it by 25 April. This meant that, thanks to Kerr's discretion, the Admiralty had sure Intelligence of Villeneuve having passed the Straits of Gibraltar just seventeen days after he did so – very good going for those days.[2]

When the news arrived the political crisis was at its height; Barham was still Sir Charles Middleton, his appointment as First Lord not yet

being confirmed, but the cool authority and the continuity of the Admiralty's responses indicate that he was to all intents and purposes in charge. The first reactions were straightforward: the government and the Admiralty had been anxious about the West Indies, especially Jamaica, for some time. A junction of Villeneuve and Missiessy would create a fleet of seventeen French ships of the line in that area, to say nothing of the Spanish. The Admiralty, accordingly, concerned itself chiefly with the security of Jamaica: a concentration of the ships of the line already in the West Indies (Cochrane's squadron and Dacres's) on Jamaica would produce eleven, including a three-decker. This might be enough to make Villeneuve hesitate, but more would be required to defeat him, and there was no reason for the Admiralty yet to doubt that more would soon arrive. The naval system, hammered out across a century of war, would see to that. Corbett writes: 'It was an old but now forgotten tradition which throws much light on Nelson's great movement, that in such an eventuality as had occurred the Commander-in-chief in the Mediterranean should send or follow with a proportion of his force large enough to make the British squadron in the threatened area superior to that of the enemy.' In the eighteenth century it was normal to spell this instruction out, but by the French Revolutionary Wars it had come to be taken for granted. As we have seen, it was Nelson's declared intention to do precisely this in 1798, and again in 1803 and 1804, and equally precisely what he desired to do now. But, of course, it all depended on whether he knew which way to go.

During the next two days doubts began to arise on this vital point. The emphasis with which Nelson defended his move to Egypt in January must have contributed to them. If, through one of the many mischances which always had to be reckoned with, he was doing the same thing again, the system would break down. Fears grew that, in the words of a contemporary, 'his only eye is directed eastward, and we shall find ourselves in a great scrape'. The bold decision was taken to reinforce the West Indies from the Western Squadron (which we see here in its rôle of strategic naval reserve) by detaching at least part of the 'Flying Squadron' under Collingwood which had

'At the centre of all military transactions is Intelligence . . .

Villeneuve's passage through the Straits of Gibraltar, and departure for the West Indies, were observed by two British warships: the frigate *Fisgard*, of the Mediterranean Fleet, then refitting at Gibraltar, and the sloop *Beagle*, of Sir John Orde's squadron. The following table shows how each dealt with the important Intelligence that had come her way.

Date	Main event	Fisgard	Beagle
1805			
8 April	Villeneuve passes Gibraltar, enters Cadiz Bay	Observes Villeneuve	At Cape Spartel
9 April	Villeneuve sails for West Indies	Reports Villeneuve's position to Nelson by hired vessel	Observes strange fleet
10 April		Leaves Gibraltar for England	At Tangier; learns strange fleet was Villeneuve
11 April	Orde tries to inform Nelson of Villeneuve's position	Making for Ushant	Observes Villeneuve again; finds Cadiz empty; searches for Orde
12 April	Orde detaches frigate *Sophie* to inform Admiralty	,,	Watches Villeneuve; searches for Orde
13 April	Orde at Cape St Vincent	,,	Searching for Orde
14 April	Orde searches south for Villeneuve	,,	,,
15 April	Orde searching south	Speaks *Melampus* near Cape Finisterre	,,
16 April		Makes for Ireland; *Melampus* warns Calder	,,
17 April	Orde turns west; sends *Polyphemus* to report to Admiralty	Making for Ireland	,,
18 April	Orde turns north-west	,,	Makes for Ferrol
19 April	Craig Expedition leaves Portsmouth	,,	,,
23 April	Orde making north-east	Reports to Gardner off Ushant; sends news to Plymouth; continues to Cork	? Speaks Calder at Ferrol
24 April	,,	Making for Cork	Makes for Plymouth
25 April	Admiralty receives *Fisgard*'s report; issues first orders	,,	,,
29 April	Admiralty receives *Sophie*'s report	,,	,,
30 April	Craig Expedition at Lisbon; Nelson sights Gibraltar	,,	Arrives at Plymouth
1 May	Nelson receives *Fisgard*'s report	,,	
2 May	Admiralty receives *Beagle*'s report		
4 May	Admiralty issues new orders		

been formed at the beginning of March. However, even retaining half of this squadron (five of its ten ships) Gardner would be dangerously weak at the decisive point, and a tremendous effort was put in hand to reinforce him from the British bases by commissioning ships of the line laid up 'in ordinary'. The problem, as usual, was manpower. Pitt told Barham: '. . . I think we must not lose a moment in taking measures to set afloat every ship that by any means of extra-ordinary exertion we can find means to man. At such an emergency, I am inclined to think many measures may be taken to obtain a supply of men for the time, which would not be applicable to any case less immediately urgent.' Just what that meant in terms of redoubled press gang activities, with all their hardships and cruelties, may be imagined. But when Pitt wrote that, at the end of a terrible night in the House of Commons on 29 April, he had new information that was deeply disturbing for the security of the country.

If it was accident and discretion combined that had brought in the first Intelligence of Villeneuve, what now followed was all due to discretion. When Sir John Orde reached his decision to close in on Lord Gardner, he sent ahead the sloop *Sophie* with explanations of his intentions and thinking for Gardner and the Admiralty. It was these that arrived on 29 April, and that Pitt and Barham had to digest in the early hours of the 30th, and a very poor breakfast they must have found them. First, there was the depressing absence of any definite news of Nelson; all Orde could offer was Sir Richard Strachan's opinion that Nelson was most probably on the way to Egypt again. Secondly, there was Orde's own movement, taking him off the Cadiz station. The conjunction of these two circumstances was potentially disastrous: it meant that the expedition under Sir James Craig which had sailed from Portsmouth ten days earlier, with only two ships of the line, the *Queen* (98) and the *Dragon* (74) under Rear-Admiral John Knight as escort, would now have no cover beyond the latitude of Ferrol. If the expedition with its fifty transports fell in with Villeneuve – or even with only some of his plentiful cruisers – there was bound to be a terrible disaster, which in turn would have its own dire effects in the diplomatic field. And Orde's

suggestion, which no one appears to have considered until then, that Villeneuve might double back towards the Channel, if true would make all this only too likely. Small wonder that Pitt described this communication to Barham as 'of the most pressing importance'.

Through all that followed, whether prompted by sound intelligence or not, Barham clung without any doubt or faltering to the hard core of the naval system: the vital rôle of the Western Squadron. In the stream of orders which he issued on his first day in office, 30 April, in the various ensuing streams which fresh Intelligence, some of it true, some false, caused him to issue during the next few weeks, this is the consistent thread. Other matters, of course, varied as circumstances changed: there was the vital matter of keeping Craig's expedition safe, and how that was to be done depended very much on where it was, so alternatives had to be offered; and there was the desirability of holding on to Ferrol: Calder might be reinforced by both Orde and Knight. But in all cases of doubt, in all new dangers, the focal point was Ushant, and all would rally there to close the mouth of the Channel. In the words of Colonel Desbrière: 'All the Napoleonic plans could only dash themselves to pieces against this primordial device so imperturbably followed.'q

For a man of over eighty, Barham put in a good day's work on 30 April – and there were many that would be just as exacting ahead of him. It would have been much eased if he had known – but how could he? – that on this day Craig's expedition had reached the mouth of the Tagus. It was not yet out of trouble, but it was intact and, better still, cover was at hand. For it was also on 30 April, after a dragging voyage – 'I believe Easterly winds have left the Mediterranean. I have never been one week without one, until this very important moment. It has half killed me . . .' – that Nelson at last sighted Gibraltar, and the end of uncertainty was close.

There can be times in a man's life when everything he touches turns to gold. Nelson had known such times – the Nile and Copenhagen – and he was a national hero in consequence. But there can be times of another sort, when miscalculation (whether justifiable or not) and mischance combine against the man, and the public imagination no longer perceives its hero. This was such a time in Nelson's life, and the foul wind that had slowed his passage to Gibraltar and that continued to hold him inside the Straits even with the Rock in sight, was only the outward, physical manifestation of the foul wind blowing against his whole career. Admiral Radstock, one of his lifelong friends, wrote to his son in H.M.S. *Victory*:[3] 'Where are you all this time? for that is a point justly agitating the whole country more than I can describe. I fear that your gallant and worthy chief will have much injustice done him on this occasion, for the cry is stirring up fast against him, and the loss of Jamaica would at once sink all his past services into oblivion.'

It was on the same day (13 May) that Barham told Radstock that the Admiralty was entirely without news of Nelson. The Board was worried – had there been a disaster? It was also discontented; even granted the communications hazards of the period, this silence was particularly galling; it meant that a vital piece was missing from the great chess game. Some members of the Board wondered whether Nelson was perhaps still sulking over the appointment of Sir John Orde. Radstock added in his letter: 'I am sure that they are out of humour with him, and I have my doubts whether they would risk much for him, were he to meet with any serious misfortune.' Another week passed; fears for the West Indies grew, and the merchants of the City of London became very inflamed against Sir John Orde for not having thrown his six ships against Villeneuve's eighteen. They could be equally unreasonable to Nelson. Radstock wrote:

'You may readily guess that your chief is not out of our thoughts at this critical moment. Should Providence once more favour him, he will be considered our guardian angel; but, on the other hand, should he unfortunately take a wrong scent, and the Toulon fleet attain their object, the hero of the 14th of February[4] and of Aboukir will be – I will not say what, but the ingratitude of the world is but too well known on these occasions.'

However, all was well; by now, at last, the Admiralty had some news of Nelson. On 19 May Lord Gardner received the despatch that Nelson had sent from his position ten leagues west of the island of Toro exactly thirty days before, stating his intention to go to Scilly or join the Western Squadron. That brought at least some reassurance; what the Admiralty was not yet to know, of course, was that at last Nelson had reached certainty about Villeneuve's destination, and was on his trail. When this information came to hand it would ease many problems.

On 4 May, with the wind still foul for Gibraltar, Nelson decided to make the best use of the time that he could, and was rewatering and revictualling his fleet at Tetuan in Morocco. We can sense the high tension of frustration in the admiral and his captains by what followed in the next two days. On the 5th the wind shifted just enough to allow a course for Gibraltar to be laid. At once the revictualling stopped – in the case of the *Superb* it meant leaving a herd of cattle and other 'refreshments' actually on the beach. On the 6th they were at Gibraltar, but the wind was still foul for a westward passage. Many officers thought it a good time to send their washing ashore, but Nelson would never risk missing a wind. In the late afternoon it shifted, and in the words of his secretary, the Reverend A. J. Scott: 'Off went a gun from the *Victory*, and up went the Blue Peter, whilst the admiral paced the deck in a hurry, with anxious steps, and impatient of a moment's delay. The officers said, "Here is one of Nelson's mad pranks." But he was right.' Now at last, thirty-seven days after Villeneuve's departure from Toulon, and nearly a month after his passage through these same straits, Nelson was out of the Mediterranean.

Already his mind was moving on different lines; the further he came west, the more the western aspect of the war seemed to take hold of him, and with it the sense of a new responsibility. While at Tetuan, he wrote to Captain Otway, the Navy Commissioner at Gibraltar: 'I believe my ill luck is to go on for a longer time . . . I cannot very properly run to the West Indies, without something beyond mere surmise; and if I defer my departure, Jamaica may be lost. Indeed, as they have a month's start of me, I see no prospect of getting out time enough to prevent much mischief being done . . .' The next day, while the *Superb* was waiting for the bullocks she never received (some of which were also meant for the *Victory*)

'The high-water-mark of prosperity for the sugar trade'; sugar cultivation, West Indies

Nelson told her captain, Richard Keats: 'It is generally believed that the French and Spanish Ships are gone to the West Indies. As far as April 27th, nothing was known of them at Lisbon; therefore, I am likely to have a West India trip; but that I don't mind, if I can but get at them.'

Like the City of London, the government and the Admiralty, Nelson was casting his mind towards the Caribbean. All the significance that Egypt had once held was now transferred to the West Indies, and above all to Jamaica. This was not to be wondered at; the period of the French Revolutionary and Napoleonic Wars was the high-water mark of prosperity for the sugar trade, the greatest part of which was centred in Jamaica. During the eighteenth century British consumption of sugar had risen from an annual 10,000 tons to 150,000 tons; the wars created a scarcity which sent prices up accordingly. The sugar islands and the sugar convoys were rich prizes, as Nelson knew very well. Somewhat later he would be writing: 'I ever have been, and shall die, a firm friend to our present Colonial system. I was bred, as you know, in the good old school, and taught to

appreciate the value of our West India possessions . . .'[5] The capture of Jamaica, he became more and more certain, was 'a blow which Buonaparte would be happy to give us'. In fact, as we know, Napoleon was only using the West Indies now as a rendezvous, and if any islands were threatened by him they were in the Windward and Leeward groups. But that was beside the point; what mattered was that Nelson now had a very good idea of what to do; all he needed was certainty and a fair wind.

Certainty grew by inches. On 7 May Nelson was still writing to Sir Evan Nepean: 'I am still as much in the dark as ever . . . If I hear nothing, I shall proceed to the West Indies.' The next day, writing to Captain Keats, his determination at least seems to have grown: 'Perhaps none of us would wish for exactly a West India trip; but the call of our Country is far superior to any consideration of self.' On the evening of 9 May the fleet anchored in Lagos Bay, just east of Cape St Vincent. There it found the transports which had been victualling Sir John Orde when he was so suddenly interrupted by Villeneuve; they were a welcome sight to Nelson, who at once set about taking aboard five months' stores. And his certainty was now clinched: at Lagos, Rear-Admiral Donald Campbell of the Portuguese navy came aboard the *Victory* in great secrecy and gave Nelson the assurance he needed that Villeneuve had sailed to the West Indies.[6] But there was still a complication – the complication that had so alarmed Lord Barham on 30 April: the Craig expedition, with Knight's escort, now at Lisbon, where French pressure on Portugal was making its situation precarious. So it was on this day, 9 May, that Nelson was at last able to declare his firm intention to the Admiralty: 'I shall wait here until Admiral Knight joins, and then proceed to Barbadoes, taking care that he is seen safely inside the Gut . . .' And the next day, to his friend, Sir Alexander Ball: 'My lot is cast, and I am going to the West Indies, where, although I am late, yet chance may have given them a bad passage, and me a good one: I must hope the best.'

Already Nelson had formally handed over the Mediterranean command to Rear-Admiral Sir Richard Bickerton, 'whose zeal, abilities, and perfect knowledge both of this Country, and my sentiments upon every particular point of their Lordships' instructions render him most fully competent to this charge, and their expectations'.[7] There remained only to await Knight, and his coming was not long delayed. At 09.10 on the morning of 11 May Nelson's fleet weighed; at four o'clock that afternoon Knight's ships and convoy rounded Cape St Vincent. The business between them was brief: instructions for Knight; the detachment of the *Royal Sovereign*, whose foul bottom made her a slow sailor, to help Knight see the convoy past Cadiz and Cartagena; detachment of the sloop *Martin* to go on ahead to Barbados and warn Cochrane of Nelson's coming. Then they parted company, and the *Victory*'s log tersely records: 'At 6.50, bore up and made sail. Cape St. Vincent N.W. by N., distance 7 leagues.' The West Indian chase had begun.[8]

In all these events, a contrast constantly stands out: on the one hand, the unanimity, mutual comprehension and cooperation of the British admirals and Admiralty, on the other, the everlasting cross-purposes of the French admirals and their distant, uncomprehending emperor. Villeneuve had left Cadiz on 9 April and arrived at Fort Royal in Martinique on 13 May, just two days after Nelson had begun his pursuit. His activities – or lack of activities, to be more accurate – in the West Indies were hardly more effective than Missiessy's; the feebleness of both being largely attributable to the profusion of modified or conflicting orders which Napoleon deluged upon his unfortunate naval officers.

Once again it is important to set the precise movements in what the British think of as 'the Trafalgar campaign' against the backcloth of Napoleonic policies. During these critical months – April, May and June – the forefront of Napoleon's mind was occupied with a matter far removed from the hazards of men-of-war in far-off seas, yet closely linked to all of them in its results. On 10 April he was at Lyon, a favourite city. Here he and the Empress Josephine were received with tremendous enthusiasm; they passed six days in a whirl of firework displays and receptions, founding great public works and enjoying brilliant balls. It was an interlude of excitement and enthusiasm calculated to go to the head of any man, and shortly to be followed by even more stimulating circumstances: Napoleon was on his way to Milan, where he proposed to take the crown of King of Italy in addition to the imperial crown of France. So the empire, only one year old, was already expanding; vistas of splendour unfolded before Napoleon, and with them a vista of danger, because if anything was needed to combine the powers of Europe against him, it was this.

It was while he was in the midst of the festivities at Lyon that Napoleon received news of the formation of the Craig expedition, and a similar force under Sir Eyre Coote which was intended for India. The key point, as he wrote to Arch-Chancellor Cambacérès, was that in the case of both expeditions (which he was told comprised 5,000–6,000 men each), 'They are neither militia nor volunteers they are sending: they are their best troops.' And this drew him at once to a splendid thought: 'If then, our flotilla receives the signal and is favoured by six hours of fair wind, of fog, and of night, the English will be surprised and find themselves stripped of their best troops.'

'Rear-Admiral Magon sailed to join Villeneuve';
Magon, killed at Trafalgar

The invasion of England thus took on a quite new
look, and new orders accordingly went out to the
admirals.

The limelight was now full upon the unfortunate
Villeneuve, a man 'of mild and melancholy
disposition, sad and modest behaviour'.
Ganteaume's failure to escape from Brest at the
end of March (repeated again on 15 April, though
Napoleon would not hear of this until several
days later) and the probability that Missiessy would
already be on his way home (as indeed he was)
meant that Villeneuve would have to take the main
rôle. He was now (14 April) ordered to go, not to
Cadiz, but to Ferrol, to raise the blockade there,
and then, in conjunction with Gourdon's squadron,
to go to Brest and link up with Ganteaume, force
the Channel and come to Boulogne, where
Napoleon in person would issue final orders to the

admirals; 'on their successful arrival,' he added,
'hang the destinies of the world.'[9]

This was all very rousing stuff – except for
those who had to try to carry it out – but there
was more to come. On 20 May Napoleon reached
Italy, very pleased with his triumphal progress
through the French southern provinces. He now
heard that as late as 10 April Nelson had been
seen off Sardinia, and since it suited him to hold a
low opinion of Nelson's intelligence, he was able
to persuade himself quite easily that Nelson had
gone to Egypt again and would be likely to remain
there, and could thus be counted out of the game.
To make sure of this, he proposed to create a new
Toulon squadron, to be composed of Missiessy's
ships and the Spanish ships in Cartagena.
Alternatively, the junction could be at Cadiz,
which would be just as effective in holding Nelson
down. Meanwhile, Villeneuve was given explicit
orders to spend his time in the West Indies in
capturing and pillaging the British Windward
Islands, including Tobago[10] and Trinidad. The
orders of 14 April went off from Rochefort where
two ships of the line under Rear-Admiral Magon
sailed to join Villeneuve on 1 May; the amended
orders went by the frigate *Didon* the following day.
She was the first to arrive, on 31 May, and a
woeful moment it was for Villeneuve when she
did so.

Of all those who were concerned with Nelson's
whereabouts, Villeneuve was undoubtedly the
most anxious; for him it was a matter of life and
death. Nor was his anxiety in any way allayed by
the excitement of action. His orders were to wait
for Ganteaume, and this could not be reconciled
with any of the combined operations against British
islands that were urged upon him. The most he
could consent to was frigate action against British
commerce, and an attack on Diamond Rock. This
was an islet of under a mile circumference, rising
to a height of 600 feet out of the sea less than a
mile from the south-west tip of Martinique. It
had been seized by a landing party from H.M.S.
Centaur (74), flying the broad pennant of
Commodore Samuel Hood, in January 1804. By
incredible exertions and great skill the *Centaur*
seamen then landed and placed in position a
battery of three long 24-pounder and two
18-pounder guns, one of them able to fire almost

'An attack on Diamond Rock'. Top left: H.M.S.
Centaur seamen landing their guns on Diamond Rock;
Bottom left: H.M. Sloop of war *Diamond Rock*, with
guns in position; Right: the French capture of
Diamond Rock, 2 June 1805

across the wide bay which forms the southern end of Martinique. Diamond Rock now became a British 'sloop of war', with a 'crew' of 120 men and boys under Captain James Maurice, and for nearly a year and a half had been an intolerable nuisance to the French.

On 29 May Villeneuve detached two seventy-fours, a 36-gun frigate, a corvette, a schooner and eleven gunboats, with 300 or 400 soldiers, to retake Diamond Rock. Against adverse winds, it took them two days to reach the rock, and against the firm resistance of Captain Maurice it took them the best part of three days to capture it. But by late afternoon on 2 June, according to Maurice's report, he had 'but little powder left, and not a sufficient quantity of ball cartridges to last until dark'. The next day the British 'crew' or garrison marched out with the honours of war, having lost two men killed and one wounded against a French loss estimated by Maurice at about fifty. At his subsequent court-martial he was honourably acquitted for the loss of the 'sloop' and highly complimented for his able defence. And that was all that Villeneuve had to show for three weeks' sojourn in the West Indies when the *Didon* arrived the following day with Napoleon's orders to be capturing the British islands.

It was a bad moment. Fearing imperial rebuke at the very least, Villeneuve now did what he could to make up for lost time. His new orders were to wait another thirty-five days for Ganteaume, but this was impossible because of the state of his supplies. However, he could at least harry the smaller islands in the short time that remained before he had to return, and accordingly he set sail at once for Antigua and Barbuda. On 8 June he gained his only other success apart from Diamond Rock, and suffered his worst setback. He was able, through the folly of the merchants, to capture the whole of a British sugar convoy of fourteen ships but from his prisoners he learned the news that he dreaded most: Nelson was in the West Indies.

He had, in fact, arrived at Barbados on the very day that Magon had arrived at Martinique and Villeneuve had sailed from there: 4 June. The reports that Villeneuve now received exaggerated Nelson's strength, but even if they had been exact there is little doubt that he would have acted in the same way. He wrote: 'This force, joined to that of Admiral Cochrane, which is about in these seas, would be enough to balance the combined forces, even if it were not superior, seeing the strength of the ships, of which several are three-deckers.' It did not take Villeneuve very long to realize that Napoleon's grand combination had collapsed. The only thing left for him was to save his fleet – if he could. With sickly crews (especially the Spanish) and supplies running out, he could not fight; there was only one thing for it: he had to return to Europe. On 10 June he set his course for the Azores, and once more vanished into the wide emptiness of the Atlantic.

Nelson gained ten days on the French in his passage to Barbados, despite the condition of his fleet.[11] He did not write many letters on this journey – there was little need, and equally little opportunity of despatching them. The qualities called for from him at this stage, as he recognized, were those which are not immediately associated with him. As he set out on 11 May he wrote to Lord Sidmouth:[12] 'My lot seems to have been hard, and the Enemy most fortunate; but it may turn, – patience and perseverance will do much.' A few days later, reporting to the Admiralty, the same virtues are in his mind: '. . . although it may be said I am unlucky, it never shall be said that I am inactive, or sparing of myself; and surely it will not be fancied I am on a party of pleasure, running after eighteen Sail of the Line with ten, and that to the West Indies. However, I know that patience and perseverance will do much . . .' Nelson's stay in the West Indies was very brief, but during it he had need of all the patience and perseverance that he could summon up, for his luck had by no means turned. Once again, in this long, harrowing tale of Nelson's frustrations, it was Intelligence – false Intelligence – that did the damage. What an exaggerated report of the military expedition aboard Villeneuve's ships, with its '5,000 saddles', had done before, an equally firm and precise statement, this time from an old acquaintance, was now to do again. And unfortunately it would receive ample apparent corroboration.

No sooner had Nelson arrived at Carlisle Bay, Barbados, on the late afternoon of 4 June, than he was informed by the commander-in-chief there, Lieutenant-General Sir William Myers, of a sighting of the Combined Fleet. The information came from Brigadier-General Robert Brereton, commanding at St Lucia, some ninety miles away to the north-west: a fleet of twenty-eight sail had been sighted to the windward (east) of St Lucia on the night of 28–9 May sailing southward. Brereton had served with Nelson in the Mediterranean many years earlier, when he had shown himself to be a capable, trustworthy staff officer. His information was exact; it was not to be trifled with. 'There is not a doubt in any of the Admirals' or Generals' minds, but that Tobago and Trinidada are the Enemy's objects . . .'[13]

Over seven weeks later, still full of bitterness at what ensued, Nelson indicated to Alexander Davison, his banker and confidential friend in London, that he himself had not been so sure about the destination of the French:

'When I follow my own head, I am, in general, much more correct in my judgment than following the opinion of others. I resisted the opinion of General Brereton's information till it would have been the height of presumption to have carried my disbelief further. I could not, in the face of Generals and Admirals, go N.W., when it was *apparently* clear that the Enemy had gone South. But I am miserable . . .'[14]

It is difficult to know quite what to make of this. There is nothing whatever in the Letters to support the story of him 'resisting' Brereton's information at the time. On the contrary, his letter to the Admiralty on 4 June reports that General Myers has offered to embark for Tobago and Trinidad with 2,000 troops, and Nelson continues enthusiastically: 'I cannot refuse such a handsome offer; and, with the blessing of God on a just Cause, I see no cause to doubt of the annihilation of both the Enemy's Fleet and Army . . .' That does not sound like a man who has been resisting the idea; nor does his instruction to his captains the next day, in which he explains his purpose as 'frustrating the Enemy's intentions, who, it appears have determined on an immediate attack on some of the Leeward Islands . . .' And when it comes to him 'following his own head', we have to bear in mind this, to Sir Alexander Ball, on 12 June, the day before he left the West Indies: 'In this diversity of opinions I may as

well follow my own, which is, that the Spaniards have gone to Havannah, and that the French will either stand for Cadiz or Toulon – I feel most inclined to the latter place; and then they may fancy that they will get to Egypt without any interruption.' Egypt: still harping on Egypt! No; it is clear that Nelson was not always at his best when 'following his own head', but rather when he was acting on clear information, gathered with 'patience and perseverance', that was not false.

For the time being, however, everything was false. On 5 June at 9.30 a.m. the fleet weighed, and made sail southward. The next day the brig *Curieux* (captured from the French in 1804) spoke an American merchantman who said he had been boarded a few days before off Grenada by a French fleet standing towards Trinidad. He was obviously lying. On the same day, the sloop *Pheasant* was sent on to Trinidad to look for the French there, and a special signal was arranged to report their presence. By an almost incredible misfortune, as Nelson's ships approached Tobago, a merchant sent out a schooner to find out whether they were French or English. The signal agreed to indicate an English fleet, almost unbelievably, corresponded exactly with that by which the *Pheasant* was to report the French at Trinidad, and was duly observed and recorded as such in the *Victory*'s log at 6.10 p.m. To top everything, the following morning, 7 June, approaching the coast of Trinidad at nine o'clock, the fleet observed smoke and flames going up from a British fort, 'and the Troops to abandon it'. After that there could be no further doubt; it was with complete certainty of impending battle that the fleet passed the Dragon's Mouths into the Gulf of Paria, Trinidad. In the words of Nelson's first biographers: 'The Admiral and Officers of his Squadron, after such corroboration, felt it difficult to believe the evidence of their senses, when, on entering the Gulf of Paria on the 7th, no Enemy was to be seen, nor had any been there.'[r]

We shall probably never know what the original cause of this dreadful succession of deceptions was. Corbett suggests that the watchers at the St Lucia signal station on the night of 28 May had seen Villeneuve's detached cruiser squadron, and in the dark had mistaken it for the whole Combined Fleet. It is difficult, however, to believe that even in the darkness three frigates could be counted as twenty-eight vessels, twenty of them ships of the line. Yet Brereton must have acted in good faith. The mischief, of course, lay once again in the precision: that unarguable 'twenty-eight' – like the '5,000' saddles. No doubt privately blaming himself, and excusing himself at the same time, as the weeks went by Nelson laid the blame squarely on Brereton. To Lord Fitzgerald, British Minister at Lisbon, 15 June: 'I have no reason to blame Dame Fortune. If either General Brereton could not have wrote, or his look-out man been blind, nothing could have prevented my fighting them on June 6th; but such information, and from such a quarter, close to the Enemy, could not be doubted.' To Sir Evan Nepean at the Admiralty, 16 June: 'There would have been no occasion for opinions, had not General Brereton sent his damned intelligence from St. Lucia; nor would I have received it to have acted by it, but I was assured that his information was very correct. It has almost broke my heart, but I must not despair.' To Vice-Admiral Collingwood, 18 July: 'The name of General Brereton will not soon be forgot. But for his false information, the Battle would have been fought where Rodney fought his,[15] on June 6th.' To the Admiralty, 20 July: 'I am . . . as completely miserable as my greatest enemy could wish me; but I neither blame fortune or my own judgment. Oh, General Brereton! General Brereton!' It is all very unfair – and very under-standable: Nelson, we need to remember, by the time this last letter was written, had been hunting Villeneuve almost incessantly for six months. Even the most phlegmatic temperament would be liable to crack at that.

Now to return to that shocking moment on 7 June when the fleet entered the Gulf of Paria, only to find it empty of enemy ships. Nelson anchored for the night, and at seven o'clock the next morning he was away again, heading north. On that day more news reached him, some true, some false as ever. From Captain Maurice he learned of the capture of Diamond Rock, and that the Combined Fleet had still been at Martinique on 4 June; so far so good. But from the same source (informed by Commodore Cosmao of the *Pluton* commanding the French expedition at Diamond Rock; no doubt trying to embroider his rather ragged victory with a few useful deceits) he also learned that Gourdon had joined Villeneuve from Ferrol, bringing six French and eight Spanish ships of the line with him. If true, that could have been distinctly bad news, but Nelson was not perturbed. He wrote to the governor of Barbados that day:

'I have my doubts respecting the certainty of the arrival of the Ferrol Squadron, as I have always understood that nothing could pass in or out of Fort Royal without being seen; but, my Lord, powerful as their force may be, they shall not with impunity, make any great attacks. Mine is compact, theirs must be unwieldy; and though a very pretty fiddle, I don't believe that either Gravina or Villeneuve know how to play upon it.'[16]

This was not all: Maurice also informed Nelson that the Combined Fleet was to sail on the evening of 4 June 'for an attack on Grenada and Dominica'.[17] Since Grenada lies to the south-south-west of Martinique, and Dominica to the north-north-west, this information, in turn, must have taken some digesting. However, by noon the next day Nelson himself was at Grenada, where he learned that 'all was safe', not only there, but also at St Vincent's and St Lucia. So the Combined Fleet must have gone north; and within the hour the corroboration came in: a report from Dominica that it had been seen passing that island on 6 June, and 'in the evening they were under the Saints, standing to Northward. Whether the Enemy's object is to attack Antigua, or St. Kitt's, or to return to Europe, time must show. I shall guide my movements according to the best of my judgment, for I have too [often?] unfortunately, been deceived by false intelligence.'[18]

This time it was not false – but it did mean that Villeneuve was at least 350 miles away, thanks to Nelson's wasted voyage to Trinidad. He lost no time in following, and by 12 June he was at Montserrat. Here, instead of the usual deluge of mixed nuggets and dross, he had the greatest difficulty in extracting any information at all from the islanders:

'On Sunday an American came from Guadeloupe who told them the Fleet was gone, it was supposed, against Antigua; but they did not know, nor did it seem a matter of even curiosity to the good folks of Monserrat [sic] to inquire, very particularly. If I hear nothing of the Enemy from Antigua, I shall stand for Prince Rupert's Bay[19] and form my judgment; but, I feel, having saved these Colonies, and two hundred and upwards of sugar-loaded Ships, that I must be satisfied they have bent their course for Europe before I push after them, which will be to the Straits' Mouth, when I shall leave the Command with Rear-Admiral Sir Richard Bickerton, and take their Lordships' permission to go to England, to try and repair a very shattered constitution.'[20]

Once more, containing all his natural impatience, Nelson insisted that he 'must be satisfied'. Neither in coming to the West Indies nor in leaving them would he act without certainty, risking what Winston Churchill would call, in the next great war for survival, 'the safeguard of considerable affairs'. But satisfaction now came swiftly; there is a postscript to this letter: 'The French Fleet passed to leeward of Antigua on Saturday last, standing to the Northward. All their Troops and Stores which they took from Guadaloupe are re-landed there: therefore, I am pushing for the Anchorage at St. Johns,[21] to land the Troops, and hope to sail in the morning after them for the Straits' Mouth.'

At sunset on 12 June, just two days after Villeneuve's departure from the West Indies, Nelson anchored at St John's. At eight o'clock that evening he sent off the *Curieux* to England, to bring the Admiralty all the latest information that he had of the Combined Fleet's strength and movements. The next morning was spent in landing General Myers and his soldiers who had been taken aboard at Barbados, and at noon 'I sailed in pursuit of the Enemy' once again. About an hour later he was joined by the schooner *Netley*, the sole escort of the merchant convoy which Villeneuve had captured on 8 June. She had watched the entire proceedings, unable to intervene, but able to count the Combined Fleet: thirty-two sail (and five frigates on detached duty had still to join). The *Netley's* information reassured Nelson that he was doing the right thing, but gave him food for thought. His determination to catch the enemy if he could never faltered; but catching was one thing, what to do when it happened was another altogether. During the journey back from the West Indies Nelson resumed, as often as possible, his longstanding

habit of entertaining his captains, singly or in groups, aboard the *Victory*. About 16 June he expounded his intentions to them:

'I am thankful that the Enemy has been driven from the West India Islands with so little loss to our Country. I had made up my mind to great sacrifices; for, I had determined, notwithstanding his vast superiority, to stop his career, and to put it out of his power to do any further mischief. Yet do not imagine I am one of those hot-brained people who fight at immense disadvantage, without an adequate object. My object is partly gained. If we meet them, we shall find them not less than eighteen, I rather think twenty Sail of the Line, and therefore do not be surprised if I should not fall on them immediately: we wont part without a Battle. I think they will be glad to let me alone, if I will let them alone; which I will do, either till we approach the shores of Europe, or they give me an advantage too tempting to be resisted.'[5]

As to Villeneuve's destination, Nelson was fairly clear in his mind. He wrote to Sir John Acton at Naples on 18 June: 'I am so far back on my way to the Mediterranean; for although I have not yet met the Enemy, I shall never allow them to get a superiority in the Mediterranean, so as to annoy Sicily, or the other Dominions of your good King. I am very, very unwell, and vexed . . .' The vexation, needless to say, was at General Brereton's 'wrong information'. Nelson adds: 'What a race I have run after these fellows; but God is just, and I may be repaid for all my moments of anxiety.'

On the previous day an American vessel had reported seeing the Combined Fleet definitely on its way to Europe, and on the 19th Nelson sent off the sloop *Martin* to warn Gibraltar and the Mediterranean, and the frigate *Decade* to Lisbon, which in turn could warn Ferrol and Ushant. That left him with only two frigates, and these he also detached on 30 June. The *Amphion* he sent to Tangier, to see whether the Combined Fleet had passed the Straits: 'You will keep my near approach as secret as you can . . .' The *Amazon* he sent to Cadiz, to see if the enemy 'have entered the Port of Cadiz, or gone into the Mediterranean'. By 17 July, the fleet had travelled 3,459 miles on its return journey, and despite all his efforts to trace the enemy Nelson was forced to write: 'Cape Spartel[22] in sight, but no French Fleet nor any information about them: how sorrowful this makes me, but I cannot help myself!' Two days later, 20 July, the *Victory* was back at Gibraltar. Nelson inscribed in his private diary a summary of the harrowing ordeal: 'I went on shore for the first time since the 16th of June, 1803; and from having my foot out of the *Victory*, two years, wanting ten days.'

Far removed from all these hazards, at the centre of his imperial web, Napoleon entertained himself with dreams of power on land and at sea. Italy had been the theatre of his first fame in 1796, and the scene of his last triumph, Marengo, in 1800. In 1805, amidst much other pomp and circumstance, a large imperial review ended with a gratifying re-enactment of that battle. But the peak of pageantry came on 26 May in the cathedral of Milan, when Napoleon crowned himself King of Italy with the iron circlet of the ancient kings of Lombardy, uttering the traditional challenge: 'God gave it me, woe to him who touches it!' The crowns of Italy and France were in theory to be kept separate, and in the future Napoleon's rule over Italy would be exercised through a viceroy, his stepson, Eugène Beauharnais, who succeeded in identifying Napoleonic imperialism with Italian liberalism and nationalism while everywhere else it became increasingly the enemy of such ideas. Even in Italy, this imperialism did not always respect national instincts, as was seen only nine days after the coronation, when Napoleon annexed the Ligurian Republic with the port of Genoa to France. About the same time the duchy of Parma was also incorporated in the French empire. All this, and the knowledge of intrigues to bring about a similar incorporation of the Helvetic Republic, finally resolved the mind of the vacillating tsar, and persuaded the Emperor Francis I of Austria that he would have to join Pitt's coalition.

Amidst all his Italian occupations, his stubborn island enemy still took up much of Napoleon's attention. Further news of General Craig's expedition came to him: it had reached Lisbon; it had sailed from there – where to? He thought it might be going to the Cape of Good Hope[23] or the West Indies; 'If it is destined for Malta, so much the better . . . for the English have deprived

themselves of 6,000 men and of a certain number of ships.' It is one of Napoleon's curiosities that the more England resisted him the more he despised her efforts. He told Decrès on 8 June that if Craig's expedition was really going to Malta, 'Nothing will prove more strongly the ineptitude of the English Cabinet; for these plans of continental operations based on detachments of a few thousand men are the plans of pygmies.' But supposing the pygmies were to be allied to a giant? How far was he deceiving himself when he wrote to his brother-in-law, Murat: '. . . what you write me about the conclusion of a treaty of alliance between England and Russia is nonsense: it is entirely false'? Or to Fouché, in charge of his press propaganda: 'I have already told you that the treaty of England with Russia is false. It is a trick of the English Cabinet. Their intrigues have broken down completely. Even when you see this treaty printed in the English gazette and Pitt announcing it to Parliament, you can say it is not true'? Or to Decrès: 'England is entirely abandoned by the continent, her situation is worse than ever'? These letters fall within the period 25–8 May, that is to say, the period of his coronation. Had it turned his head completely?

Certainly he was able to persuade himself without difficulty on 9 June that Nelson was still in European waters, possibly in the Mediterranean, but more likely in England where his ships would be refitting, and could be considered 'comme en très-mauvais état'. Hearing that a flying squadron had been detached from Ushant, he had equally little difficulty in concluding that it had gone to India. And it was in this condition of euphoria that he began devising fresh plans for his separated squadrons. The news that Missiessy had returned to Rochefort on 20 May meant that Villeneuve would be that much the weaker in his intended 'grand combination' in the West Indies, but it also meant that Napoleon had a new card to play in the great invasion game. Unfortunately, the elderly admiral, exhausted by his last adventure, showed no eagerness to leave his safe harbour again; all he wanted to do was to go to Paris to see his wife. Napoleon, however, had other ideas: he wanted the Rochefort squadron to draw away British ships from the mouth of the Channel by commerce raiding, perhaps even as far afield as

the mouth of the Baltic. If Missiessy would not do it, someone else would have to. Missiessy gave up his command on grounds of ill-health, and was succeeded by a much younger man, Captain Allemand of the *Magnanime* (74). Napoleon could hardly have made a better choice.

On 6 July Napoleon left Italy. During the last phase of his stay there his mind had been very full of naval schemes. General Marmont, at Utrecht, was ordered to stage deceptions by movements of soldiers and ships suggesting a descent on Ireland by the north-about route. The idea was to force the Admiralty to weaken the Western Squadron by detaching ships to the Downs, to 'compel the English to keep there a squadron of at least ten of the line and give them all kinds of uneasiness'. Accordingly, in the second week of July there was a great deal of unwonted activity on the Dutch coast, and when, later in the month, the Admiralty received information that Villeneuve was probably also returning by the north-about route to meet Marmont's expedition, considerable anxiety ensued. Cornwallis was ordered to send three 74s to Admiral Keith (despite the latter's resolute scepticism about the whole manoeuvre) and a few days later three more. But Barham was not the man to weaken Cornwallis unduly if he could help it, and no sooner had the first group arrived at the Downs than it was ordered back, so that all Napoleon achieved by this elaborate feint was a detachment of three ships, two of them only 64s in any case.

On 10 July the emperor reached Fontainebleau. Soon more orders for new combinations were pouring forth: orders for Villeneuve when he arrived at Ferrol, emphasizing that 'the fleet under your command shall carry through the great project of the invasion of England, conceived so long since by [Napoleon's] genius', [24] but at the same time giving him considerable latitude in the matter of how it should be done. In ordinary circumstances it is only correct to give such latitude to the commander of a major unit, operating in an uncertain element; if the commander in question is demoralized, however, it might prove less helpful, and Napoleon did not yet appreciate how demoralized Villeneuve was, nor could he know how much more demoralized he would shortly become. One thing he did know:

that Villeneuve must be nearing the European coastline somewhere, and the great climax must therefore be at hand. Allemand was accordingly ordered to Ferrol – but before the new order could reach him he slipped out of Rochefort to begin a journey which was as unprofitable to Napoleon as it was distracting to the British Admiralty. There remained Ganteaume; it was now his turn to be prodded towards impossible action, and derided when he failed to obey. On 20 July Marshal Berthier, the chief of staff, was told to order the immediate embarkation of the four assault corps of the Grand Army. Ganteaume received a final prod – towards Boulogne: 'There all is prepared; and there, master of the sea for three days, you will enable us to end the destiny of England . . . When you receive this letter we shall be in person at Boulogne-sur-Mer.'

—————————————————

'The uncertainty and confusion that the London Admiralty is in,' Napoleon told Decrès, 'declares itself on all sides. Orders and counter-orders and the greatest indecision – that is the actual state of things.' [25] Certainly there was a marked contrast between his own firm commands, irrespective of wind, tide or weather, and the flurries of activity which took place at the Admiralty whenever the vicissitudes of wind, tide and weather permitted more information to come to hand. We have noted the brisk business which surrounded Barham's first day in the First Lord's office. There was another bustle only two days later, on 2 May, when the sloop *Beagle*, one of Sir John Orde's cruisers, brought more precise and up-to-date news of Villeneuve's movements. The Admiralty became more than ever convinced that his westward course was taking him towards Jamaica, and Barham now had to weigh three necessities against each other for priority.

First, there was Jamaica: the Flying Squadron under Collingwood [26] (which Napoleon supposed was meant for India) had not yet been detached; now was the time, and Gardner was told to order it away. He received a packet of sealed orders for Collingwood, who was to go to Madeira, find out whether Nelson was in pursuit of Villeneuve, and if not go on to Barbados and Jamaica. Before this instruction could reach Gardner, however, a fresh and potentially very serious crisis arose – the last of the tsar's vacillations, which threatened to undo all that had been achieved by the Treaty of St Petersburg. The reason for the tsar's change of mind was the apparent failure of the British government to make good its promise of military cooperation in the Mediterranean: the non-appearance of General Craig's expedition, in other words. So once more command of the Mediterranean became a vital factor. And for Barham, of course, the Western Squadron was always the most vital of all. He saw it as 'the mainspring from which all offensive operations must proceed', and consequently at all times 'it shall be my care to keep it as strong and effective as possible'. Gardner was told that all other orders should be interpreted in terms of the necessity to keep the Western Squadron up to a strength of not less than eighteen of the line.[27]

Meanwhile Ushant was living up to its reputation: on 10 May Gardner and Collingwood were driven off the blockade station by a gale which sent Gardner to the Lizard and Collingwood to Plymouth. Still worried about the West Indies, Barham now decided that Collingwood's squadron should be brought up to the strength originally intended – ten of the line – and new orders accordingly went out. Then Barham learned that the two admirals were no longer together, which required more redrafting, another bustle for Napoleon's spies to note and for him to mis-interpret, and then, on top of all, that bane of the times for everyone: false information. From Lisbon came the news that Craig's expedition was in the Tagus (satisfactory only inasmuch as it showed that the expedition was so far safe) and that Villeneuve was back in Cadiz!

It may be imagined what a shock this extra-ordinary error produced. It was not lessened by the realization that the expedition would by now most probably have no escort, since Commodore Knight had been ordered to reinforce Sir Robert Calder's squadron at Ferrol. Once more there was a press of activity: a frigate was sent off immediately to Cadiz to find out the truth, and Collingwood was ordered to the same destination with a squadron expanded to sixteen of the line. But now there was another complication, just as Colling-wood was about to set off: Missiessy returned to

Rochefort. Neither the admirals nor the Admiralty could know that this was purely fortuitous; Missiessy's return had to be regarded as a deliberate manoeuvre, most likely part of another of Napoleon's grand combinations. It was soon established that Missiessy's ships were in a very poor state, but they were back at their base and could be repaired – a significant increase of enemy strength in home waters. Together Gardner and Collingwood decided that the detachment of sixteen ships was now no longer safe, and accordingly it was with only nine that Collingwood finally sailed for Cadiz on 23 May. A new piece thus appeared on this vast chessboard, a piece of very great importance. Once in position it would remove all the uncertainties about Craig's expedition, and see it through the Straits on a safe run to Malta; and the observation of Cadiz, which had lapsed with such confusing results from the time that Villeneuve drove off Orde, would be resumed, and it would be Collingwood, not Bickerton as he expected, that Nelson would find when he came back to Gibraltar in July. By then, however, the whole game would be taking another turn.

Collingwood arrived at Cadiz with his nine ships on 8 June. It was characteristic of the Royal Navy's sense of shared responsibility and mutual support that the first thing he did on arriving (and finding that Villeneuve had *not* returned) was to detach two of his ships to Nelson, in case the latter should be weakened by Cochrane following Missiessy back to Rochefort. Nelson himself, of course, was trying to make up for lost time, and four days later he left Antigua on his return chase. We have seen that as he did so he sent ahead the brig *Curieux* to give the Admiralty all his informa-tion. She arrived in Plymouth on 7 July, with even more comprehensive intelligence than Nelson had possessed: she had sighted and shadowed the Combined Fleet. The sighting had taken place on 19 June, some 900 miles north-north-east of Antigua, and the shadowing had established that Villeneuve was still on a northerly course. When Barham heard this, it at once became clear that Cadiz was not the enemy's most likely destination: they must be making for the Bay of Biscay, and a new hazard at once arose. If, as seemed to be most probable, Ferrol was Villeneuve's destination, Sir

'A new piece appeared on this vast chess-board';
Cadiz in 1805, as it appeared when Collingwood
took station there in June

Robert Calder, with his squadron of ten, would be in great danger.

Once more the centre of gravity of the war swung back to the Bay of Biscay and became the responsibility of the Western Squadron. At Ferrol five French and nine Spanish ships of the line were ready to put to sea; Rochefort would soon be able to supply another five; Ganteaume, stirring restlessly in Brest under Napoleon's prods, had his twenty-one; and now Villeneuve was heading in this direction with twenty. It must have been with profound relief that Barham noted the return to duty of his most experienced and trusted Ushant admiral, Cornwallis, on 7 July. Even so, with Calder urgently needing reinforcement,[28] the Western Squadron, facing this potential combination, was, as Mr James says, 'rather critically situated'.

Yet, though evidently anxious, Barham was not unduly alarmed. He knew that Nelson had left the West Indies only three days after Villeneuve, and would either catch him or precede him in European waters.[29] He was making for Cadiz, where he would find Collingwood, giving him not less than fourteen ships of the line. Once the two admirals were sure that Villeneuve's destination was not Cadiz, they could be depended on to close in on the Western Squadron, conforming to the naval system. The squadron itself, Cornwallis and Calder combined, would number thirty-three, so the final concentration might amount to forty-seven or more (with ships from home ports) in the vital area. And what of the French? The Rochefort squadron could be discounted, at least for the moment. If Villeneuve released the Ferrol ships and came north, he would have only thirty-four against Cornwallis's thirty-three of which as many as seven might be three-deckers. But would not Ganteaume more than offset this advantage? The answer is interesting, because it throws much light on the faults of Napoleon's naval strategy throughout the whole campaign.

What Napoleon (and many others at the time and subsequently) never understood was the

world of difference between raising a blockade and raising the siege of a land fortress. In the latter case, unless the garrison was *in extremis* through starvation or disease, it could and almost certainly would cooperate with the relieving force, if only by holding down a substantial part of the besieging army. The opposite was the case with a blockade; Corbett goes so far as to say: '. . . there is no recorded case in sailing days of a blockaded squadron having been able to take effective part in an action between a relieving force and the blockaders.' A moment's thought shows why this is so; there are, fundamentally, two reasons. First, the wind that would carry the relief to the blockaded port would almost certainly be foul for the ships inside to come out and join their friends. Secondly, the main body of the blockaders was generally out of sight of land, with only an inshore squadron of cruisers actually watching the port. Even if the relief force was able to draw off the blockaders and open the port, it would generally take a couple of days to establish the fact, and

naturally it would be the entire object of the blockaders to use that time to defeat the two separated divisions of their enemy in detail. The French admirals understood this as well as Barham and Cornwallis did; Napoleon did not. The junction of Villeneuve and Ganteaume was always a far more difficult and chancy matter than he was prepared to allow.

It was this knowledge, all part of the great fund of naval lore that had been accumulated since the days of Drake, that sanctioned the daring movements that now followed. On 12 July Admiral Stirling uncovered Rochefort, and set out to join Calder; the two were then ordered to look for Villeneuve to the west of Cape Finisterre, in case he was making for Ferrol. But in case he was aiming at Brest, Cornwallis was also to cruise in search of him – even at the cost of opening Brest itself. He, too, began his movement on 12 July, first making a wide sweep to the south-west; on the 16th he was as far south as the latitude of Rochefort, but there was no sign of the enemy. The following day

'The guns thundered at last . . .'; Vice-Admiral Sir
Robert Calder, and (below) a general view of the
action of 22 July 1805

Commodore Allemand slipped out of Rochefort,
taking advantage of Stirling's absence, but, as we
have seen, thwarting by his very speed Napoleon's
attempt to weave his squadron into the grand
design. And this, also, was the day that Nelson
arrived at Cape St Vincent.

On 18 July Collingwood wrote a percipient letter
of greeting to his old friend, now returned as his
superior officer. He was certain, he told Nelson,
that the ultimate destination of the Combined
Fleet was Ireland, but in the meantime,

'they will now liberate the Ferrol Squadron from
Calder, make the round of the Bay, and, taking the
Rochefort people with them, appear off Ushant –
perhaps, with thirty-four sail, there to be joined by
twenty more. Admiral Cornwallis collecting his out
Squadrons may have thirty and upwards. This appears
to be a probable plan; for unless it is to bring their
great Fleets and Armies to some point of service –
some rash attempt at conquest – they have been only
subjecting them to chance of loss, which I do not
believe the Corsican would do, without the hope of an
adequate reward. This summer is big with events.'[30]

No part of the summer was bigger with events
than the week that followed. On this very day
General Craig's expedition reached Malta, and
the grand strategy of the war was thus transformed
by the possibility of an 'offensive return' on the
part of the coalition. And Napoleon, through
Decrès, was intensifying the prodding that was
supposed to bring Ganteaume out of Brest.

The next day, 19 July, Sir Robert Calder
received the news contained in the despatch which
Nelson had sent to Lisbon precisely a month
earlier, and realized that he might soon have to
face twenty ships with his fifteen, while fourteen
more from Ferrol might strike him in the back – an
inconvenient situation. Commodore Allemand
brought off the first of a series of providential
escapes from his surrounding enemies by con-
triving to place himself precisely where Cornwallis
had been three days before. The 20th was the day
on which Napoleon ordered the embarkation of
the Army of England, and made yet one more
attempt to make Ganteaume move. Nelson, having
digested Collingwood's letter, was reorganizing
the Mediterranean command, in anticipation of
his own departure to Ushant. Cornwallis, on his
way back to Brest, was taking the opportunity of

looking into Rochefort and Lorient. On the 21st
all was quiet. On the 22nd the guns thundered at
last, as ships of the line of the Royal Navy sailed
into battle against the Combined Fleet.

The action of 22 July, so long awaited, so much
desired, so full of consequence, does not even
have a name. It took place some 120 miles north-
west of Cape Finisterre, a scrambling, disjointed
scuffle, mostly in fog so thick that at times the
opponents could only fire at each other's gun
flashes, but which nevertheless had a
disconcerting trick of clearing suddenly for short
spells, so that ships first of one side then of the
other would find themselves caught at painful
disadvantages.

It would seem to have been the Combined Fleet,
during one of these brief clearings of the weather,
that first became aware of enemies approaching:
they proved to be Sir Robert Calder's squadron,
fifteen of the line with two frigates. It was not long
before Calder's look-out ship, the *Defiance* (74),
was also signalling a strange fleet bearing south-
west. At noon Calder made the signal to prepare
for battle, and shortly afterwards the frigate *Sirius*
made the full count of the Combined Fleet,
twenty of the line with seven frigates, a superiority
estimated by Mr James at four to three, taking
into account the qualities of the various types of
ship present. Sir Robert Calder appears to have
been entirely unperturbed by this; his squadron
continued to run down towards the enemy as fast
as the light and adverse wind permitted. It was
not until 5.15 that the action began, and in the
conditions of the day it was inevitably very
confused, with neither admiral able to do much to
influence its course. The battle continued into the
hours of darkness; Calder made the signal to his
by now well scattered squadron to break off action
at 8.25 p.m., but few ships saw it, and firing did
not die away until half past nine.

The tally of those four hours is curious. In
material terms it is very straightforward: Calder's
squadron captured outright the Spanish *San-Rafael*
(80) and *Firme* (74), and so badly damaged the
French *Atlas* (74) and three more Spanish ships
that they took no further part in the campaign.
On the British side the *Windsor Castle* (98) and

Malta (80)[31] were both damaged enough to have to return to England, though the former was at sea again in three weeks, and the latter would have been out of action for even less time if she had not also needed coppering. The casualties in the British squadron were 41 killed and 158 wounded; the Combined Fleet lost 155 killed and 341 wounded besides the unwounded prisoners in the two Spanish ships. And Villeneuve's route into Ferrol was firmly barred. Yet before the year was out, Sir Robert Calder faced a court-martial on his conduct, and received a severe reprimand.

It is with understandable wonder that Captain Infernet of the 74 *Intrépide*, captured at Trafalgar, said to his captors on board H.M.S. *Orion*: 'It is very well for you gentlemen that you can feel justified in finding fault with an admiral who, when in command of fifteen sail of the line, fights a battle with twenty, because he only makes two of them prizes!' And Villeneuve himself, also a prisoner: 'I wish Sir Robert and I had fought it out that day. He would not be in his present situation, nor I in mine.' The crux of the matter, of course, lies in the renewing of the action. This was precisely what Calder had intended to do, and he reported as much to Cornwallis as soon as the battle was over: 'They are now in sight to wind-ward; and when I have secured the captured ships and put the squadron to rights, I shall endeavour to avail myself of any opportunity that may offer to give you a further account of these combined squadrons.' But he added: 'At the same time it will behove me to be on my guard against the combined squadrons in Ferrol, as I am led to believe they have sent off one or two of their crippled ships last night for that port; therefore, possibly I may find it necessary to make a junction with you immediately off Ushant, with the whole squadron.' Unfortunately, this sentence was omitted when Calder's despatch was published, so that the public was left with a sense only of unfulfilled promise – for daylight on the 23rd persuaded Calder that discretion was the better part of valour. The weather was still hazy, so that a clear view of the situation was not possible for either fleet. The Combined Fleet still held the weather gauge, as on the 22nd, which meant that Villeneuve could have attacked at any time, and it is significant that he did no such thing. The

British fleet was at first very divided, with an advanced squadron about five miles from the main body (and about six miles from the nearest enemy) with another group of ships including the *Windsor Castle*, the *Malta* and the two prizes about five miles off in the opposite direction. The first thing to do was to concentrate, and then get the cripples and prizes away without interference, and this Calder duly did, interposing himself between them and Villeneuve, and preparing to offer battle if necessary – but despite some boastful talk of the British 'fuyant en désordre' the Combined Fleet never came any nearer than about nine miles. The next day the wind shifted, and Calder now found himself to windward of the enemy, which meant that he could have attacked them had he wished. He did not do so, satisfied, it appears, to get his prizes away. Slowly, throughout the day, the two fleets drew away from each other, and by 6 p.m. both were lost to the other's sight. It was for this inaction on the 23rd and 24th that Calder received his reprimand.

In his defence Calder said:

'Circumstanced as I was, it appeared to me to be impracticable to force the enemy to action with such advantage as would justify me, even if I had nothing to apprehend but the opposing squadron. But when I reflected that sixteen sail were at Ferrol, who might have come out to the assistance of the combined fleet, or . . . be pushing to England, the invasion of which was an event daily expected, I felt by renewing the action I should run too great a hazard and put my fleet in a state of danger which I could not have been justified for doing. I therefore thought it best to keep my squadron together and not to force the enemy to a second engagement till a more favourable opportunity.'

There are various comments to be made on this, most of them adverse. Corbett says that Barham's object had been 'to establish an abiding dread that though hostile squadrons might slip out of their blockaded ports, the penalty of their success would be never to return. At the cost of a sacrifice admirably judged he had placed Calder in a position to secure that end, and Calder had not secured it.'

In other words, Calder was expendable, as Nelson had supposed himself to be when he pursued Villeneuve to the West Indies against even greater odds. It must be remarked, however, that it requires a special temperament to be able to regard oneself as expendable without being explicitly told so, and Calder should not be blamed too much for not having it. Nelson himself, sympathizing deeply with Calder when the public outcry against him later came to a head, nevertheless put his finger on a real reason for criticism: 'He appears to have had the ships at Ferrol more in his head than the squadron in sight . . .' Mr James, also, traces a fatal preoccupation of Calder's on the two days after the battle – his prizes: 'Considering the little value of the vessels, the *San-Rafael*, a ship of 34, and the *Firme*, a ship of 51 years old, and both battered to pieces, their destruction would have been not only a justifiable measure, but, under the circumstances, the most eligible that could have been devised.'

Such are the criticisms of Calder, and, of course, there is weight in them all. Yet there is another verdict on his action, trenchantly expressed by General Fuller:

'The moral effect of this action was decisive, for the little faith Villeneuve had in his fleet now oozed out of the soles of his shoes. On August 6 he wrote: "In the fog our captains, without experience of an action or of fleet tactics, had no better idea than to follow their second ahead, and here we are the laughing-stock of Europe." The action palsied him.'

And since it was on Villeneuve and no one else that Napoleon now depended, this palsy spelt the true finish of his 'grand combination'; for which Vice-Admiral Sir Robert Calder might be considered entitled to more thanks than blame.

Footnotes

Ch V

1 See p. 34.
2 The frigate *Decade* made the run from England to Malta in the same time – seventeen days – in March–April, but this was an extraordinary feat.
3 Actually, his son had transferred to the frigate *Hydra*, but Radstock did not know this.
4 The Battle of Cape St Vincent, 14 February 1797.
5 Nelson to Simon Taylor, Jamaica, 10 June 1805.
6 Not to be confused with Rear-Admiral George Campbell, Nelson's third-in-command in the Mediterranean, who had gone home sick. Corbett and James say that Admiral Donald Campbell came aboard the *Victory* at Gibraltar. That would have been on the 6th, making it impossible to understand why Nelson should say 'I am as much in the dark as ever' on the 7th. Certainly he had to preserve

all the secrecy he could for Campbell's sake (he is not mentioned in the Letters), but he did not need to be as emphatic as that. Mahan says Campbell saw him at Lagos on the 9th, and it is certainly on that date that Nelson made his first firm statement of intention to go to the West Indies. Despite all precautions, the Spaniards found out about Campbell's visit and brought pressure on Portugal to get him dismissed, and he died in poverty in England.
7 Nelson to Admiralty, 6 May.
8 Nelson's fleet consisted of: *Victory* (100), *Canopus* (80), *Belleisle* (74), *Conqueror* (74), *Donegal* (74), *Leviathan* (74), *Spencer* (74), *Superb* (74), *Swiftsure* (74), *Tigre* (74) and the frigates *Amazon* (38), *Decade* (36), *Amphion* (32).
9 Napoleon to Villeneuve and Decrès, 14 April.
10 Tobago, recently taken from the French, was to be considered a French island and spared the pillage.
11 *Canopus*, *Belleisle* and *Donegal* needed coppering, *Superb* needed a full dockyard overhaul, in default of which, despite all the efforts of her captain, she inevitably slowed down the fleet. (Nelson to Admiralty, 19 April.)
12 Henry Addington, ex-Prime Minister.
13 Nelson to Admiralty, 4 June.
14 Nelson to Alexander Davison, 24 July.
15 The Battle of the Saints, 12 April 1782, named after the islands Les Saintes in the channel between Guadeloupe and Dominica; French historians call it the Battle of Dominica.
16 To Lord Seaforth, 8 June.
17 Nelson to Admiralty, 11 June.
18 Ibid.
19 Dominica.
20 Nelson to Admiralty, 12 June.
21 Antigua.
22 Morocco.
23 Restored to Holland by the Treaty of Amiens, recaptured in January 1806.
24 Decrès to Villeneuve, 13 July.
25 Napoleon to Decrès, 14 June.
26 See p. 73.
27 Barham to Gardner, 9 May.
28 Which Barham in fact supplied by ordering Rear-Admiral Stirling, who was watching Rochefort with five of the line, to join Calder; this was a calculated risk; in the event it led to much trouble but no serious damage.
29 Nelson arrived at Cape St Vincent on 17 July; Villeneuve was off Cape Finisterre on 22 July.
30 A curious echo of Nelson's own phrase to Sir Alexander Ball in 1804: 'The times are big with great events' (see p. 45).
31 See p. 28.

'...the really decisive battle of the Napoleonic War'

Below: 'This army was at its most parade-ground magnificent'. The Army of England drawn up for the distribution of the Legion of Honour at Boulogne, 16 August 1804

Right: 'A famous 64 was the *Agamemnon*': in Nicholas Pocock's painting of Nelson's ships she is on the extreme left. Next comes *Captain* (74) in which he fought at Cape St Vincent, then *Vanguard* (74) his flagship at the Nile, and *Elephant* (74) to which he transferred his flag, with *Victory* (100) on the right

'Their great size and weight ... the solidity of their build' well illustrated in J. M. W. Turner's famous painting of 'A First Rate Taking On Stores'

Following pages: 'Stations are assigned at the guns ...' The lower gun-deck of H.M.S. *Victory*, showing a Mess Deck table and utensils between two gun-ports, where hammocks were slung, and the crew made the only home it knew

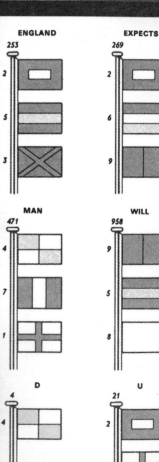

'England expects . . .' Nelson's famous signal, as it
was flown at the mastheads of *Victory*, and as it was
composed by Lieutenant Pasco with the numbered
flags (see p. 141)

Left: 'A day of elation in the Grand Army.' Napoleon takes the surrender of General Mack and the Austrian army at Ulm

Below: 'A day of elation off Cadiz.' Nelson explains his battle plans to his officers

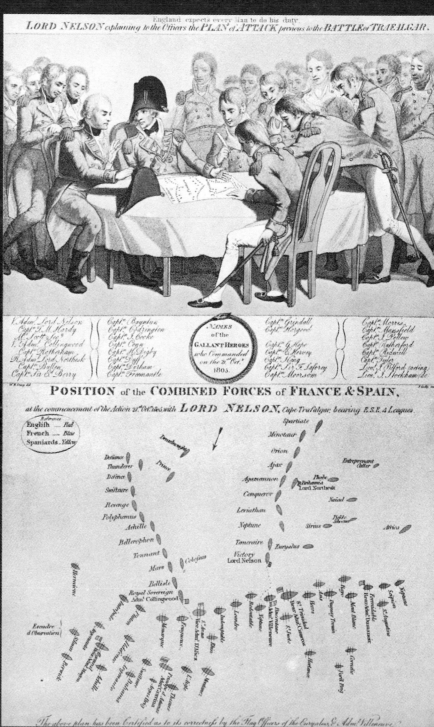

England expects every Man to do his duty.

LORD NELSON explaining to the Officers the PLAN of ATTACK previous to the BATTLE of TRAFALGAR.

NAMES of the GALLANT HEROES who Commanded on the 21st Oct. 1805.

POSITION of the COMBINED FORCES of FRANCE & SPAIN, at the commencement of the Action 21st Oct. 1805, with LORD NELSON, Cape Trafalgar, bearing E.S.E. 4 Leagues.

The above plan has been Certified as to its correctness by the Flag Officers of the Euryalus & Adm. Villeneuve.

THAT		EVERY	
863		261	
		2	
		6	
		1	

DO		HIS	
220		370	
		3	
		7	
		0	

T		Y	
9		24	
		2	
		4	

'...a pell-mell battle...is what I want.' The Battle of Trafalgar by C. Stanfield, showing *Redoutable* trapped between *Téméraire* and *Victory*

Overleaf: 'Nelson was hit by a musket-ball from *Redoutable*'s tops'. Turner's impression of the scene as Nelson fell, with the ships of the weather column coming up behind *Victory*

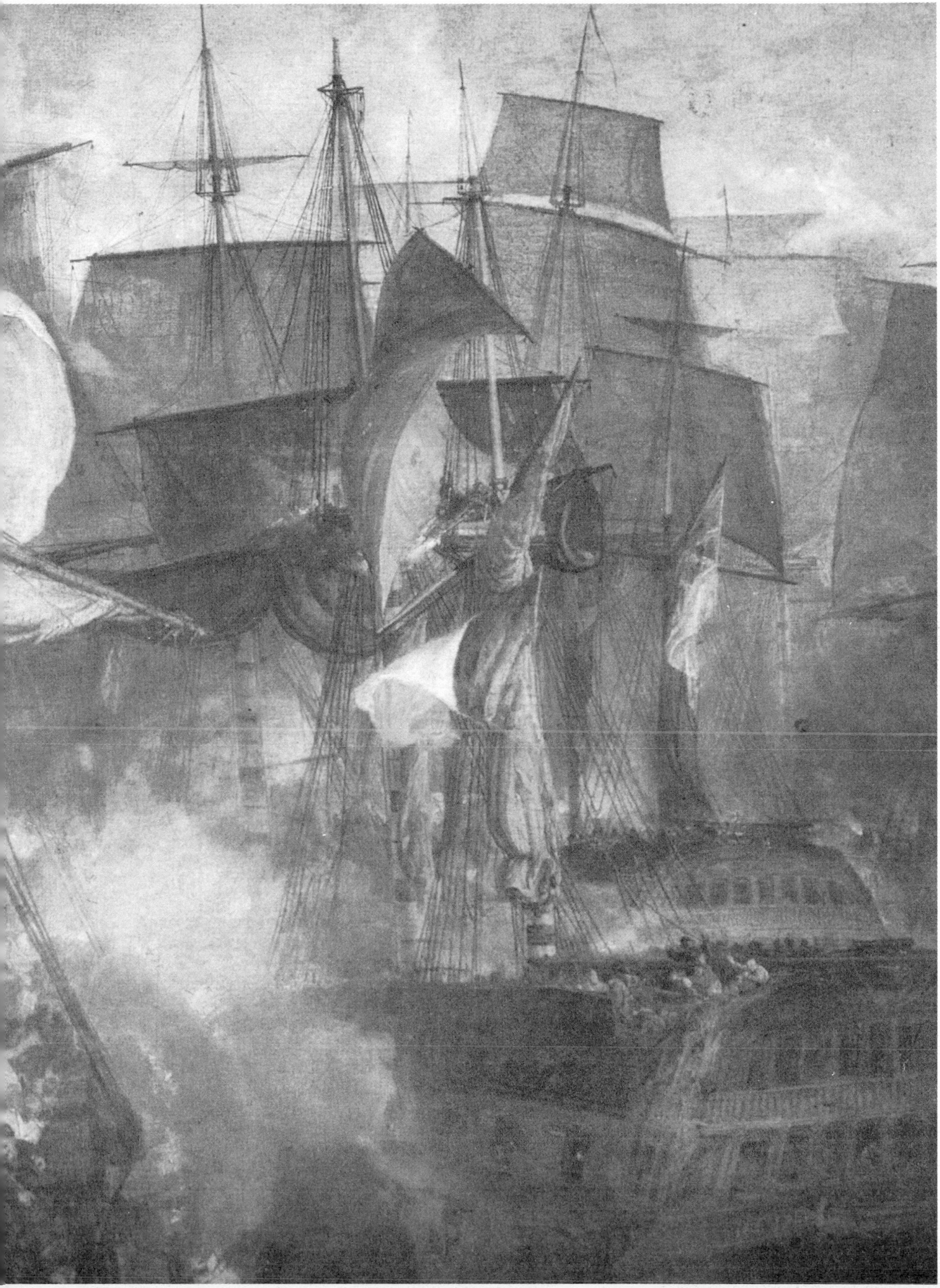

'...her masts came down with a tremendous crash...' *Neptune* pours a broadside into *Santissima Trinidad*, while on the right *Conqueror* finishes off the dismasted *Bucentäure*

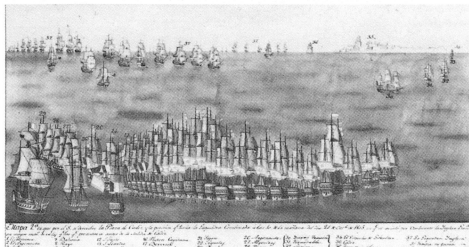

Left: '. . . lying on the water an unmanageable wreck . . .' *Santissima Trinidad* strikes to *Neptune*

Right: 'Three well-marked phases . . .' A Spanish impression of the development of the battle: the approach of the British fleet, the 'pell-mell', and the retreat of the remnants of the Combined Fleet into Cadiz

Opposite above: 'An awful finale to an awesome
scene': the French *Achille* blows up at the end of the
battle
Below: 'The tally of the gale's victims . . .': Spanish
officers and seamen washed ashore after the wreck
of their ship in the great storm after the battle

6. CONSUMMATUM EST

'Let the battle be when it may, it will never have been surpassed': *Victory* engages *Redoutable* at Trafalgar

Villeneuve had returned to Europe and been defeated; Napoleon's 'grand combination' had collapsed; the crisis of the Trafalgar campaign had passed – but no-one knew it. Indeed, the five weeks that followed Sir Robert Calder's action must have seemed to the British government and Admiralty the most critical of the war; certainly they produced two of its most dramatic occasions: Napoleon's return to the cliff-tops of Boulogne at the head of the Army of England, and the concentration of the Royal Navy at its pivot, the Western Squadron.

Villeneuve's destination, when he met Calder, had been Ferrol; it was there that Napoleon had sent his orders to await the admiral's return; it was to Ferrol that Villeneuve tried to go when he lost sight of Calder. If any further indication were required of the extent to which he felt himself defeated by Calder, it would lie in the fact that he was unable to reach that port. The damage that his fleet had sustained made it impossible for him to fight the rising wind and sea, and on 25 July, the day after parting from Calder, he gave up the attempt to reach Ferrol and turned south, hoping to make Cadiz. Even this proved impossible, and on the 26th he put into Vigo, an impossible resting place: the harbour was undefended, there was no dockyard for repairs, and supplies were extremely difficult to obtain. Surrounded by enemies, with three ships unfit for further service, and his crews weakened by scurvy and dysentery, he certainly did not exaggerate when he spoke of himself as being in 'a most distressing situation'.

The British, of course, were unaware of the extent of Villeneuve's misfortunes; for a time they did not even know where he was. All that they could assume was that he had gone to Ferrol, threatening the Bay of Biscay, and they acted accordingly. Cornwallis was by now back on his Brest station – he arrived there on 24 July, depriving Ganteaume of his last chance of slipping out unhindered. On the following day Nelson, outside Tarifa, learned at last that Villeneuve had not, as he had supposed, been making for the Straits, but for Ferrol: He immediately began to close in on Cornwallis, against a wind which held him in the latitude of Cadiz for the next five days. Calder, anticipating this movement, went to look for Nelson off Cape Finisterre, but finding no sign of him turned back to Ferrol on the 27th. Allemand, the following day, enjoyed another of the almost miraculous strokes of luck that favoured his squadron. He, in turn, was looking for Villeneuve, and arrived at the Cape Finisterre rendezvous only a matter of hours after Calder's departure. On the 29th the latter was back at Ferrol, surprised to find it empty; it would not remain so for long.

His position in Vigo being quite impossible, and hearing that Ferrol was uncovered, Villeneuve set out for there on 30 July, hoping to make the port without another battle. He was forced to leave behind three ships: the *Atlas* and two Spanish 64s, the *America* and the *España*; a neutral merchant captain who rowed round these ships in Vigo harbour said that the engaged side of the *Atlas* 'was like a riddle', and that there were innumerable shot-holes in the hulls of the two Spanish ships. The Spanish 74 *Terrible* was also badly damaged, but able to go to sea, giving Villeneuve fifteen ships in all. Calder, even when he had sent the *Malta* home for repairs on the 31st, had thirteen – so substantially had he reduced the odds in his previous action. There is little reason to doubt what the outcome of another fight would have been: even if not destroyed in the manner of the Nile, Villeneuve's fleet would have been placed out of action for months to come, with heavy losses of ships. In that event there would have been no question of court-martial for Calder, no Trafalgar for Nelson. But it was not to be: a gale on 1 August drove Calder far off his station, and Villeneuve was able to enter Ferrol unopposed later that very day. On the 2nd, obedient to Admiralty orders, Calder sent Rear-Admiral Stirling back to Rochefort with his five ships, leaving himself with only eight. If he found Rochefort empty, Stirling was to join Cornwallis. Meanwhile Calder took up station some forty to sixty miles north of Ferrol, and it was in that position that he learned that Villeneuve had entered the port, and that Allemand was also in the vicinity. He had no doubt whatever about what he should do; the next day, 10 August, he set course for Ushant, and four days later joined Cornwallis. Stirling had already done so, and on the next day, 15 August, Nelson appeared. The concentration was complete.

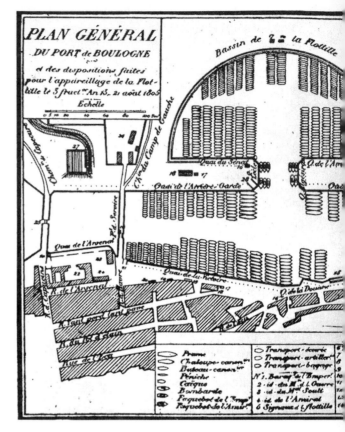

'A grand review followed by an embarkation rehearsal': a general plan of Boulogne Harbour, showing the arrangement of the invasion flotilla in the harbour

It is not to be wondered at if, at the time, the climactic moment in the campaign's high drama seemed to come in the first weeks of August. It was on 3 August that Napoleon himself arrived at Boulogne, and marked the occasion by holding a grand review in the spectacular style for which he was famous, followed, according to Mr James, by an embarkation rehearsal, repeated for good measure. We may judge how much this impressed his contemporaries, on both sides of the Channel, by the tone in which Mr James writes about it, just over thirty years later. He first gives the strength of the flotilla, as stated in the return of 20 July: 1,339 armed vessels of all types, with 954 unarmed transports, the whole being capable of carrying 163,645 men (of whom 16,783 were sailors) and 9,059 horses. He continues:

'It would be entering too much into detail, to explain all the regulations that contributed to perfect the system of this armament: suffice it that every thing was adopted which ingenuity could devise and ability execute, without much regard to the labour or the expense.

Anxious to have ocular proof of the degree of celerity with which the army could be embarked, Napoleon . . . ordered the operation to be executed twice in his presence. The result surpassed his belief. Although the troops had to march from camps, the extremities of which were more than two miles from the point of embarkation, one hour and a half after the beating of the *générale*, men and horses, all were on board.

This, as well it might, excited the admiration of the generals and other officers present, and all were elated at the prospect it held out; all, save the prime mover himself, and he, although he did not appear so, was filled with regret. His fleets were not in the Channel, and without them, he knew full well, that his plan could not succeed.'t

Propaganda was always as much a weapon in the Napoleonic armoury as the Old Guard or the Reserve Cavalry, and it would appear that Mr James was taken in by it on this occasion. Although the review was no doubt very splendid, it is most dubious whether the rehearsal took place at all – let alone twice in one day. On the contrary, Colonel Desbrière's research brought to light a report of this selfsame date, 3 August, which, while it outlines plans of elaborate detail and perfect symmetry, nevertheless shows that out of the 150,000 soldiers who were intended to embark,

only 90,000 were actually ready, and only 3,000 horses instead of over 9,000, while the harbours were choked with far too much shipping ever to get out on one tide, and Boulogne was blocked with transport for soldiers who were not there. No one, says this report, had the faintest idea how long it would take to get the invasion flotilla to sea. It was, in all probability, precisely to mask these unpalatable truths, that Napoleon caused the fabrication of the successful rehearsal to be publicized. Colonel Desbrière is so struck by the contrast between the plans and the reality that he poses a question as intriguing as it is impossible to answer:

'If, then, in an organisation essential for the success of his enterprise, where order and rapidity of embarkation were factors of the first importance, his genius indulged itself in systems simply symmetrical, bearing no relation either to the actual state of the troops and their service, or to the means of embarkation

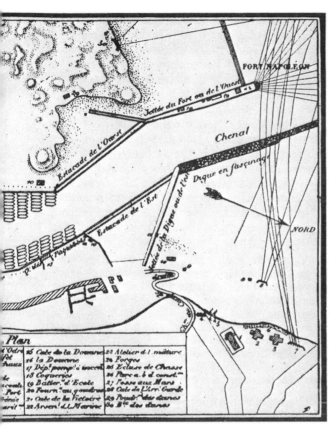

accumulated in the ports, we must surely ask ourselves if he ever seriously intended to make a sudden departure.'[u]

It would certainly appear that Napoleon was now in two minds. He knew that troop movements were taking place in Austria, provoked by his flaunting policy in Italy. General St Cyr also reported a secret call-up of the Neapolitan militia, suggesting the possibility of combined actions with the Russians in Corfu and the British in Malta. On the day before he set out for Boulogne Napoleon ordered ultimatums to be prepared for both Naples and Vienna, and on 4 August he approved the texts. Afterwards he said that he had been convinced that these threats would be effective, and leave him free to carry out his invasion of England. Yet it was on this very day that Talleyrand was reporting Nelson's return to Gibraltar, and forecasting a concentration of over fifty English ships in the Channel. 'This unfore-

seen concentration,' he added, 'leaves no doubt that the project of invasion is impracticable for the moment.'

Nevertheless, for a few days longer, Napoleon continued to play with the idea. 'Everything here is going well,' he wrote, 'and certes if we are masters of the passage for twelve hours, England has lived.' Ganteaume was once more ordered to be ready for instant departure from Brest. Then came Villeneuve's report of his action against Calder, containing the words: 'The enemy then made off. He had had several vessels crippled aloft, and the field of battle remained ours. Cries of joy and victory were heard from all our ships.'

Needless to say, Napoleon found no difficulty in translating this into a famous victory, brushing aside the tiresome detail that it was two of Villeneuve's ships, not Calder's, that had been captured. Villeneuve was ordered to continue his mission, collecting the Ferrol squadron and immediately coming north to the Channel. Marmont was ordered to redouble his deception ploy, to 'do the impossible' and tie down at least twelve ships of the line. So strong was the sense of imminent action on both sides of the Channel, that on 9 August the Admiralty warned Cornwallis: '. . . the enemy have it in contemplation to attempt immediately the invasion of this country from the ports of Holland and Boulogne.' Barham backed this with a private note saying: 'I take it for granted you will take a near station during the spring tides in order to reinforce the Eastern force[1] if necessary.' What neither the British government nor Napoleon yet knew was that on this very day Austria, so far from being cowed by Napoleon's ultimatum, had joined the Russo-British coalition.

Villeneuve's 'victory' soon turned to ashes. Admittedly, he had at last made his junction with the Ferrol squadron, but even as he did so every-thing began to go wrong. As he entered Corunna bay, facing Ferrol eight miles away, he received peremptory orders from Napoleon not to enter that port. It was too late; Admiral Gravina was already too far in to stop, and the French ships themselves found the anchorage at Corunna so confined that they ran aboard each other. All their supplies had to come from Ferrol – another difficulty; and to cap it all, the commander of the

Ferrol squadron, Rear-Admiral Gourdon, was apparently dying. All in all, Villeneuve had plenty to worry about without the news that Calder was not far away. The only encouragement was that Allemand was also near, with a further potential reinforcement. On 6 August Villeneuve sent out the 40-gun frigate *Didon* to find Allemand and bring him to Ferrol. He himself remained in Corunna bay until the 11th, trapped by contrary or failing winds.

It was with utter disgust that Napoleon, on 13 August, learned that his admiral had (seemingly) disregarded his orders not to enter Ferrol, and had anchored instead of coming straight on. General Daru, the intendant-general of the army, was present when the news arrived, and recorded Napoleon's explosion of rage: 'What a navy! What an admiral! What sacrifices for nothing!' And then, according to Daru, a dramatic sequel occurred. 'My hopes are frustrated,' said Napoleon. 'Daru, sit down and write.' And then and there he dictated the marching orders which constituted the plans of campaign for the Battles of Ulm and Austerlitz. It is, to say the least, a tall story; Napoleon was not in the habit of dictating military plans far in advance of events. As we shall see, the Ulm campaign was Napoleon's retribution for an unwise manoeuvre by the Austrians – and that manoeuvre did not begin until 8 September. As to Austerlitz, there could have been no conceivable preparation for that battle until after the victory at Ulm. So General Daru's entertaining reminiscence has to be dismissed; but it is more than likely that it was this news of Villeneuve that undermined Napoleon's last vestiges of hope of invading England. In any case, as we have seen, at this very moment the Royal Navy was completing its concentration at Ushant; remorseless pressures were deciding Napoleon's actions and the fate of Europe.

Remorseless pressures were also impelling Villeneuve towards his doom. From the moment he left Toulon until he reached Ferrol, the spectre of Nelson had haunted his waking and sleeping hours. As General Lauriston, commanding the soldiers in the fleet, reported to Napoleon, 'the fear of Nelson has got the upper hand of him'. Nelson's implacable chase to the West Indies and back, the action with Calder, and now, above all,

the fear of having to meet Nelson and Calder combined, all contributed to his lamentable condition. Not even the accession of fourteen fresh ships (five French and nine Spanish) in Ferrol had brought him any cheer; all his belief in his ability to fulfil the rôle allotted to him by his imperial master had evaporated. As he said later: 'Seeing that I had no confidence in the condition of my ships, in their sailing, and in their power of manoeuvring together, the concentration of the enemy and the knowledge they possess of all my movements since I reached the coast of Spain leave me no hope of being able to fulfil the grand object for which the fleet was destined.' Villeneuve was already a defeated man; even as he finally put to sea on 13 August his mind was full of doubts:

'I am about to sail, but I don't know what I shall do. Eight of the line keep in sight of the coast at eight leagues. They will follow us; I shall not be able to get contact with them, and they will close on the squadron before Brest or Cadiz, according as I make my course to the one port or the other . . . I do not hesitate to say [to Decrès] that I should be sorry to meet twenty of them. Our naval tactics are antiquated. We know nothing but how to place ourselves in line, and that is just what the enemy wants.'

The 'eight of the line' which alarmed him so much were, of course, fictitious; the only English ship of the line in the vicinity at this stage was the fast seventy-four, *Dragon*, left behind by Calder, and she observed Villeneuve's squadron at sea the following day. But there were frigates. Villeneuve was making for the Cape Finisterre rendezvous where he hoped to find Allemand – who was, in fact, less than 100 miles away to the north at this time. Allemand had already been sighted by the 32-gun British frigate *Aeolus*; it was she who took the news to Calder that sent him off to Ushant. Two days later she sighted Villeneuve's *Didon* and chased her for a time, but neither captain was anxious for a fight at this stage. Two days later, however, one of the most famous single-ship actions of the war occurred, when the 36-gun frigate *Phoenix*, under Captain Thomas Baker, came up with the *Didon*. So anxious was Captain Baker to bring on a fight that he persuaded an American merchant captain, in the event of his meeting the *Didon*, to say that the *Phoenix* was only a 20-gun ship, with such a high opinion of herself that she would almost certainly offer a challenge. The American played his part, and, accordingly, when Captain Milius of the *Didon* saw the *Phoenix* approaching, he believed that he had a fine opportunity of teaching at least one over-confident Englishman a lesson. Even without Captain Baker's deception, the French ship possessed the advantages of size, crew, number and weight of broadsides,[2] and there were some moments when it looked as if Captain Milius might well have his wish. But seamanship, good gunnery and morale worked their magic once more, and after a struggle lasting over four hours it was the *Didon* that surrendered. Villeneuve's chance of making contact with Allemand had gone, barring only miracles.

The frigates were everywhere: as the Combined Fleet left Ferrol it was seen and shadowed by the 32-gun *Iris*. Soon the *Iris* was joined by the 38-gun *Naiad*, and the two captains came to the conclusion that Villeneuve must be making for Cadiz. They were quite right, although in fact he did not make the decisive turn to the south until they had gone – the *Naiad* to inform Cornwallis, the *Iris* to warn Collingwood. It was during the night of 15–16 August that Villeneuve set his course for Cadiz. The state of his fleet was pitiful; Lauriston told Napoleon: 'The captains have no heart left to do well. Attention is no longer paid to signals, which are kept flying on the masts two or three hours. Discipline is completely gone.' Evidently, the desire for a safe harbour had now become obsessive, and it was not far away. But still there was no eluding the English cruisers. The *Iris*, running south, had fallen in with Captain Henry Blackwood in the *Euryalus*, who decided that the two must find and shadow the Combined Fleet together. On the 18th they heard from a neutral that a large fleet was nearing Cape St Vincent; there was no doubt what it was. Blackwood at once sent off the *Iris* to Ireland and, if possible, Cornwallis, while he himself waited for Villeneuve.

Meanwhile the whole pattern of the naval war was changing once again. It is one of the most surprising facts, and one of the most daring moves in the entire campaign, that Cornwallis, having concentrated a fleet of some thirty-six sail (after detachments) in the Channel, immediately broke it up again. Recognizing the absolute necessity to

find and fix Villeneuve, on 16 August Cornwallis detached Calder with eighteen of the line, including five three-deckers, to do just that. On the 19th the *Naiad* brought Cornwallis her news of Villeneuve's probable destination, and was promptly sent off after Calder with orders for him to pursue and if possible fight the enemy before they could reach port. But that was too much to ask; the next day the Combined Fleet appeared off Cadiz. Blackwood had found it impossible to pass through this throng of vessels to warn Collingwood, who was nearly caught at anchor. 'I must tell you,' Collingwood wrote to his wife, 'what a squeeze we had like to have got yesterday. While we were cruising off the town, down came the Combined Fleet of 36 sail of men-of-war. We were only three poor things with a frigate and a bomb, and drew off towards the Straits.' But in fact neither Villeneuve nor his captains had any stomach for a fight; the admiral was convinced that Nelson was nearby, and all he wanted to do was find refuge in Cadiz – a refuge which very soon became a prison. Collingwood was back on watch the following day, although with only four ships of the line, but six days later Bickerton joined him with his four ships, and on the 30th Calder arrived. Now only Allemand was at large. The combination had finally collapsed – but it did not matter, because by now Napoleon had abandoned it in any case.

Long before he discovered where Villeneuve had gone, Napoleon had made up his mind. On 22 August he learned that Villeneuve had left Corunna, and this day saw the last flicker of his hope that the Combined Fleet would come north.

Ganteaume was ordered to be ready to leave Brest the moment Villeneuve appeared; his whole fleet was already at the Bertheaume anchorage, closely observed by Cornwallis, who took his own flagship *Ville-de-Paris* (112) close in to reconnoitre. The next day there was a brief, brisk action between the advanced squadrons of the two fleets, and the French shore batteries did some damage to the leading English ships, Cornwallis himself being slightly wounded. For another week Ganteaume kept up similar shows of activity every day, but in fact they were only a deception. On 23 August Napoleon wrote to Talleyrand:

'. . . the more I reflect on the situation of Europe the more I see it is urgent to take a decisive line. I have, in reality, nothing to expect from Austria's explanation. She will only reply with fair phrases, and gain time to prevent my doing anything this winter . . . and in April I shall find 100,000 Russians in Poland, supplied by England with equipment, horses, artillery, &c., and 15,000 to 20,000 English at Malta, and 15,000 Russians at Corfu. I shall then find myself in a critical situation. My decision is made.'

The decision was still a painful one, but it was fortified by a letter from Decrès:

'. . . I know no situation more painful than my own. I beg your Majesty will consider that I have no interest but that of your flag and the honour of your arms. If your fleet is at Cadiz, I implore you to regard this event as a decree of destiny, which is reserving you for other operations. I implore you not to make it come back from Cadiz into the Channel . . .'

On 25 August Napoleon told Talleyrand that he had definitely abandoned his invasion of England. On the 26th Marshal Berthier, the chief of staff, received marching orders for the army. On the 28th the great camp at Boulogne and all the other camps of the Army of England began to break up. The soldiers saluted the watchful English cruisers with shouts of 'Vive l'Empereur!' The truth was, as one officer admitted, that 'there wasn't one of them who would not have preferred to go to the depths of Siberia, rather than the expedition to England'. So, long before Trafalgar, the threat of invasion vanished; yet history would not be cheated of its spectacular finales.

On 18 August, 1805, H.M.S. *Victory* anchored at Spithead; it was two years and two months (all but two days) since she had left England in May 1803. The next day the ship's log tersely records an historic moment: 'At 9, P.M., hauled down Lord Nelson's flag.' Nelson was home again – and in some doubt about what sort of reception he would have. As he came in he heard 'the account of Sir Robert Calder's Victory, and the joy of the event; together with the hearing that *John Bull* was not content, which I am sorry for'. The criticism of Calder grieved him by its unfairness, and prompted the thought: 'Who can command all the success which our Country may wish?'[3]

He was very conscious of his own lack of success during the past months: of having missed Villeneuve in the Mediterranean, missed him again in the West Indies, and missed him yet again off the coast of Spain when Calder found him. His ill-luck – and General Brereton – were still on his mind, and he would not admit that his health was more than 'so-so – yet, what is very odd, the better for going to the West Indies, even with the anxiety'.

The new anxiety was whether his motives would be understood, or whether he might not have to share blame with Calder – with, indeed, better reason. And this was no idle fear; on the very day that Nelson struck his flag, Lord Radstock, who would have called himself a friend, was remarking querulously that nothing had been heard from him since 27 July:

'I confess I begin to be fearful that he has worried his mind up to that pitch, that he cannot bear the idea of showing himself again to the world, until he shall have struck some blow, and that it is this hope that is now making him run about, half-frantic, in quest of adventures. That such unparalleled perseverance and true valour should thus evaporate in air is truly melancholy.'

If a friend could have misjudged him so much, we may imagine what enemies might have been saying.

It did not matter what they were saying; public opinion, so cruel to Calder, was bursting with kindness to Nelson. A vast crowd watched the *Victory* come in, and when Nelson's barge brought him ashore he received a tremendous ovation. In London it was the same. A possibly chastened Lord Radstock wrote: 'Lord Nelson arrived a few days ago. He was received in town almost as a conqueror, and was followed round by the people with huzzas. So much for a great and good name most nobly and deservedly acquired.' Lord Minto gives us an even more vivid picture of the hero's return:

'I met Nelson in a mob in Piccadilly, and got hold of his arm, so that I was mobbed too. It is really quite affecting to see the wonder and admiration, and love and respect of the whole world; and the genuine expression of all these sentiments at once, from gentle and simple, the moment he is seen. It is beyond anything represented in a play or in a poem of fame.'

There was undoubtedly a degree of hysteria abroad in England at that time, expressing itself as much in this adulation of Nelson as in the persecution of Calder. It can only be explained by the very real fear of invasion which possessed the people at that time. The spy mania which swept through Britain in the early months of the First World War, causing hallucinations of the liveliest kind, was also a manifestation of hysteria linked to fear of invasion. In 1940 nerves were steadier; even so, there were those who saw German paratroops all around them, who treated every minor blackout infringement as a case of high treason, and, indeed, saw traitors everywhere. The mood of 1805 has to be assessed in the light of these comparisons – with the additional reflection that in 1805 the government enjoyed none of the means of communicating with and calming the people that existed in 1914 and 1940. The people needed a miracle; Calder failed to provide it, and so was castigated. They needed a hero: Nelson was cast for the rôle.

Nelson himself was aware of the hazards involved. On 24 August he wrote to his friend Captain Keats of the *Superb* (now at last receiving her much needed repairs):

'Yesterday the Secretary of State,[4] which is a man who has only sat one solitary day in his Office, and of course knows but little of what is passed, and indeed the Minister,[5] were all full of the Enemy's Fleet, and as I am now set up for a *Conjuror*, and God knows they will very soon find out I am far from being one, I was asked my opinion, against my inclination, for if I make one wrong guess the charm will be broken . . .'

Yet he was prepared to say one thing which illuminates his own thinking about the nature of the whole campaign: '. . . but this I ventured without any fear, that if Calder got fairly close alongside their twenty-seven or twenty-eight Sail, that by the time the Enemy had beat our Fleet soundly, they would do us no harm this year.' It is perhaps in this understanding of what Mahan, in a lapidary phrase, calls 'a battle wisely lost, as contrasted with what Jomini calls the sterile glory of fighting battles merely to win them', that Nelson's true genius resides. This was what he meant when he spoke of having made up his mind 'to great sacrifices' when he pursued Villeneuve's eighteen ships to the West Indies with only ten.[6]

This was what he meant when he said: 'we won't part without a battle.'[7] This was, in fact, the difference between him and Calder: 'this realization of the possible fruitfulness of a defeat' in the crippling of the enemy's power to carry through a larger enterprise. When Barham, who scarcely knew him, and may well have thought him something of a poseur, read his journal of the two pursuits of Villeneuve, he at last appreciated the breadth and depth of Nelson's mind in forming his own plans of operations, and all doubt vanished as to the command-in-chief of the Mediterranean.[8]

The result, of course, was what would have been for any other man a deep personal tragedy. Nelson himself wryly summed it up in a later letter: 'I was only twenty-five days, from dinner to dinner, absent from the *Victory*.'[9] The worry of his health, his deep and long-felt need for recuperation in the English scene and climate, his love for his family, his mistress and the four-year-old daughter whom he hardly knew, the necessity of putting his financial affairs in better order: all were thrust aside at the knowledge that the Prime Minister 'is pleased to think that my service may be wanted'. This was when he had been home less than ten days. On 31 August he wrote: 'my stay is very uncertain.' The *Victory* had been ordered out again, and Nelson seemed to take it for granted that he would be in her, though in fact at this stage she was meant to join Cornwallis. Then, on 1 September, the *Euryalus* hove to off the Needles, having made the journey from Cape St Vincent in just ten days to announce that Villeneuve was safely in Cadiz. Passing Nelson's house at Merton the following morning, on his way to the Admiralty, Captain Blackwood gave him the news. Shortly afterwards it was in Barham's possession, and soon after that it was all over London. The relief was intense. So Villeneuve would not be coming up the Channel; almost as important, he would not be intercepting the priceless East and West India convoys, now approaching the English coast.[10] On 3 September Lord Radstock wrote to Nelson: 'Thank God! Thank God a thousand times that these Jack o'Lanterns are once more safely housed without having done that mischief which was justly dreaded. The papers tell us you will shortly be after them.' This was correct: Nelson's orders are dated 3 September, and the next day we find

'Hoisted the Flag of the Right Honourable Lord
Viscount Nelson': Nelson's last departure from
Portsmouth, 14 September 1805; painting by
Christopher Ridley in the Royal Exchange

Lady Hamilton writing to his niece: 'My dear
Friend, I am again broken-hearted, as our dear
Nelson is immediately going. It seems as though
I have had a fortnight's dream, and am awoke to
all the misery of this cruel separation. But what
can I do? His powerful arm is of so much consequence to his Country. But I do, nor cannot say
more. My heart is broken.'

Among the first orders that now streamed out
from Barham's office at the Admiralty in one of its
heaviest periods of business (2–4 September) was
one stopping the *Victory*: she would be Nelson's
flagship after all. Now the remainder of his time
ashore was to be occupied with preparations
for departure, and thoughts about what it might
lead him to. He wrote to Alexander Davison on
6 September:

'I hope my absence will not be long, and that I shall
soon meet the Combined Fleets, with a force sufficient
to do the job well; for half a victory would but half
content me. But I do not believe the Admiralty can
give me a force within fifteen or sixteen Sail of the
Line of the Enemy; and therefore, if every Ship took
her opponent, we should have to contend with a fresh
Fleet of fifteen or sixteen Sail of the Line. But I will
do my best; and I hope God Almighty will go with me.
I have much to lose, but little to gain; and I go because
it's right, and I will serve the Country faithfully.'

On the night of Friday 13 September, he wrote in
his private diary:

'At half-past ten drove from dear dear Merton, where
I left all which I hold dear in this world, to go to serve
my King and Country. May the Great God whom I
adore enable me to fulfil the expectations of my
Country; and if it is His good pleasure that I should
return, my thanks will never cease being offered up
to the Throne of His Mercy. If it is His good
providence to cut short my days upon earth, I bow
with the greatest submission, relying that He will
protect those so dear to me, that I may leave behind.
His will be done. Amen, Amen, Amen.'

He arrived at Portsmouth at six o'clock on 14
September, and at two o'clock he went aboard the
Victory. A great crowd watched him embark, as
they had watched him come ashore, cheering him
all the way as his barge pushed off. Sentries who
tried to hold them back were wedged helplessly
in the throng.

It was England's farewell to her champion.
Seeing this demonstration of affection, Nelson
said to Captain Hardy of the *Victory*: 'I had
their huzzas before – I have their hearts now!'
Indeed he did – to an extent not known by any
other naval or military commander before or since.
The navy itself does not express emotions on such
occasions, however much it may be conscious of
them; there is just a hint – no more – of a proper
emotion in the *Victory*'s log: 'September 14.
A.M. at 11.30, hoisted the Flag of the Right
Honourable Lord Viscount Nelson, K.B. Sunday,
15th. 8, A.M., weighed and made sail to the
S.S.E. *Euryalus* in company.'

The two setpieces of the great European drama
rolled towards their conclusions with what, at
this distance of time, looks like remorseless
precision, but in the fog of war never seemed quite
like that to the participants. Yet the sense of
mastery was present in both elements, land and
sea, and only accident – never to be ignored –
could have halted its exercise. The beginning
came on land, marked by the birth of an instrument
of power that would dominate Europe for the
next ten years. On 29 August the Army of England
ceased to exist: it became 'The Grand Army', a
legend in its own lifetime and ever since. The poet
Alfred de Vigny, a schoolboy during the last days
of the empire, wrote:

'. . . our teachers' voices were drowned in my ears by
the roll of drums . . . It was impossible to concentrate
for any length of time while our heads were awhirl
with the thunder of cannon and with bells pealing out
the *Te Deum* . . . Indeed, the masters themselves read
out to us the bulletins of the Grand Army, and Tacitus
and Plato were interrupted by our cries of "Long live
the Emperor!" 'v

The triumphs and sorrows of the Grand Army are
inscribed on the Arc de Triomphe, in the street
names of Paris, and in a thousand other similar
memorials throughout France; and this was the
beginning of them all, August 1805, when the
camps broke up, and the long, long march began.

The seven army corps were quickly on the move.
An officer of Marshal Davout's III Corps describes
the scene:

'The seven army corps were quickly on the move'.
Left: The Grand Army leaves Boulogne; Right:
'We shall not rest until we have planted our eagles
on the territory of our foes' – the Grand Army
crossing the Rhine

'The camps at Boulogne, Ambleteuse, Amiens and St. Omer are all in movement to the sound of drums, trumpets and bands. It is an unimaginable hubbub, uproar, enthusiasm. The opening of the campaign fills the army with inexpressible contentment. Splendid army, well disciplined, admirably turned out and equipped . . . We flood through the towns and all the villages that we pass with joy on our faces and in our hearts; our line of march is through Lille and Belgium, and we reach the Rhine at Mannheim . . .'

From Boulogne to the Rhine is over 300 miles; the Grand Army had lined up along the river by 24 September – a leisurely pace compared with what was to come. On 26 September Napoleon himself arrived, and issued one of his characteristic proclamations:

'Soldiers!
Your Emperor is amongst you. You are only the advance-guard of the mighty people. If necessary it will rise in its entirety at my call to confound and break up this new league woven by English hatred and English gold. But, soldiers, we have forced marches to make, every kind of fatigue and privation to endure. Whatever obstacles we meet, we shall conquer, and we shall not rest until we have planted our eagles on the territory of our foes!'

The Grand Army crossed the Rhine in a fever of excitement, wearing green twigs as though they were laurels; the scene was set.

Slow to join the coalition, and far from recovered from the blows they had sustained at Marengo and Hohenlinden in the previous war, the Austrians now displayed a strange temerity that gave Napoleon a rare chance. They counted on his movements being as slow as their own – an extraordinary self-deception after the whirlwind of his campaign in Italy in 1796, and the very similar display in 1800. Instead of waiting for the three Russian armies, totalling nearly 100,000 men, who were to support them, and instead of

taking the offensive with their main army, 95,000
men in north Italy under the Archduke Charles,
the Austrians made a premature push into Bavaria
with what should have been primarily a covering
force. This was the army of the Archduke
Ferdinand, numbering 70,000; its function should
have been to discourage the Elector of Bavaria
from siding with Napoleon, and to cover the
Russian advance. Only when the allies were united
was this army supposed to take the offensive,
towards Strasbourg, under the command of the
Emperor Francis. Meanwhile, the Archduke
Ferdinand's authority was purely nominal; the
real commander of his army was Quartermaster-
General Mack.

General Mack was the only Austrian general
who had suffered no great defeat; his reputation
was accordingly high – in some circles. A recent
French writer[w] calls him one of Austria's 'most
celebrated generals, of great valour though greyed

in harness'. Neither Napoleon nor, interestingly,
Nelson would have agreed. It so happened that
Nelson had met Mack in Naples in 1798, when he
had come to command the Neapolitan army, and
hearing that he was once more to hold an important
position in 1805 Nelson wrote to his friend the
Duke of Clarence: 'If your Royal Highness has
any communication with Government, let not
General Mack be employed, for I know him to be
a rascal, a scoundrel and a coward.' Napoleon also
appears to have thought him a charlatan – and it
was certainly Mack who made Napoleon a present
of the opening phase of the campaign. He was a
firm believer in the old eighteenth-century style
of positional warfare, and believed that he had
found a master position near the junction of the
Danube and the Iller, inside Bavarian territory at
Ulm. No doubt he believed that he had stolen a
march on Napoleon when he accordingly invaded
Bavaria as early as 8 September; in reality he had

thrust the head of his army into the jaws of a greedy lion. Once Napoleon knew where Mack had gone, he knew what to do. He was on the very peak of his warrior form, and what followed is the classic of all his campaigns for speed and decision.

No sooner was the Grand Army across the Rhine than Napoleon hurled it towards the Danube. Now was the time of the forced marches; now, as the weather changed to cold and pelting rain, was the time of the 'moaners', '*les grognards*', the old soldiers who were, in truth, the backbone of the Grand Army. In long, miserable columns, the bright uniforms turning filthy and filthier, it poured through the defiles of the Black Forest towards the rear of the Austrians.

'Never did anyone make such a fearful march. They didn't give us one hour's sleep. Night and day we marched by platoons. We held each other up in the ranks so as not to fall over. If anyone did fall over, nothing could wake him.'x
'The regiment marched night and day, and in this campaign I saw for the first time men asleep while they marched, something I would never have thought possible.'
'I saw the Emperor looking like a devil. You'd have said he'd been dragged through mud. He was unrecognisable, he was so covered in muck.'

In ten days they reached the Danube, and the toils began to close around the foolish Mack. Convinced of the strength of his position at Ulm, he chose to believe that it was he, and not Napoleon, who was gaining the advantage. Had he been Frederick the Great, at the head of his veteran army, or Wellington, with the men of 1814 behind him, he might indeed have struck mortal blows at the French lines of communication, and turned the tables on them. But it was 1805, and he was Mack. He did nothing. By 6 October the French had reached the Danube. In all the opening skirmishes and combats they proved their superiority. On the 14th Marshal Ney forced the river crossing at Elchingen, from which he later took the title of a dukedom long before he became Prince of the Moskva. The next day Ney stormed the Michelsberg defences outside Ulm, and at last Mack realized that he was trapped. On the 17th he signed a convention by which he would surrender on the 25th unless relieved, but in fact he accepted the necessity to do so on the 20th. On 21 October

27,000 Austrian infantry and cavalry with sixty cannon, forty stands of colours and eighteen generals surrendered to Napoleon. Marshal Marmont described the scene: 'Such a spectacle can never be again, and my memory of it is still vivid. What transports of delight among our soldiers! What a reward for a month of travail! What ardour, what self-confidence a result like that instils in an army! And with that army there was nothing you could not undertake, no enterprise that would not succeed.' Napoleon himself said, in his 'Bulletin de l'Armée': 'The day of Ulm has been one of the best days in the history of France.'

Not entirely; for something else was happening that day. The Royal Navy was winning its crowning victory.

'Sunday, September 28th, 1805.
Fresh breezes at N.N.W. At daylight bore up, and made sail. At nine saw the *Aetna* crusing. At noon saw eighteen sail. Nearly calm. In the evening joined the Fleet under Vice-Admiral Collingwood. Saw the Enemy's Fleet in Cadiz, amounting to thirty-five or thirty-six Sail of the Line.'

So Nelson's private diary records his arrival at the climactic rendezvous of his career. He came in without fuss or panoply; Collingwood had been warned not to give him the customary gun salute, or hoist colours, 'for it is as well not to proclaim to the Enemy every Ship which may join the Fleet'. In any case, Nelson by now had the measure of Villeneuve's nervousness; he urged General Fox, the Governor of Gibraltar, to forbid the *Gibraltar Gazette* to mention the strength of the fleet, or the names of ships, 'For I much fear, that if the Enemy know of our increased numbers, we shall never see them out of Cadiz'.

Only twenty-three days would separate Nelson's arrival in the fleet from the great consummation which he had so ardently desired and sought for so long. They were days of great activity; in the relevant volume of his Letters and Despatches there are over 100 separate documents from his hand during this period, ranging from diplomatic papers to a famous tactical memorandum, from friendly exchanges of views with Collingwood to instructions on the procedure of investigation of a suspected embezzling boatswain.[11] They were days of worry; the Combined Fleet might yet give him the slip. He did not think they would, but it could not be ruled out, and once more he was plagued by the everlasting shortage of frigates: 'I have only two Frigates to watch them, and not one with the Fleet. I am most exceedingly anxious for more *eyes*, and hope the Admiralty are hastening them to me. The last Fleet was lost to me for want of Frigates; God forbid this should.'[12]

It was his firm opinion that he needed eight frigates 'to be constantly with the Fleet off Cadiz', and two more to convoy store ships to and from Gibraltar; instead he had for the time being only two, increased later to five, though the number fluctuated constantly, and on the day of battle would be four. Admittedly, out of a total of twenty-two which he considered necessary for the Mediterranean command (stretching from Cape St Vincent to the Dardanelles) the Admiralty had, with unusual generosity, allocated twenty-one – but only fourteen were actually on the station. On the other hand, he did have Blackwood – the Hon. Henry Blackwood, captain of the *Euryalus*, who was in command of all the cruisers watching the enemy in Cadiz. Nobody understood such a business better than Blackwood, and the communication between them was close, although the main body of the fleet was generally at least fifty miles from land. 'I should never wish to be more than forty-eight hours without hearing from you,' Nelson told Blackwood on 9 October, and the next day, '. . . let me know every movement. I rely on you, that we can't miss getting hold of them, and I will give them such a shaking as they never yet experienced; at least I will lay down my life in the attempt.'

Fortunately, there was not only Blackwood; reporting his arrival in the fleet to Ball on 30 September, Nelson wrote: 'I find them as perfect as could be expected . . .' and to Alexander Davison on the same day: 'Nothing can be finer than the Fleet under my command.'[13] This was partly an acknowledgment of the presence of trusted friends, men whom he knew to be masters of their profession; it was also a tribute to the work of Vice-Admiral Collingwood, whom he relieved. It was a piece of great good fortune that his old friend Collingwood ('My dear Coll') should now be his second-in-command. The understanding between them was complete, their minds entirely in tune, as the brisk correspondence between them during these three weeks shows.[14] Collingwood may not have aroused in the fleet the devotion that Nelson could command, but he had its full respect, and that also was a hopeful factor.

Curiously, this last phase of the long campaign seems to have been reserved for these two men, as though by a deliberate destiny. Bickerton had gone home. Vice-Admiral Sir Robert Calder, much broken down in health as was the fate of admirals in these gruelling times, left for England to face his court of enquiry on 14 October. 'He has an ordeal to pass through which I fear he little expects,' Nelson told Collingwood. Collingwood replied: 'I am grieved whenever I think of Sir Robert Calder's case.' It was characteristic of Nelson that when Calder protested at having to leave his three-decker, the *Prince of Wales*, Nelson allowed him to go home in it, disobeying the Admiralty's orders and risking their Lordships' displeasure at his parting with a 98-gun ship before a battle: 'but I trust that I shall be considered to have done right as a man, and to a Brother Officer in affliction – my heart could not stand it, and so the thing must rest. I shall submit to the wisdom of the Board to censure me or not, as to them may seem best for the Service . . .'[15]

There were two other flag officers with the fleet: Rear-Admiral Thomas Louis, and Rear-Admiral the Earl of Northesk. Louis was an old friend; he flew his flag in the *Canopus*, herself part of the Mediterranean Fleet since 1803. But Louis was out of luck; on 3 September, with four other ships of the line (including the three-decker *Queen*) he was detached to Gibraltar to take in water and provisions. Taking leave of Nelson the previous evening, Louis said: 'You are sending us away, my Lord – the Enemy will come out, and we shall have no share in the Battle.' Nelson replied: 'My dear Louis, I have no other means of keeping my Fleet complete in provisions and water, but by sending them in detachments to Gibraltar. The Enemy *will* come out, and we shall fight them; but there will be time for you to get back first. I look upon *Canopus* as my right hand; and I send you first to insure your being here to help beat them.'

But it was not to be; so two out of four flag

officers would be absent on the day. The fourth, Lord Northesk, is a somewhat shadowy figure. He does not appear to have been an intimate; Nelson refers to him in a letter to Collingwood as 'the Earl'. He did not hold a separate command, which, as we shall see, may have been a pity when the time of action came.

And there were the captains, the 'band of brothers'. As was his custom, Nelson lost no time in meeting them, and sharing his thoughts with them. On 1 October he wrote to Lady Hamilton:

'. . . I believe my arrival was most welcome, not only to the Commander of the Fleet, but also to every individual in it; and, when I came to explain to them the "*Nelson touch*", it was like an electric shock. Some shed tears, all approved – "It was new – it was singular – it was simple!" and, from Admirals downwards, it was repeated – "It must succeed, if ever they will allow us to get at them! You are, my Lord, surrounded by friends whom you inspire with confidence." Some may be Judas's; but the majority are certainly much pleased with my commanding them.'

This letter, and the secret memorandum dated 9 October in which he outlined his tactical intentions, have, between them, been responsible for a great deal of nonsense. The 'Nelson touch' has been interpreted in a hundred ways; sailing instructions and fleet formations have been analysed and re-analysed to give it meaning; pedantry has feasted upon it. The simple truth, as we shall shortly see, is that the 'Nelson touch' never really lay in a system of tactics, formations, or theoretical propositions; it lay in personal magnetism. Captain Duff of the *Mars*, writing to his wife on the same day as Nelson's letter to Lady Hamilton, spoke for many when he said: 'I dined with his Lordship yesterday, and had a very merry dinner. He certainly is the pleasantest Admiral I ever served under.' And a few days later: 'He is so good and pleasant a man, that we all wish to do what he likes, without any kind of orders.' At the root of this magnetism, this quality that bound his subordinates to him, was trust. As General Fuller says, writing of the tactical memorandum: 'The novelty in this memorandum does not lie in the "modes" of attack . . . but in the liberty of action delegated to subordinates to carry them out. Nelson, as a subordinate, had

displayed the highest initiative at the battle of St. Vincent, and he expected his captains to model themselves upon him.' The secret of his victory lay, not in theory, but in the degree to which they did so.[16]

In the memorandum itself, it is the offensive spirit that comes through, as vigorously today as in 1805, though the tactical dispositions are no longer of any practical significance. The whole object of the paper, indeed, firmly stated in the first sentence, is to make the offensive effective: 'Thinking it almost impossible to bring a Fleet of forty Sail of the Line into a Line of Battle . . . without such a loss of time that the opportunity would probably be lost of bringing the Enemy to Battle in such a manner as to make the business decisive, I have therefore made up my mind . . .' Nelson saw with complete clarity the absurdity – indeed, the sheer impossibility – of the old-fashioned linear battle formation. The answer, as he saw it, was to divide his fleet into three squadrons or divisions, in such a manner as to be able, without loss of time, to concentrate at least twenty-four ships against any part of the enemy's line. And this, naturally, would require the utmost subordinate initiative: 'The Second in Command will, after my intentions are made known to him, have the entire direction of his line to make the attack upon the Enemy, and to follow up the blow until they are captured or destroyed.' A lifetime of experience had taught Nelson that 'Something must be left to chance; nothing is sure in a Sea Fight beyond all others', and so he gave his captains a piece of broad advice whose meaning was unmistakable: '. . . in case Signals can neither be seen or perfectly understood, no Captain can do very wrong if he places his Ship alongside that of an Enemy.'

And in that fashion he proposed to pass the hostile fleet, section by section, through a mincing machine, beginning with the rear twelve ships, on which the second-in-command's division would concentrate: 'The remainder of the Enemy's Fleet, 34 Sail, are to be left to the management of the Commander-in-Chief, who will endeavour to take care that the movements of the Second in Command are as little interrupted as possible.'

As we have said, the reader may make what he will of it: parts of the memorandum read like a blueprint of Trafalgar, other parts seem to have

Capt. JOHN COOKE, of the BELLEROPHON.

Killed at Trafalgar

Capt. GEORGE DUFF, of the MARS.

Killed at Trafalgar

Capt. THOS. M. HARDY, of the VICTORY.

as an Admiral. After R. Evans.

Capt. HENRY BLACKWOOD, of the EURYALUS.

as a Captain. After J. Hoppner.

Vice Admiral COLLINGWOOD.
After C. Turner. About 1804.

Capt. Edw. CODRINGTON, of the ORION.

Commander in Chief at Navarino. After G. Hayter.

Capt. Sir E. BERRY, of the AGAMEMNON.

as a Junior Captain, about 1798. After H. Singleton.

Rear Admiral Lord NORTHESK.
After H Patterson About 1811.

'The majority are much pleased with my commanding
them'; some of Nelson's captains at Trafalgar

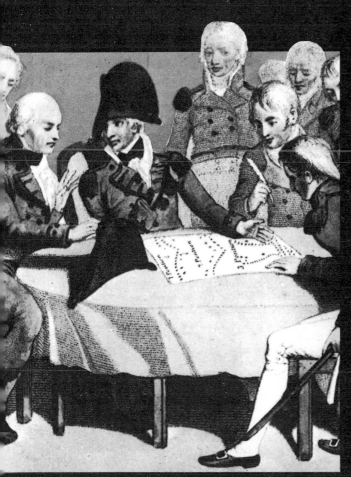

Nelson's Battle Fleet at Trafalgar

The 'Flying Squadron', arrived 8 June at Cadiz
*Dreadnought (98) T Vice-Admiral Collingwood
Colossus (74) T
Achille (74) T
Mars (74) T
*Queen (98)   Rear-Admiral Sir Richard Bickerton
Tonnant (80) T
Bellerophon (74) T
Minotaur (74) T

Sir Robert Calder's Squadron, joined 30 August
*Prince of Wales (98) Vice-Admiral Sir Robert Calder
*Britannia (100) T   Rear-Admiral the Earl of Northesk
Téméraire (98) T
Prince (98) T
Neptune (98) T
*Canopus (80)   Rear-Admiral Thomas Louis
Revenge (74) T
Spartiate (74) T
Conqueror (74) T
Defence (74) T
Orion (74) T
Swiftsure (74) T
Spencer (74)
Tigre (74)
Zealous (74)
Donegal (74)
Polyphemus (64) T
Africa (64) T

Nelson, 29 September
*Victory (100) T
Thunderer (74) T
Ajax (74) T

From England, 7 October
Defiance (74) T

From Gibraltar, 8 October
Leviathan (74) T

9–13 October
*Royal Sovereign (100) T   Collingwood, transferred
Belleisle (74) T
Agamemnon (64) T

Less:

To Gibraltar, 2 October	To England, 14 October
*Canopus	*Prince of Wales
Queen	**To Gibraltar, 17 October**
Spencer	Donegal
Tigre	
Zealous	

*Flagship of the officer named
T   — Fought at Trafalgar
Number in brackets   = number of guns

Top: Nelson greets Collingwood; Bottom: 'I...explain to them the "Nelson touch"; it was like an electric shock'

no connection with what ultimately happened. The spirit of the occasion breathes through every line, and yet it is not in this memorandum that one finds the epitome of Nelson's approach to the Battle of Trafalgar. That is to be discovered in the account of a conversation he held at Merton before he set out for Cadiz. He was talking to his favourite captain, Keats of the *Superb*,[17] and outlined his intentions very much on the lines of the later memorandum: the three divisions, the absolute initiative of the second-in-command, the concentration on a selected part of the enemy's line. Then he asked: 'What do you think of it?' Keats recalled: 'Such a question I felt required consideration. I paused. Seeing it, he said, "but I'll tell you what *I* think of it. I think it will surprise and confound the Enemy. They won't know what I am about. It will bring forward a pell-mell Battle, and that is what I want."'

In other words, he meant to achieve surprise, that eternal blessing in war, by what a later generation would call an '*attaque brusquée*', and a close-quarters fight in which the general superiority of his fleet would more than compensate for any inferiority in numbers. And that is, indeed, a blueprint of Trafalgar.

Pondering all these thoughts, and well occupied with the daily business of the fleet, Nelson composed himself in a frame of mind nowhere better expressed than in a letter to his friend, Alexander Davison:

'Day by day, my dear friend, I am expecting the [Combined] Fleet to put to sea – every day, hour, and moment; and then you may rely that, if it is within the power of man to get at them, that it shall be done; and I am sure that all my brethren look to that day as the finish of our laborious cruise. The event no man can say exactly; but I must think, or render great injustice to those under me, that, let the Battle be when it may, it will never have been surpassed. My shattered frame, if I survive that day, will require rest, and that is all I shall ask for. If I fall on such a glorious occasion, it shall be my pride to take care that my friends shall not blush for me. These things are in the hands of a wise and just Providence, and His will be done! . . . Do not think I am low-spirited on this account, or fancy anything is to happen to me; quite the contrary – my mind is calm, and I have only to think of destroying our inveterate foe.'[18]

Coincidence, the jester of history, was hard at work throughout this last phase of the long campaign. It was a coincidence which no novelist would dare, that on the day before Nelson sailed from Portsmouth, Napoleon was drafting the orders to Villeneuve that would cause him to do the very thing that Nelson and his 'brethren' most desired.

It was another such coincidence that Villeneuve should receive those fatal orders on the exact day that Nelson joined the fleet outside Cadiz. And it is a curiosity – but by no means a coincidence – that it should be a land force, the Craig expedition, that prompted the manoeuvre which brought the destruction of the Combined Fleet. The 'plans of pygmies' achieved that much, after all.[19]

It was on 14 September, ten days before he set out for the Rhine, that Napoleon made his last attempt to weave Villeneuve effectively into his plans:

'Having resolved to make a powerful diversion by directing into the Mediterranean our naval forces concentrated at the port of Cadiz, combined with those of his Catholic Majesty, we would have you know that our intention is that, immediately on receipt of these presents, you will seize the first favourable opportunity of sailing with the Combined Fleet and proceeding to that sea. . . . You will first make for Cartagena to join the Spanish squadron which is in that port; you will then proceed to Naples and disembark on some point of the coast the troops you carry on board to join the army under the orders of General St. Cyr. If you find at Naples any English or Russian ships of war, you will seize them. The fleet under your command will remain off the Neapolitan shores so long as you may judge necessary to do the utmost harm to the enemy, *and to intercept an expedition which they intend to send from Malta* [my italics]. Our intention is that wherever you meet the enemy in inferior force you will attack them without hesitation, and obtain a decision against them. It will not escape you that the success of these operations depends essentially on the promptness of your leaving Cadiz.'[20]

The next day, which was the day that Nelson set sail from Portsmouth, Napoleon had second thoughts. Villeneuve, as he saw it, had let him down time and time again; all the latest reports indicated that the man was more or less unnerved.

Could he be depended on to extract the Combined Fleet from Cadiz under the eyes of a strong British fleet, and get it into the Mediterranean? The answer was evidently 'no', and accordingly Villeneuve was superseded by Vice-Admiral Rosily, who was ordered to set out forthwith for Cadiz, take command of the fleet, and send Villeneuve home to give an account of his 'excessively pusillanimous' conduct.

Villeneuve's orders to sail far outstripped Rosily with his supersession, and found him in one of his rare moods of optimism. He issued one of those Orders of the Day with which he favoured his fleet from time to time, and which seem to apply to entirely different people, even to a different campaign.[21] He announced his intention to sail on the 30th, and to 'strike down England's tyrannical domination of the seas'. But then came news that

the blockading squadron had been reinforced, and uncertainty set in again. On 2 October it was much increased by the definite news that Nelson was now present, and that he intended to burn the Combined Fleet in its harbour by distant bombardment.[22] This placed Villeneuve in several dilemmas: on the one hand, he had Napoleon's definite orders to sail at once – but was that any longer feasible in view of Nelson's arrival and the increase of the British fleet to 'from thirty-one to thirty-three of the line, of which eight are of three decks'? On the other hand, if he did not sail, the only way to protect the Combined Fleet against distant fire was to form a large flotilla of gun-boats and bomb-vessels to keep the British out of range – and these could only be manned by taking sailors and soldiers from the fleet. Which was it to be?

It is indicative of Villeneuve's abject state that

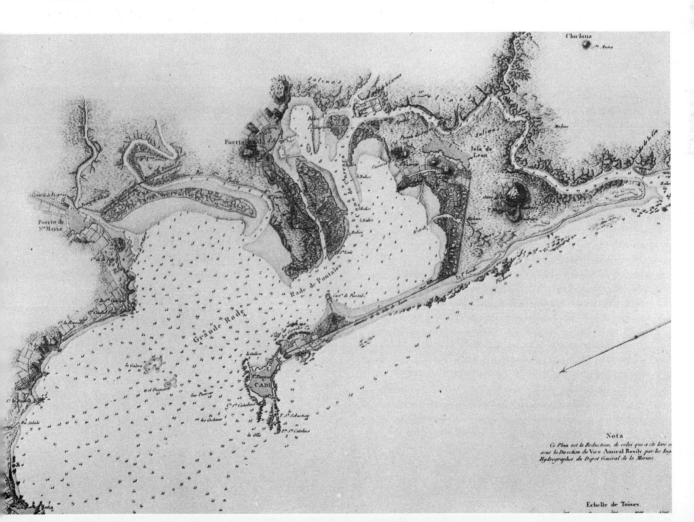

he now adopted the worst possible procedure in such a case: he summoned a council of war. It is an old adage that 'Councils of War never fight', and this one, held on 8 October, was no exception. The question was put: 'Ought or ought not the Combined Squadron to put to sea, seeing that it is not in such superiority of force as to balance its inherent inferiority?' The very wording is that of beaten men, and it is no surprise to learn that the result of the vote was a decision not to sail, and to use the fleet's personnel to build up a defensive flotilla. It must be said that, taking all circumstances into account, the decision was probably correct, providing (a) that the defensive flotilla could really be made strong enough and efficient enough to keep the British at a safe distance, and (b) that the defensive stance was resolutely maintained, without wavering between one policy and the other. The first of these conditions might have been fulfilled, though that does not seem likely. The second, in view of Napoleon's imperative orders (repeated to Rosily, though the council could not know this), seems quite impossible. So, inevitably, the effect of the council of war was further indecision – with the added mischief of bad temper and high words exchanged between the French and Spanish officers, to the grave harm of discipline and cooperation.

So matters rested for a week or more; as Nelson put it: 'I have thirty-six Sail of the Line looking me in the face; unfortunately there is a strip of land between us . . .' Behind that 'strip of land' all was doubt and hesitation, until suddenly, amazingly, they were dispersed, as a final fit of boldness took hold of Villeneuve. What prompted it was this: Admiral Rosily arrived at Madrid on 12 October; from there to Cadiz at that time was a ten-day journey, part of it through country infested with brigands. The French ambassador in Madrid warned him not to continue without an adequate escort; while this was being collected, however, the news of his arrival sped before him. It is not quite certain when Villeneuve received it, but when he did he understood it instantly. He knew that he would now be superseded, more or less in disgrace. This knowledge must have come to him some time between 16 and 18 October, and with it came two more items. The first was noted by

Nelson on 16 October: 'Fine weather, wind Easterly; the Combined Fleets cannot have finer weather to put to sea.' The second item was that Admiral Louis's detachment had been observed escorting a convoy for Malta eastwards to pass Cartagena, which meant that Nelson could be short of six ships. Impending disgrace, good sailing weather, a weakened enemy – it was enough; on 18 October Villeneuve made the signal to prepare to weigh anchor, and for the last time addressed his fleet. With sound discernment he warned them what Nelson's tactics were likely to be: an enveloping attack on the rear. He warned the captains not to wait for signals, but rather to be guided only by their courage and their love of glory. He concluded:

'There is nothing to alarm us in the sight of an English squadron; their 74s have barely 500 men on board; they are worn out by a two-years' cruise; they are not braver than us, and they have infinitely less motive to fight well, less love of country. They can manoeuvre well. In a month we shall be as good as them. So everything joins to give us confidence in a glorious success, and a new era for the Imperial Navy.'

General Mack had already accepted that his game was up: on 19 October came the first of the Austrian surrenders, which culminated with his own on the following day – 8,000 men who attempted to escape encirclement, but were rounded up by Marshal Murat. It was a day of elation in the Grand Army.

It was also a day of elation off Cadiz. At six o'clock in the morning the frigate *Sirius* made the signal to *Euryalus*: 'Enemy have topsail yards hoisted.' At seven o'clock *Sirius* made the signal that every blockading squadron had yearned to see for nearly two and a half years, No. 370: 'The enemy's ships are coming out of port.'

From *Euryalus* the signal passed to *Phoebe*, from *Phoebe* to *Mars*, in which Captain Duff was commanding the Advance Squadron, and from *Mars* it was received by *Victory*, fifty miles from Cadiz, at 9.30 a.m.[23] Nelson, without an instant's delay, made the signal 'General chase, south-east', and stood away for the Straits of Gibraltar.

In fact, thanks to light land breezes, it was only twelve ships under Rear-Admiral Magon that managed to clear Cadiz that day, watched all the time by Blackwood's inshore cruiser squadron. Blackwood wrote to his wife: 'The day is fine, the sight of course beautiful.' The next day found Nelson at the mouth of the Straits; the weather was no longer fine, and the sight that greeted him at dawn very far from beautiful: no sign of the enemy, and no sign either of Rear-Admiral Louis, whom Nelson had hoped to find there. Captain Edward Codrington of *Orion*, writing to *his* wife that morning, struck a very different note: 'All our gay hopes are fled, and instead of being under all sail in a very light breeze and fine weather, expecting to bring the enemy to battle, we are under close-reefed topsails in a very stormy wind with thick weather and the dastardly French we find returned to Cadiz.' The last statement, however, was quite wrong; the truth was that it was not until this day, the 20th, that Villeneuve was able to assemble his whole fleet outside Cadiz, and really put to sea, watched without intermission by Blackwood's frigates, and by afternoon, when the weather cleared, Nelson was receiving their signals again. But it had been an anxious morning.

The Combined Fleet[21] was an unwieldy force: eighteen French ships of the line and fifteen Spanish, with five French frigates and two brigs. The most impressive-looking vessels of all were Spanish, *Principe de Asturias* (112), picked up in Ferrol, now Admiral Gravina's flagship, and also from Ferrol the 80-gun *Neptuno*. From Cadiz itself came *Santissima Trinidad* (130), flagship of Rear-Admiral Cisneros, a four-decker, the largest warship afloat, *Santa-Ana* (112), flagship of Vice-Admiral Alava, *Rayo* (100), flying the broad pennant of Commodore Macdonel, and *Argonauta* (80), last survivor of the six Spanish ships which had gone with Villeneuve to the West Indies and back. The French had four 80-gun ships: Villeneuve's flagship *Bucentaure*, *Formidable*, flagship of Rear-Admiral Dumanoir, *Neptune* and *Indomptable*; all the rest were 74s. Strangely enough, in view of differences of type, age and condition, to say nothing of language, the French and Spanish ships were in mixed formation.[25] They carried 21,580 officers and men (including soldiers) – about the equivalent of a standard army corps of the Grand Army. Their broadsides totalled 2,626 guns.

It was not until between two and three o'clock in the afternoon of the 19th that the whole fleet was out, and Villeneuve then ordered it to form five sailing columns (as previously agreed), and in that formation they steered westward as best they could with a wind which had shifted to west-north-west. Shortly afterwards one of the French frigates signalled that she had eighteen sail of British ships in sight to the south. At five o'clock Villeneuve turned south-east, towards the Straits of Gibraltar, a collision course with Nelson's fleet. He also detached some of his faster sailers under Gravina to drive off the British frigates and act as an observation squadron. At 7.30 one of these ships, *Aigle*, also made the signal for eighteen British ships to the south. At this, with the light failing, Villeneuve turned north-west. Shortly after that Nelson, whose great fear was that he might be forced through the Straits by a strong westerly wind, turned south-west, so that for some hours the two fleets were sailing away from each other. At 4 a.m., however, the British fleet turned north by east, and at some time during the night Villeneuve again turned towards the Straits, so that when, at about six o'clock on 21 October, the fleets came in sight of each other, they were again converging, at a distance of ten to twelve miles according to Mr James, eight or nine according to Sir Julian Corbett. Cape Trafalgar bore east by south 'distant about seven leagues'. Nelson wrote in his private diary:

'At daylight saw the Enemy's Combined Fleet from East to E.S.E.; bore away; made the signal for Order of Sailing, and to Prepare for Battle; the Enemy with their heads to the Southward: at seven the Enemy wearing in succession. May the Great God, whom I worship, grant to my Country, and for the benefit of Europe in general, a great and glorious Victory; and may no misconduct in any one tarnish it; and may humanity after Victory be the predominant feature in the British Fleet. For myself, individually, I commit my life to Him who made me, and may his blessing light upon my endeavours for serving my Country faithfully. To Him I resign myself and the just cause which is entrusted to me to defend. Amen. Amen. Amen.'

The Combined Fleet

From Toulon, 30 March

*Bucentaure (80) FC	Vice-Admiral Villeneuve; wrecked on 22 October
*Formidable (80) F	Rear-Admiral Dumanoir; captured by Sir Richard Strachan on 3 November
Neptune (80) F	Escaped
Indomptable (80) F	Escaped; wrecked on 24 October
Pluton (74) F	Escaped
Mont-Blanc (74) F	Captured by Sir Richard Strachan, 3 November
Swiftsure (74) FC	
Atlas (74) F	Left in Vigo after Sir Richard Calder's action, 22 July
Intrépide (74) FC	Later burned
Scipion (74) F	Captured by Sir Richard Strachan, 3 November
Berwick (74) FC	Later wrecked

From Cadiz, 9 April

Aigle (74) F	Escaped
Argonauta (80) SC	Later scuttled
San-Rafael (80) S	Captured by Sir Robert Calder, 22 July
Firme (74) S	Captured by Sir Robert Calder, 22 July
Terrible (74) S	Damaged on 22 July; left in Cadiz
America (64) S	Damaged on 22 July; left in Vigo
España (64) S	Damaged on 22 July; left in Vigo

From Rochefort, joined at Martinique, 4 June

*Algésiras (74) FC	Rear-Admiral Magon; recaptured on 22 October and escaped to Cadiz
Achille (74) F	Blew up

From Ferrol, 11 August

Argonaute (74) F	Escaped
Duguay-Trouin (74) F	Captured by Sir Richard Strachan, 3 November
Fougueux (74) FC	Wrecked 22–3 October
Héros (74) F	Escaped
Redoutable (74) FC	Wrecked 22 October
*Principe de Asturias (112) S	Vice-Admiral Gravina; escaped
Neptuno (80) SC	Recaptured on 23 October
Monarca (74) SC	Later burned
Montañez (74) S	Escaped (captured on 24 October and wrecked?)
San-Augustino (74) SC	Later burned
San-Idelfonso (74) SC	
San-Juan-Nepomuceno (74) SC	
San-Fulgencio (64) S	Left in Cadiz
San-Francisco de Asis (74) S	Escaped

From Cadiz, 19 October

*Santissima Trinidad (130) SC	Rear-Admiral Cisneros; later burned
*Santa-Ana (112) SC	Rear-Admiral Alava; recaptured on 23 October
Rayo (100) S	Captured on 24 October; wrecked
Bahama (74) SC	
San-Justo (74) S	Escaped
San-Leandro (64) S	Escaped

*Flagship of the officer named
F — French ship   S — Spanish ship
C — Captured at Trafalgar, 21 October 1805
Number in Brackets — number of guns

'Captain-General' (Spanish style) Gravina, Villeneuve's second-in-command at Trafalgar

Summary

French ships present at Trafalgar	18
Spanish ships present at Trafalgar	15
Total	33
French ships captured or destroyed on 21 October	8
Spanish ships captured or destroyed on 21 October	10
Total	18
French ships recaptured after the battle	1
Spanish ships recaptured after the battle	2
Total	3
Net loss	15
French ships wrecked or captured after the battle	5
Spanish ships wrecked or captured after the battle	2
Total	7
Net loss	22

Daylight on 21 October showed the fleets to each other, like two great flocks of white sea birds. The day was fine but at first hazy; the wind was westerly, light, dropping away at times almost to calm; a heavy swell from the west gave warning of an approaching storm. The Combined Fleet had lost its five-column sailing formation, and was shaking out into two lines for which the word 'parallel' would be a very misleading description; the best that one can say is that there were ships sailing side by side, in some places three abreast.

According to the various authorities, the fleet stretched along three to five miles of sea. Dawn found Nelson's fleet also in a shapeless huddle, which soon resolved itself into two divisions, or crude 'columns,' as *Victory*'s signal flags took effect: first No. 72,[26] 'Form the order of sailing in two columns', then No. 76, 'Bear up and sail large on the course signalled', with the course signal at east-north-east, followed by No. 13, 'Prepare for battle', and somewhat later No. 76 again with the course signal east.

Already there was a significant departure from the tactical memorandum: instead of the three divisions envisaged there, now there were only two: a Weather Column under Nelson himself, and Collingwood's Lee Column. Some authorities account for this change by the fact that the fleet did not consist of the forty ships referred to in the Memorandum, but only twenty-seven. General Fuller says it was 'because of the absence of Louis's squadron' – i.e. because Nelson had only twenty-seven ships instead of thirty-three. Was it perhaps rather because of the absence of Admiral Louis himself? We have seen that Nelson had high regard for him; possibly he did not care to entrust to the less well known Earl of Northesk the responsibility for leading a line that he would have given to Louis. Whatever the reason, the result was unfortunate. It meant that Lord Northesk's flagship, the 100-gun *Britannia*, instead of being quickly in the thick of things, did not, if her log is to be believed, pass through the enemy line until the battle was three hours old. Not only that, but it meant that the rear ships of both columns were only briefly engaged, so that during the decisive phase of the battle Nelson was deprived of a quarter, perhaps a third, of his ships.

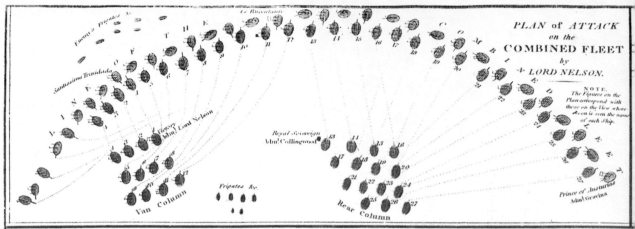

PLAN of ATTACK
on the
COMBINED FLEET
by
LORD NELSON.

NOTE.
The Figures on the
Plan correspond with
those on the View where
& can is seen the name
of each Ship.

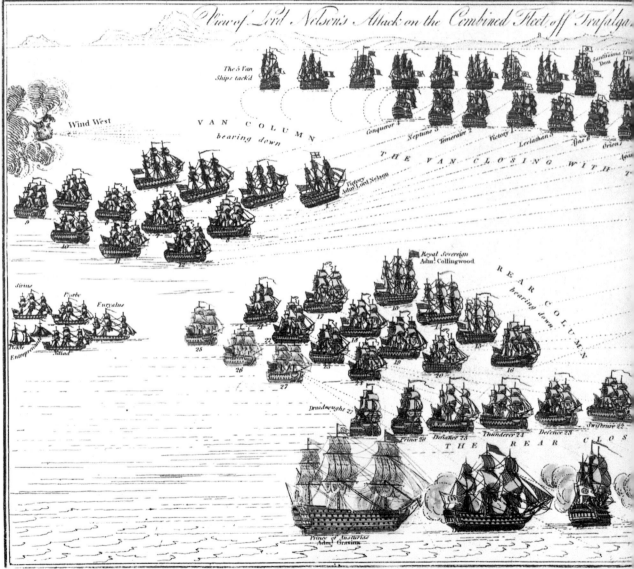

View of Lord Nelson's Attack on the Combined Fleet, off Trafalgar

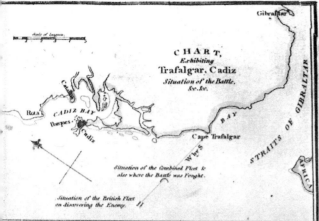

A general, but somewhat fanciful view of the battle on 21 October 1805; the arc of the Combined Fleet would have been much flatter, though the 'coveys' of the British approach are well shown

As a French officer remarked: 'This manner of engaging was contrary to the most simple prudence...'[27] That it did not produce a disaster was due entirely to the immense superiority in seamanship, gunnery and morale of the British fleet – and Nelson, of course, was fully aware of all those factors. He was asking a lot, and he knew it; he took a big risk, but it was calculated. As General Fuller says: 'The differences between the Secret Memorandum and what occurred are those between idea in mind and idea in action.'

The two British columns – or, to use Fuller's expressive image, 'coveys' – strung themselves out one to two miles apart as they made towards their enemy. Nelson's Weather Column consisted of twelve ships, Collingwood had fifteen. But, as usual, a mere count of hulls is misleading: four of the three-deckers were with Nelson, and one of Collingwood's three three-deckers was such a slow sailer that she only just got into battle at all. The relative strengths of the two divisions were therefore roughly equal. The feature of Nelson's column was the massing of three three-deckers, *Victory* (100), *Téméraire* (98), and *Neptune* (98)[28] at its head. This formidable aggregate of gun-power seems strangely placed to modern eyes, used to naval actions beginning with light craft, and reserving the dreadnoughts for the later stages, but it was in keeping with the rôle that Nelson had reserved for himself: smashing through the enemy's centre, where their own heavy ships would almost certainly be. Northesk's 100-gun *Britannia* was sixth in Nelson's line, but worked her way up to fifth as the fleets closed. One of Nelson's ships, the 64-gun *Africa*, very nearly missed the battle altogether; she had lost touch with the fleet in the night, and held her northward course when the rest turned south, with the result that she was by this time far away to larboard of the Weather Column. If the Combined Fleet had not gone about, *Africa* would have been out of it, but when they did so she found herself isolated in a most dangerous position – accepted by her captain, Henry Digby, with complete phlegm.

Collingwood's column was formed quite differently from Nelson's. At the head of it was his flagship, *Royal Sovereign*, with 100 guns. Luckier than the *Superb*, she had gone home in

July, her foul bottom having made her an impossibly slow sailer. She had rejoined the fleet on 8 October, spick and span for Collingwood's flag, and with a fine new copper bottom which now made her the fastest sailer in the fleet; we shall shortly see the result of this. Behind *Royal Sovereign* came two seventy-fours, *Belleisle* and *Mars*, and then the 80-gun ship *Tonnant*. Collingwood's old flagship, the three-decker *Dreadnought*, a poor sailer, was eighth in the line, and the worst sailer of all, *Prince* (98), was right at the rear. What this meant was that the gun-power of the Lee Column was far more evenly spread than Nelson's – not by any particular design, but because of the sailing properties of the ships concerned, made worse, as Collingwood reported, by the light wind.

Following their leaders in loose formation, under full sail but with few of them managing more than three knots, in the bright sunshine which came when the haze cleared, the British ships narrowed the gap. Seeing that battle was inevitable, and that on his present course there was a clear risk that he might not only be cut in two, but also cut

off from Cadiz, at some time between 7.15 and 8.30[29] Villeneuve made the signal for his fleet to wear together – that is, for each ship simultaneously to go about with the wind and proceed on the opposite course. It was a manoeuvre which invariably produced confusion in any fleet, and in the Combined Fleet at that stage it did not fail to do so. All accounts agree that it took about two hours to complete the manoeuvre, or until about ten o'clock. During that time the spectacle presented to the telescopes in Nelson's fleet must have been one of complete disorder. It is most likely that Nelson himself believed that the Combined Fleet was turning tail and making for Cadiz, and this would account for the sheer impetuosity of his attack. The impression was certainly present in the British fleet that they were now engaged in a chase. Perhaps misinterpreting Signal No. 307 – 'Make all sail possible with safety to the masts' – which was flown by *Victory* for particular ships, and later as a general signal, an officer of *Royal Sovereign* wrote in his journal: 'The signal was made to chase', while the master of *Conqueror* logged: 'Bore

'England confides that every man will do his duty';
Nelson gives his instructions for the famous signal
to Lieutenant Pasco. Painting by Thomas Davidson

up and made all sail in chase.' This aspect of the onset emphasized its imprecision: the object was to get between the enemy and Cadiz as soon as possible, without regard to nice formations. In the words of Captain Codrington of *Orion*: 'We all scrambled into battle as soon as we could.' Captain Robert Moorsom of *Revenge* was even more graphic: 'Admiral Collingwood dashed directly down, supported by such ships as could get up, and went directly through their line. Lord Nelson did the same, and the rest as fast as they could.'[30] One interesting result of Villeneuve's wearing together, not much noticed, is that it meant that Collingwood would, after all, play the part designed for him in the tactical Memorandum, and attack the enemy's rear; but if Villeneuve had held his course, it would have been Nelson who would have done so, quite contrary to the intention stated in the Memorandum – yet a further reason for seeking in it only the spirit of the event, and not its detail.

At three knots and less it takes a long time to close ten miles; the hours passed slowly. It was not so bad on the upper decks, with the whole imposing panorama to inspire one; down below, beside the big guns, with only restricted vision through the gun-ports, it was a testing time. Few were found wanting. Nelson, dressed in his 'threadbare frock uniform-coat' with, stitched to the left breast, 'the same four weather-tarnished and lack-lustre stars always to be seen there', visited every deck of the *Victory* and addressed a few words to the men on each.[31] Then he returned to the quarter-deck, singled out by his honours among all who stood there. Blackwood of *Euryalus* was with him, and related:

'About ten o'clock, Lord Nelson's anxiety to close with the Enemy became very apparent: he frequently remarked that they put a good face upon it; but always quickly added, "I'll give them such a dressing as they never had before," regretting at the same time the vicinity of the land. At that critical moment I ventured to represent to his Lordship, the value of such a life as his, and particularly in the present battle; and I proposed hoisting his Flag in the *Euryalus*, whence he could better see what was going on, as well as what to order in case of necessity. But he would not hear of it, and gave as his reason the force of example; and probably he was right. My next object, therefore, was

to endeavour to induce his Lordship to allow the *Téméraire*, *Neptune*, and *Leviathan* to lead into Action before the *Victory*, which was then headmost.'

To this Nelson appeared to consent. He said to *Victory*'s captain, Thomas Hardy, 'Oh yes, let her go ahead.' But it would appear that what he meant was 'let her, if she can'. He refused to allow *Victory* to shorten sail, and the result was that *Téméraire*, although sailing abreast at that time, was never able to pass her. Westminster Abbey was, indeed, his objective.[32]

The mast-heads were busy all the time. At some time between 11.32 and 12.15, according to the logs of no less than thirteen ships (though Mr James says 11.30), Nelson made the signal that shows the instinctive seaman in him, no doubt prompted by the ominous swell that many noticed. With No. 8 as preparative – 'The Signal made herewith is to be carried into execution at the end of the day' – he hoisted No. 63: 'Anchor as soon as convenient.' He felt the coming storm, and this was his warning to the fleet. With that done, at some time between 11.25 and 12.10, logged by seven ships (Mr James says 11.40), according to Flag Lieutenant Pasco of the *Victory*:

'His Lordship came to me on the poop, and after ordering certain signals to be made, about a quarter to noon, he said. "Mr. Pasco, I wish to say to the fleet, ENGLAND CONFIDES THAT EVERY MAN WILL DO HIS DUTY;" and he added, "you must be quick, for I have one more to make, which is for Close Action." I replied, "If your Lordship will permit me to substitute the *expects* for *confides* the signal will soon be completed, because the word *expects* is in the vocabulary, and *confides* must be spelt." His Lordship replied, in haste, and with seeming satisfaction, "That will do, Pasco, make it directly." When it had been answered by a few Ships in the Van, he ordered me to make the signal for Close Action, and to *keep it up*: accordingly, I hoisted No. 16 at the top-gallant mast-head, and there it remained until shot away.'

Now the fleets were almost within gun-shot. The Combined Fleet had shaken itself out into a vast arc, a concave bow into which the two British columns were determinedly thrusting themselves. The distance between the columns had greatly diminished – so much so that one Spanish account says that they were in wedge formation, i.e.

Victory and *Royal Sovereign* both aiming at the same point. This was not true – certainly it was not intended – but it is a strange fact that in the Franco-Spanish outer line only the lengths of five ships and the intervals between them separated Collingwood's point of impact from Nelson's. Collingwood by now was well ahead of the whole fleet; *Royal Sovereign*'s new copper bottom was carrying her admiral and all his crew into a position of supreme danger which it appeared he could hardly wait to take up. It was, accordingly, on *Royal Sovereign* that fire first opened, ranging shots from *Fougueux* beginning at a time variously stated by the ships' logs,[33] but probably just before noon. Immediately all three British admirals flew their respective flags, and in obedience to Nelson's orders (10 October) every ship hoisted a White Ensign and a Union Jack. The Battle of Trafalgar had begun.

Under the eye of history, this long awaited event has an Aeschylean quality, a remorselessness like the vengeance of the gods; and for once one senses that this was felt by the participants. Making all allowances for the hazards of timing already noticed, it can be safely said that all the effort, all the endurance, all the hopes, of nearly two and a half years of war were resolved in about five hours, and never at any time did the issue seem to be in doubt.

The battle falls into three well marked phases: first, a period of about two hours during which those British ships which were to play a decisive part (about two thirds of the whole fleet) made their way into action one by one, discovered their particular opponents and engaged them; this was followed by a similar period of about two hours during which the rewards of proficiency were gathered – twelve out of the total of seventeen prizes – and the solitary attempt at a counter-stroke was brushed aside; finally, there was a 'mopping up' period of about an hour and a half, during which the British took their remaining prizes while the survivors of the Combined Fleet made their escape, a conclusion marked by the awful drama of a French ship blowing up. From beginning to end the battle pursued a relentless progression, in which all the penalties of weakness were mercilessly exacted.

It began as it was to continue. At noon, according to her own log, 12.04 by that of *Belleisle* some distance behind her, *Royal Sovereign* cut through the weather line of the Combined Fleet under the stern of Vice-Admiral Alava's 112-gun flagship *Santa-Ana*, and across the bows of *Fougueux*, somewhat more distant. As she passed, *Royal Sovereign* poured her port broadside, double-shotted, into *Santa-Ana*, killing or wounding about 400 of her crew and immediately disabling fourteen of her guns. The stamp of ruthlessness was firmly planted. As this tremendous prelude thundered out, Collingwood called to his captain: 'Rotheram, what would Nelson give to be here!' And practically at that very moment, observing the majestic scene, Nelson was saying: 'See how that noble fellow Collingwood carries his ship into action!'

And now the cost of the new copper bottom had to be met. 'For upwards of 15 minutes,' says Mr James, 'the *Royal Sovereign* was the only British ship in close action.' Needless to say, inspection of the logs produces an immediate challenge to this statement: *Belleisle* claims to have passed through the enemy line at 12.13, only nine minutes after the flagship. Whatever the precise period of her solitude may have been, there is no doubt that *Royal Sovereign* now endured a very trying time. Having fired her broadside, she at once ranged up alongside *Santa-Ana*, so close that the guns of the two ships were almost muzzle to muzzle, and began a long duel which reflects most highly upon the courage of the Spanish sailors, after the fearful loss they had already sustained. Meanwhile *Fougueux*, saved by distance and smoke from the worst effects of *Royal Sovereign*'s starboard broadside, began to rake her astern, while the 64-gun *San-Leandro* did the same ahead; and to starboard, on her bow and quarter, the 74-gun *San-Justo* and the 80-gun *Indomptable* gave her their broadsides. *Royal Sovereign* was thus engaged with five ships simultaneously, and so hot was the fire that people aboard her often saw shots hit each other in the air, while others went past her to injure friendly ships. Small wonder that Collingwood wryly remarked much later: 'I thought it a long time after I got through their Line before I found my friends about me.'

'Friends were on their way': *Belleisle* comes to the aid of *Royal Sovereign*. **Left to right:** *Fougueux, Belleisle, Indomptable, Santa Ana, Royal Sovereign*

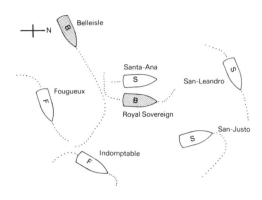

down her mizenmast, whose fall masked *Belleisle*'s aftermost guns. Meanwhile the 74-gun *San-Juan-Nepomuceno* was engaging her on the starboard beam. *Mars* came up and drove off *Fougueux*, but the French *Achille* (74) took up a position to fire into *Belleisle* where she could make no reply. Soon *Aigle* (74) joined in, while *San-Justo* and *San-Leandro* added a passing fire as they drew away from *Royal Sovereign*; finally the French 80-gun *Neptune* came up to rake the hard-pressed British ship. Wonderful to relate, *Belleisle*'s final losses, 126 officers and men killed and wounded, were by no means the highest in the British fleet, but, to conclude her story now, her damage was naturally most severe: all three masts were brought down, her bowsprit and figurehead were shot away, her hull knocked almost to pieces. She was, in fact, no more than a hulk – but a fighting hulk, as she indicated by holding up a Union Jack on the end of a pike for all to see, thus earning a cheer from the English *Swiftsure* as she passed close by. It is pleasant to be able to relate that it fell to the shattered *Belleisle* to take possession, with her last surviving boat, of the Spanish 80-gun *Argonauta*, the first British prize of the day.

Friends were on their way. *Belleisle*, coming in at an angle, suffered some loss before she even entered the enemy line, but when she did so she drove away *Indomptable* and closely engaged *Fougueux*. Very quickly she found herself in the same predicament as *Royal Sovereign*, without the advantage of three decks. Her first opponent, *Fougueux*, succeeded in bringing

'Her damage was most severe'; *Belleisle* at the end of the battle, with, (right) *Santa Ana* (dismasted), *Royal Sovereign*, *Victory* and *Achille* (on fire)

The Problem of Logs
(See also Appendix B, p. 204)

Ship's Log	Royal Sovereign Engaged	Victory Engaged	Self Engaged	Cease Fire
Royal Sovereign	Noon	—	Noon	5.00 pm.
Belleisle	11.55 starts firing 12.04 cuts enemy line	—	12.05 starts firing 12.13 cuts enemy line	5.30
Mars	Noon	—	Noon	5.30
Tonnant	—	—	Noon	5.40
Spartiate	12.09	12.59	3.07	5.20
Bellerophon	12.10 starts firing 12.20 cuts enemy line	12.28	12.30	5.07
Colossus	12.30	—	12.50 starts firing 1.00 cuts enemy line	—
Achille	Noon	—	¼ past noon	—
Victory	11.40 starts firing	12.04	12.04	4.30
Polyphemus	—	shortly after 11.40	—	6.00
Téméraire	—	12.25	As for *Victory*	4.30
Leviathan	11.55	—	—	Soon after 5.20
Neptune	11.57	Noon	12.10	4.30
Conqueror	12.20	12.45	1.35	6.05
Africa	11.32	—	1.30	
Prince	12.10	12.30	3.00 (approx.)	—
Orion	12.35 cuts enemy line	shortly after *Royal Sovereign*	2.00	—
Ajax	12.18	12.32	1.12	—
Agamemnon	—	—	1.30	—
Britannia	12.30	12.40	12.50 starts firing 3.00 cuts enemy line	5.30
Minotaur	12.20	—	3.10	—
Dreadnought	12.10 starts firing 12.40 cuts enemy line	12.55	1.25	—
Swiftsure	12.15	—	—	—

('at half past Noon the whole of the Fleets in action, and the *Royal Sovereign* cut through the Line of the Enemy, which was done soon after by several of our Ships')

Ship's Log	Royal Sovereign Engaged	Victory Engaged	Self Engaged	Cease Fire
Revenge	12.02	—	12.35	6.15
Defence	12.10	12.40	2.20	5.00 ('about')
Thunderer	12.15	12.40	'soon after' 1.10	'soon after' 5.15
Defiance	12.25	1.00	1.40	—
Euryalus	12.17 starts firing 12.22 cuts enemy line	12.23 starts firing 12.24 cuts enemy line	3.30	5.25 ('about')
Sirius	12.20	12.35	2.40	5.10
Phoebe	'shortly after' 12.05	12.17	4.00	5.10
Naiad	12.10	—	4.00	5.00
Pickle	12.30	—	—	—
Entreprenante	'At 1 observed the van of our Fleet bring the Enemy's Fleet to action.'			

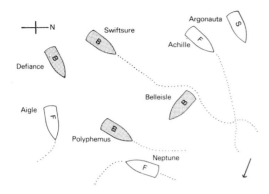

So Collingwood's line engaged: the next in was *Mars*, severely raked as she came by *San-Juan-Nepomuceno* and three 74s, *Pluton*, *Monarca* and Rear-Admiral Magon's *Algésiras*. The two last named were soon driven off by the arrival of *Tonnant*, leaving *Pluton* as *Mars*'s chief opponent. The latter was by now unmanageable, owing to damage to her sails and rigging; her captain, George Duff, was beheaded by a cannon-ball, and her final loss amounted to ninety-eight officers and men. Yet she never ceased to give better than she received – *Pluton*, at the end of the day, having only 400 men on their feet out of 700. *Tonnant*, meanwhile, had hit *Monarca* so hard that the Spanish ship pulled down her colours, but as no one was available to take her surrender, she later rehoisted them and fought a little longer. *Tonnant* herself engaged in a fierce duel with *Algésiras*.

There, with the head of his column well engaged, each ship dealing out pitiless and unflagging destruction all around her, and his own still locked in mortal combat with the Spanish vice-admiral, we must leave Collingwood to observe the fortunes of the Weather Column. At once the familiar timing difficulties arise: it is impossible to say precisely when *Victory* cut through the enemy line.[34] Admiral Mahan gives the time of *Royal Sovereign*'s breaking into the Combined Fleet as 12.10, and says that *Victory* 'still had a mile and a half to go'.[35] He also tells us, following Mr James, that *Bucentaure* fired the first shot

at *Victory* at 12.20, which fell short. Ranging shots continued as *Victory* held her course, at a speed which had now dropped to one and a half knots – which meant a very long approach, soon under the heavy fire of several vessels. It was as *Victory* came within the enemy's range that Nelson sent away the two frigate captains, Blackwood of *Euryalus* and William Prowse of *Sirius*, who were with him. Blackwood shook hands and said: 'I trust, my Lord, that on my return to the *Victory*, which will be as soon as possible, I shall find your Lordship well and in possession of twenty prizes.' Nelson replied: 'God bless you, Blackwood, I shall never speak to you again.'

For forty minutes, according to Mahan, *Victory* remained under a fire to which she could make no effective reply: this was the penalty of the perpendicular attack. It meant, in effect, that Nelson had deliberately accepted the crossing of his 'T' (and Collingwood's too, of course), the worst possible situation in which to find oneself against an enemy who could bring his broadsides to bear, as the French and Spanish now did. All the ships near *Bucentaure* were now firing at the British admiral, doing considerable damage to *Victory*'s rigging, and causing many casualties. Nelson's secretary, Mr Scott, was killed while standing near him; a double-headed shot killed

eight marines on the poop, and wounded several more; another shot passed between Nelson and Captain Hardy, causing splinters, one of which bruised Hardy's left foot. 'This is too warm work, Hardy,' said Nelson, 'to last long.' It must have seemed to many that it lasted quite long enough, though Nelson declared that he had never in any battle seen cooler courage than *Victory*'s crew now displayed. Fortunately, gunnery in the Combined Fleet was poor, and made more inaccurate by the swell; even making that allowance, however, the French and Spanish officers must have been furious to see this wonderful target missed so often, and the British attack pressed home with such apparently irresistible deliberation.[36]

It is difficult to see exactly what was in Nelson's mind as he made this headlong assault. The best part of an hour must have elapsed since *Royal Sovereign* had struck the enemy's line; the effect of her doing so was already making itself apparent. Her opponent, *Santa-Ana*, was stopped in her tracks; immediately ahead of that ship was a gap in the line which should have been filled by *Indomptable*, but she lay to leeward and was unable to take her proper station. Next ahead was *San-Leandro*, and we have seen that she had turned to rake *Royal Sovereign* and give support to Admiral Alava. The result of all these factors was a gap in the Combined Fleet's weather line which widened, according to Mr James, to 'at least three quarters of a mile'. Nelson, says Corbett, 'clearly intended to seize the opportunity of this break in the line to pass through it and then to run up the van and engage it from to leeward, crippling each unit as he passed with his massed three-deckers, and leaving them a prey to his weaker following.' That may well have been the intention; it has a 'Nile' ring about it, and leaves plenty of scope for Collingwood to hammer the enemy's rear. But what actually happened was nothing like that. Nelson's first aiming point had been *Santissima Trinidad*, whose great size and strength seemed to single her out for the flag of the commander-in-chief. *Bucentaure* sailed immediately behind her, then, well closed up, came *Redoutable*, doubled by the French *Neptune* – a formidable, tight cluster of ships just ahead of the gap. As soon as Villeneuve showed his flag in *Bucentaure*, Nelson made for the cluster

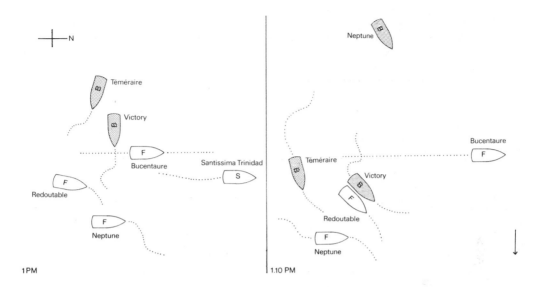

just under her stern, and totally ignored the gap. Hardy warned him that if he held this course he was bound to run on board one of the enemy ships. Nelson replied: 'I cannot help it, it does not signify which we run on board of. Go on board which you please: take your choice.' It was a strange answer: it meant that *Victory* and her immediate follower, *Téméraire*, certainly, and probably others as well, would be brought to an absolute halt very close to the head of Collingwood's column – which at this distance in time looks like a great waste of gun-power. But so it was: a further factor in establishing the character of the battle, well summed up by Collingwood afterwards: 'a severe Action, no dodging or manoeuvring.'

Whatever the motives of this onset may have been, there was no doubt about its impact. 'At 1 P.M.,' says Mr James, with firm and enviable assurance, 'the 68-pounder carronade on the larboard side of the *Victory*'s forecastle, containing its customary charge of one round shot and a keg filled with 500 musket balls, was fired right into the cabin windows of the *Bucentaure*.' This friendly offering was then followed, at a distance so close that the French ensign practically hung over *Victory*'s deck, by the whole of her larboard broadside, each gun as it bore, all double- and some treble-shotted. This was a handsome retort

to all that *Victory* had had to bear with impunity during her approach, and the effect was very much the same as that achieved by *Royal Sovereign*'s first broadside into *Santa-Ana* – a loss of nearly 400 men and twenty guns immediately dismounted. *Bucentaure* was practically put out of action by this one terrible blow.

Before the smoke and the dust from *Bucentaure*'s shattered woodwork could clear, *Victory* herself received heavy and destructive fire from the French *Neptune*, a powerful vessel in echelon behind her admiral. *Victory* could make no reply to this, but very soon she was able to deliver her full starboard broadside into *Redoutable*, while her larboard guns fired into the stern of *Santissima Trinidad*, some distance away. A moment or two later she fell alongside *Redoutable*, and the two ships locked together in a fight which may in two ways be called 'to the death'.

Redoutable, though only a 74, was one of the best ships in Villeneuve's fleet, commanded by a remarkable officer, Captain Jean Jacques Etienne Lucas. Full of Gallic fire and eagerness for battle, Lucas also had a full measure of French logic inside his head. Our *Witness* (p. 188) shows him castigating the gunnery of the Combined Fleet as the British made their approach. Long before, he had come to the conclusion that the French

'They have done for me at last, Hardy': Nelson
falls to a marksman of *Redoutable*, an engraving
from a picture by Turner

and Spanish ships could not compete with the
British in gunnery, and short of training facilities
which they did not possess never would be able
to do so. What the crews could be trained for,
however, was close-quarter musketry and boarding
tactics, and these Lucas had constantly instilled
into his men. He had raised their morale to such a
pitch that they never questioned the feasibility
of capturing the great British three-decker as it
came alongside. *Redoutable*'s tops were full
of trained marksmen; some small brass mortars
also up aloft poured small shot down onto *Victory*'s
decks; and to strengthen the boarders when the
moment came, Lucas, to the astonishment of the
British gunners, closed his lower deck gun-ports
and ceased fire from there altogether – something
no British captain would have dreamed of doing.

Nevertheless, it was *Victory* that got in the
first blow in the close-quarter fight – clearing
the Frenchman's gangway with her starboard
carronade, loaded like the twin which had fired
into *Bucentaure*. And so, for some fifteen
minutes, the two ships blasted each other, the
French concentrating on the British officers and
men, the British steadily blowing their ship from
underneath them as they did so. It was 1.25, or
thereabouts, when, in the midst of the steady
pacing up and down some twenty-one feet of
deck which was, at this stage, the sole activity of
Nelson and Captain Hardy, just as he was about
to turn, Nelson was hit by a musket-ball from
Redoutable's tops. He fell forward onto his knees,
and then right down on the deck, exactly where his
secretary had been killed, the blood still fresh
enough to stain the admiral's clothes. Hardy,
seeing him fall, uttered the hope that the wound
was not serious. Nelson replied at once:

'They have done for me at last, Hardy.'

'I hope not,' said Hardy.

'Yes,' said Nelson, 'my backbone is shot
through.'

He was carried down to the cockpit in the
orlop deck where the surgeon, Dr Beatty, was at
work; so as not to discourage the crew, he covered
his face with a handkerchief, which fell off as he
arrived below. He said to the surgeon:

'Ah, Mr. Beatty! you can do nothing for me.
I have but a short time to live: my back is shot
through.'

Swift inspection revealed that the ball was,
indeed, lodged in the spine; Nelson's life would
not out-run the battle.[37]

The first phase of the action was now reaching
its climax. Very soon after Nelson was taken
below, seeing *Victory*'s decks almost stripped
of men, Lucas believed that his opportunity had
come, and his men made a determined attempt to
get aboard her. Whether or not he could have
succeeded, and what the outcome might have
been, we cannot know. The curve of the ships'
hulls prevented a quick rush; Captain Adair of the
marines with some other officers and a party of
men from below stood off the first boarders; and
before they could be reinforced, a new combatant
appeared on the scene. *Téméraire*, damaged
(though not so much as *Victory*) during her
long run in, was now rendered practically unmanageable by a raking fire from the French
Neptune. She could, however, fire into
Redoutable, and did so while the French crew was
assembled on deck for their attempt to board
Victory, with fearful effect – nearly 200 men were
hit, among them Captain Lucas wounded,
though he remained on deck. Almost immediately
afterwards, *Redoutable* ran (or rather, drifted)
on board *Téméraire*, and the extraordinary
spectacle was seen of a French two-decker
sandwiched between two British three-deckers,
none of them able to move. What this also meant
was that these two powerful British ships could
only engage whatever came to them; they could
not look for quarries like the beasts of prey they

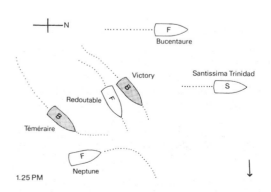

should have resembled. Trafalgar is certainly a difficult battle to admire tactically.

The pressure of battle, the shifts of wind, the moods of captains, did nevertheless bring to the crippled British giants some of the prey they wanted. While *Téméraire* was dealing with *Redoutable* on her larboard side, to starboard another opponent came into view. This was *Fougueux*, which we last saw doing considerable damage to *Belleisle* in Collingwood's battle, and being driven off by *Mars*; she had now passed across the gap in the line, and may well have supposed, from the appearance of *Téméraire*, that she had an opportunity of boarding and capturing the three-decker while she was already engaged on her other beam. But *Téméraire* was crippled only in movement; she allowed *Fougueux* to come in very close, then gave her the full starboard broadside, still undischarged for lack of targets. A moment later the French ship ran on board *Téméraire*, making the 'sandwich' now double. The damage and confusion caused by the British broadside were enormous, and *Téméraire*'s first lieutenant, Thomas Kennedy, who was fighting the starboard side of the ship, determined to take immediate advantage of it. At the head of a small party of seamen and marines he boarded *Fougueux*, drove her crew off the deck, and very shortly afterwards took possession of her. With that success, the second part of the battle may be considered well begun.

It was now about two o'clock. Collingwood's duel with Alava had been going on for nearly two hours, and the Spanish ship was in a dreadful state; all her masts had gone, and her starboard side was, in Mr James's words, 'nearly beaten in'.

At about 2.15, Vice-Admiral Alava being dangerously wounded and her other losses most severe, *Santa-Ana* struck to *Royal Sovereign*. The loss aboard the British ship was 141 officers and men killed and wounded, and her damage was also considerable, including her mizen- and main-masts over the side. Other successes followed: it was at about the same time that *Santa-Ana* struck that *Tonnant* satisfactorily concluded her duel with *Algésiras*. Rear-Admiral Charles Magon was mortally

'Her losses were naturally high'; H.M.S. *Belleropho*
(third from right) engaged against a group of
enemy ships

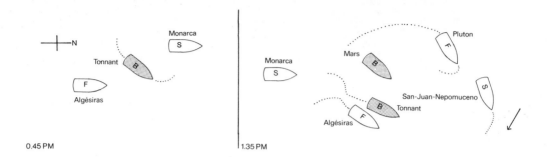

0.45 PM   1.35 PM

wounded (though he would not quit the deck)
and over 200 of the French crew were casualties;
Tonnant lost seventy-six. Receiving the
larboard fire of *Tonnant* lay *San-Juan-
Nepomuceno*, and very shortly she too surrendered,
but the boat sent from *Tonnant* (with only one
officer and two men) was damaged by a shot, so
that it was *Dreadnought*, not *Tonnant*, that
took the Spanish ship a little later (certainly not
at two o'clock, as her log states).

So it continued. By four o'clock Collingwood's
column had taken five more enemy ships. The
process was steady and relentless, as the British
captains singled out their opponents and set to
work; but it was often hard going. In Collingwood's
line the two heaviest sufferers have yet to be
mentioned: *Bellerophon* and *Colossus*.
Bellerophon was one of the smallest British 74s,
but according to Mr James 'one of the best
manned'. He places her entry into the Franco-
Spanish line at one o'clock, though the log says
12.30; the later time is more probable, since there

was a considerable distance between her and her
next ahead, *Tonnant*. She came in under the
stern of *Monarca* (74) and was soon engaged
also with the French 74 *Aigle*. Three more 74s
were shortly giving her the benefit of their
attention: the French *Swiftsure*, *Montanez* and
Bahama.[38] Her losses were naturally high, partly
due to the fire of soldiers on *Aigle*, partly to
explosions of loose powder on her gun decks:
Captain John Cooke was killed, 150 of his officers
and men killed and wounded. Nevertheless, at
three o'clock (log time) she took possession of
Monarca.

To *Colossus* falls the sad distinction of the
highest loss in the whole British fleet; with no
particular reason to account for it except her
brave and resolute enemies. She was engaged first
by the French 74 *Argonaute*, then by *Swiftsure*
and *Bahama*. After a fight lasting (according
to her log) about two hours and with a little
passing help from *Orion*, she took them both –
but at a price: 200 killed and wounded, including

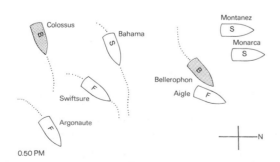

0.50 PM

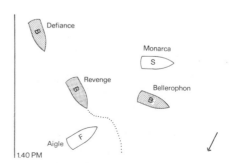

1.40 PM

her captain, James Morris, badly wounded in the leg. Her hull, says Mr James, 'in every part of it was much shattered'.

At about four o'clock the British *Achille* took the French seventy-four *Berwick* after a fight lasting about an hour, and at about the same time *Defiance* captured *Aigle* after an incident which shows how difficult a brave French crew could be to beat. A British boarding party captured the poop and quarter-deck of the French ship, hauled down her colours, and hoisted their own. But they had only been there five minutes when a fierce small-arms fire from the forecastle and tops forced them back to their own ship. *Defiance* sheered off to 'half-pistol-shot distance' and resumed her broadside firing with such effect that after twenty-five minutes the French ship really did strike her colours. When, shortly afterwards, *Defiance* took the 74-gun *San-Idelfonso*, Collingwood's tally of prizes rose to ten. By now all his ships were in action, but the decision of the day was clearly won by the leaders. The latecomers all had their parts to play, and valuable they were; Collingwood himself wrote: 'People who cannot comprehend how complicated an affair a Battle at sea is, and who judge an Officer's conduct by the number of sufferers in his Ship, often do him a wrong. Though there will appear great difference in the loss of men, all did admirably well . . .'[39] It is with no disposition to deny this that one nevertheless draws the conclusion, observing the very great differences in losses between the head of the column and the rear, that the function of the first was to win the fight, and of the second to make sure of it.[40]

And now what of Nelson's line? We left it as

Téméraire was taking possession of *Fougueux* at about two o'clock. At roughly the same time *Bucentaure*, having been raked successively by the British *Neptune*, *Leviathan* and *Conqueror* as they came up, surrendered to *Conqueror*. A curious episode now occurred, which shows how intermingled all the ships were in this part of the battle. *Conqueror*'s prize crew consisted of a corporal and two privates of marines and two seamen, commanded by Captain James Atcherly of the marines. To this relatively junior officer suddenly fell the honour of receiving the surrender of the enemy commander-in-chief and his two captains. Modestly deciding that this would not do, Captain Atcherly took off Villeneuve and the French captains in his boat to surrender to his superior, Captain Israel Pellew,[41] leaving only two sentries aboard *Bucentaure*. But *Conqueror* meanwhile had gone on to look for other foes, and it was aboard *Mars*, which had worked her way over from Collingwood's column, that Villeneuve was taken.

While this little drama, which marked the end of Admiral Villeneuve's unfortunate career, was being played out, a conclusion was also reached in the central group of antagonists. It was just after *Fougueux*'s surrender that *Victory* by immense efforts managed to disentangle herself from *Redoutable* and pull away. No sooner had she done so than the latter's main- and mizen-masts crashed down, the main-mast across the poop of *Téméraire*. After that, of course, there would be no more musketry from up above, and furthermore the great mast now made a fine bridge for a boarding party, which was away at once under the command of *Téméraire*'s second lieutenant

John Wallace. *Redoutable* had fought a tremendous fight – none better – but this was the end. Her damage, as may be supposed after such an ordeal, was very great: two masts down, bowsprit gone, rudder destroyed, her hull 'shot through in every direction, above and below water'. Two of her guns had burst, and twenty others were dismounted. But her worst loss was in the ship's company: her captain wounded, nearly all her other officers casualties, 300 men killed and 222 wounded out of a complement of 643 – in other words, only 121 unhurt. She was, in truth, a dead ship, and in dying had caused the death of Britain's hero admiral – the doubly mortal combat.

Her two great opponents were also severely damaged, though much of *Victory*'s material damage had been sustained during the run in; the bulk of her 159 casualties, however, were due to *Redoutable*, a tribute to the proficiency with small arms that Lucas had instilled in his men. *Téméraire*'s damage was partly from the long run in, but also in part from the two French ships on either side of her. She had to thank *Fougueux* for eight feet of her lower deck stove in abreast of the main-mast. Her losses were 123 officers and men, a number swollen by an explosion on the main

deck caused by a grenade from *Redoutable*. It must be said that two seventy-fours, no matter how excellent, seem inadequate prizes for a 100-gun ship and a ninety-eight. It is hard to resist the thought that if Nelson had gone for the gap in the enemy line instead of for Villeneuve's flag, like a knight in a tournament, *Victory* and *Téméraire* would have had these two prizes and others besides.

Meanwhile, with *Bucentaure* captured, the hounds were after another stag: the mighty *Santissima Trinidad*. First *Neptune*, then *Leviathan*, then *Conqueror* together poured their raking broadsides into her; her masts came down 'with a tremendous crash', and soon she was lying on the water an unmanageable wreck. While she was in this condition an episode occurred which savoured of comedy, if it is possible to think of such a thing in such a scene. We have noted that the little 64-gun *Africa*, having missed her course, found herself near the head of the Combined Fleet in the morning when it wore. Nelson at once signalled her to 'make all possible sail' (No. 307), obviously meaning 'in order to rejoin the fleet'. Captain Digby, however, seems to have interpreted this as 'in order to get into the battle', and proceeded to exchange

'The solitary attempt at a riposte': an impression
of Dumanoir's attempt to renew the battle, with
his flagship *Formidable* on the left

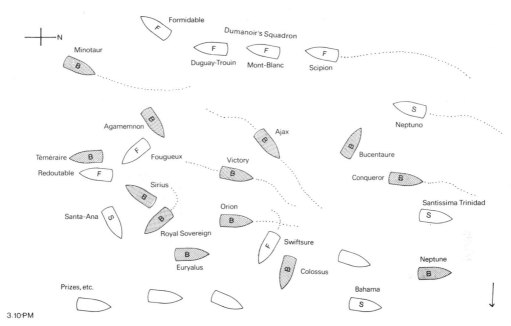

broadsides with every French and Spanish ship
that he passed until he arrived at the *Santissima
Trinidad*. Unhesitatingly he let fly at this ship
which held more than twice as many guns as his
own, and when she did not reply he sent a
boarding party from his pygmy to take the giant.
The boarders were courteously told that the
Spanish ship had no intention of striking – and
were permitted to return to their own ship!

By now the mêlée was general, with little left of
formation in either fleet. *Africa* passed on to fight
Intrépide; *Leviathan* captured *San-Augustino*
after a brief and brisk action; Lord Northesk's
Britannia engaged first *San-Francisco-de-Asis*,
then the three-decker *Rayo*; *Agamemnon*, *Ajax*
and *Orion* entered the fight. For the rear ships of
the Lee Column, the principal objective was
Admiral Gravina's flagship, *Principe de Asturias*.
She was engaged first by *Revenge*, on whom she
inflicted heavy casualties until *Dreadnought* and
Thunderer gave her fresh occupation; later
Defiance and *Prince* also fired on the Spanish
flagship, which drew out of the battle badly
damaged, and with casualties of nearly 150, including Admiral Gravina himself severely wounded.

Meanwhile, the solitary attempt at a riposte to
the British attack had come to nothing. Ahead of

Santissima Trinidad were six French and four
Spanish ships which, apart from *Africa*
passing them on the opposite tack earlier in the
day, had no opponents. Villeneuve had signalled
to Rear-Admiral Dumanoir, commanding this
division of the Combined Fleet, to bring these
ships back into the action, and this order they all
tried to obey, but the light winds made the
process slow – some of them, indeed, having to
use their boats to tow them round. In the end
four French and one Spanish ship, under
Dumanoir himself in the 80-gun *Formidable*, came
down on the weather side of the British fleet,
while the rest tried to do the same thing on the
lee side. It was a moment of some danger for the
badly damaged ships in the centre of the line,
Victory, *Téméraire* and *Royal Sovereign*;
the first two were able to show that despite their
damage they still had a sting in them; *Royal
Sovereign* was by now being towed by *Euryalus*, and
in spite of the efforts of both, she could not bring
her broadsides to bear. It fell chiefly to *Ajax*,
Agamemnon, *Minotaur* and *Spartiate* to fend off
Dumanoir's counter-attack, which they did to such
effect that the two latter were able to cut off the
Spanish 80-gun *Neptuno* from the rest of the squadron, which sailed on to the south-west, having

achieved precisely nothing. French writers have blamed Dumanoir harshly, and though it is too much to say that his conduct was what lost the battle, there certainly remains something abject about this abandonment of his stricken friends.

The final phase of the battle brought its famous individual tragedy. As the guns roared above him, shaking the very timbers on which he lay, Nelson clung to life through mounting pain and delirium all through the afternoon. 'Oh, *Victory, Victory*,' he called out, after one broadside, 'how you distract my poor brain!' And a little later: 'How dear is life to all men!' In his more lucid moments, his mind was with the battle and with the fleet. He wanted to see Hardy, and feared at one stage, when his captain did not come to him, that he was dead. But Hardy was only occupied with the pressing business of the day; he came as soon as he could, and they shook hands.

'Well, Hardy,' asked Nelson, 'how goes the battle? How goes the day with us?'

'Very well, my lord; we have got twelve or fourteen of the enemy's ships in our possession; but five of their van have tacked, and show an intention of bearing down upon the *Victory*. I have therefore called two or three of our fresh ships round us, and have no doubt of giving them a drubbing.'

'I hope none of our ships have struck, Hardy.'

'No, my lord, there is no fear of that.'

Then, after a pause, Nelson said: 'I am a dead man, Hardy. I am going fast: it will be all over with me soon.'

He lived long enough to hear of the defeat of Dumanoir; Hardy returned with that news, and told him that fourteen or fifteen enemy ships had now surrendered. Nelson said: 'That is well, but I bargained for 20.' And then, the seaman in him asserting himself again: 'Anchor, Hardy, anchor!'

Hardy replied: 'I suppose, my lord, Admiral Collingwood will now take upon himself the direction of affairs?'

'Not while I live, I hope, Hardy,' and trying to pull himself up, Nelson added: 'No, do *you* anchor, Hardy.'

Hardy asked: 'Shall *we* make the signal, sir?'

'Yes, for if I live, I'll anchor.'

What Nelson no doubt meant was that, if he lived until the end of the battle, he would anchor.

But that was not permitted. At 4.30, according to *Victory*'s suspect log, but about a quarter of an hour later according to Mr James, Nelson died. Dr Beatty's dubious narrative tells us that his last words were: 'I have done my duty; I praise God for it.' The *Victory*'s chaplain, the Rev. A. J. Scott, however, was leaning over the dying admiral, trying to alleviate his pain by massage of the chest, and records the moment somewhat differently. Amidst obvious great pain, Nelson said distinctly: 'Thank God, I have done my duty.' He repeated this several times, his voice growing fainter, and finally, as the chaplain bent forward to catch the whisper: 'God and my country.' And then he was gone.

The battle itself was to all intents and purposes over. Not long after Nelson's death, *Intrépide* struck to *Orion*; a little later *Neptuno* struck *Minotaur*, and shortly after that *Prince* took possession of the helpless *Santissima Trinidad*. Somewhat earlier the British ship had set fire to the French *Achille*, already badly damaged by *Swiftsure* and *Polyphemus*. Once more, it is impossible to fix a time, even for so dramatic an occurrence, but somewhere around 5.30 – say, about an hour after Nelson's death – *Achille* blew up, making an awful finale to an awesome scene.[42] The reverberations of the explosion died away, and silence fell across the heaving waters.

So the two accounts of this October day were rendered. Far off in Bavaria, Napoleon watched the defile of his captured enemies, uttering, it is said, 'a ceaseless tirade against British intrigue and corrupting gold'. He wrote, in the fullness of satisfaction, to the Empress Josephine: 'I have carried out my plan; I have destroyed the Austrian army just by marching; now I shall throw myself on the Russians; they are lost.' Off Cape Trafalgar, Admiral Collingwood opened his report to the Admiralty in a different vein: 'The ever to be lamented death of Vice-Admiral Lord Viscount Nelson, who, in the late conflict with the Enemy, fell in the hour of victory, leaves me the duty of informing my Lords Commissioners . . .' and he continued: 'The Enemy's Ships were fought with a gallantry highly honourable to their Officers, but the attack on them was irresistible; and it

pleased the Almighty Disposer of all events to grant His Majesty's arms a complete and glorious victory.'

Neither at Ulm nor at Trafalgar was there the slightest possibility of any mistake; the issue of the day was evident. Apart from *Achille*, blown up, eight French and nine Spanish ships were captured on 21 October.[43] Four out of the remaining fifteen, under Dumanoir, escaped to the south, relatively undamaged; the remainder, in various states of injury, returned to Cadiz – a melancholy sight, eleven battered survivors out of thirty-three. No British ship was lost. In the British fleet the commander-in-chief and 449 officers and men were dead, just over 1,200 wounded. In the Combined Fleet, the dead numbered over 4,500, the wounded 2,405, and probably another 7,000 French and Spanish officers and men were prisoners. These are the statistics of annihilation.[44]

The works of man were now for a while concluded; Nature still had a say. The British gathered in their prizes as best they could, and did what they could to patch and mend their own ragged and broken ships. Everyone now felt the coming storm, but there was little that some of those wounded vessels could do. Nelson's solution was to anchor – but for some this was not possible: *Belleisle*, for instance, had no anchors left; *Victory* herself had two disabled, and even those that had them could not always use them. Collingwood, who was now flying his flag in *Euryalus* to give himself mobility, reported: 'The whole fleet were now in a very perilous situation; many dismasted; all shattered; in thirteen fathoms water, off the shoals of Trafalgar; and when I made the signal to prepare to anchor, few of the Ships had an anchor to let go, their cables being shot . . .' It was in this condition that the storm found them all.

The wind came up that very night, freshening through the next day to gale force. Every scrap of professional expertise in the British fleet was needed to keep the ships afloat and give aid to the prizes in their even more miserable condition – but there was no way of saving them all. First to go was *Redoutable*, a sad sequel to her brave fight; Captain Lucas and 170 of his men, seventy of them wounded, were saved by *Swiftsure*;

Chronology of the Day of Battle
(all times approximate)

0600	Opposing fleets in sight, about 10–12 miles distant
0640	*Victory* makes signals 72, 13
0650	*Victory* makes signal 76
0830	Combined Fleet wears (N.B. Surgeon Beatty says 7.20; Admiral Gravina says 8 o'clock)
1000	Combined Fleet completes wearing
1130	*Victory* makes signal 63
1140	*Victory* makes signal 'England expects . . .' followed by No. 16

Geographically, the action divided into three sectors, as below:

Lee Column	Weather Column	Dumanoir's action
Phase I		
1200 *Fougueux* opens fire on *Royal Sovereign*		
1204 *Royal Sovereign* cuts enemy line		
1213 *Belleisle* cuts enemy line		
1220	*Bucentaure* opens fire on *Victory*	
1230 *Tonnant* cuts enemy line		
1235 *Bellerophon* cuts enemy line		
1259	*Victory* cuts enemy line	
1300 *Colossus* cuts enemy line	*Téméraire* cuts enemy line	
1310	*Victory* alongside *Redoutable*	
1325 *Santa-Ana* dismasted	NELSON SHOT	
Belleisle unmanageable, captures *ARGONAUTA*		
Dreadnought cuts line		
1335	*Redoutable* attempts to board *Victory*	
1340	*Téméraire* alongside *Redoutable*	
1345	*Neptune* rakes *Bucentaure*, then *Leviathan* rakes *Bucentaure*, *Conqueror* rakes *Bucentaure*	

all the rest were drowned. *Bucentaure* ran on the rocks, her crew and the British prize crew being saved by the French frigates. *Fougueux* was less fortunate; she, too, ran ashore, and only twenty-five of those on board her were saved. *Algésiras* was lucky: she was in an almost unmanageable condition, her French crew of 600 locked below while a British prize crew of only fifty tried to keep her from drifting onto the shore where *Fougueux* was already breaking up. At last, considering the task impossible, the British officer in charge ordered the prisoners to be brought up so that they could try to save themselves. What they did, however, was to rush him and retake possession of the ship, which then, with great difficulty, made its way into Cadiz. The French, to their honour, released the British prize crew, and sent them back to the fleet in a

frigate – a gesture of thanks for Collingwood's offer to put all his wounded prisoners ashore. Nelson's prayer for 'humanity after Victory' was granted in good measure during these nights and days of dreadful danger for victors and vanquished alike.

The last acts of the campaign were now played out. On 23 October Commodore Cosmao-Kerjulien bravely came out of Cadiz with five ships of the line and five frigates to try to recapture some of the British prizes. It was an ill-starred enterprise. They managed to repossess themselves of *Santa-Ana* and *Neptuno* – but at a price: returning to harbour, *Indomptable* ran ashore. She had aboard some 500 survivors of *Bucentaure*, as well as her own crew of about 600; only some 100 all told were rescued. Later *San-Francisco-de-Asis* also grounded, but most

Phase II

1400	*Dreadnought* takes *SAN-JUAN-NEPOMUCENO*	*Fougueux* alongside *Téméraire*	
1405		*Conqueror* takes *BUCENTAURE*	
1410	*Mars* 'hard pressed'	*Téméraire* takes *FOUGUEUX*	
1415	*Royal Sovereign* takes *SANTA-ANA* *Tonnant* takes *ALGESIRAS*		
1420		*Téméraire* takes *REDOUTABLE*	
1430			Begins to put about
1500	*Euryalus* takes *Royal Sovereign* in tow; *Colossus* takes *SWIFTSURE* and *BAHAMA* *Bellerophon* takes *MONARCA*	*Britannia* cuts line *Leviathan* engages *San-Augustino*	Engaged by *Ajax* and *Agamemnon*
1510	*Thunderer* engages *Principe le Asturias*		Engaged by *Minotaur* and *Spartiate*
1520		*Africa* engages *Intrépide*	
1525	*Belleisle* ceases firing *Swiftsure* engages French *Achille*		
1530		*Leviathan* takes *SAN-AUGUSTINO*	*Minotaur* and *Spartiate* cut off *Neptuno*

Phase III

1600	*Achille* takes *BERWICK* *Defiance* takes *AIGLE* Villeneuve taken aboard *Mars*	*Orion* engages *Intrépide*	*Minotaur* and *Spartiate* alongside *Neptuno*
1615	*Defence* takes *SAN-IDELFONSO*		
1630	*Prince* sets *Achille* on fire	DEATH OF NELSON *Orion* takes *INTREPIDE*	
1700			
1715			*Minotaur* takes *NEPTUNO*
1730	*Prince* takes *SANTISSIMA TRINIDAD*		
1745	*Achille* blows up		

of her company were saved. The 100-gun *Rayo* had the misfortune to meet *Donegal*, freshly returned from Gibraltar, and was captured; two days later, however, *Rayo* went ashore, as did the prize *Monarca*. Nor was the tally of the gale's victims yet full: Collingwood, under the mistaken impression that Cosmao-Kerjulien had brought out ten ships of the line, concluded that there must be enough seaworthy vessels in Cadiz to make matters very difficult if he tried to keep all his prizes in such weather. Accordingly, he gave orders for those nearest the Spanish coast to be scuttled or burned; among these was the greatest of them all, *Santissima Trinidad*. In the end only one French ship (*Swiftsure*) and three Spanish survived out of the rich haul on 21 October.

There remained only Dumanoir's detachment and it had but a short course to run. Trying to reach the sanctuary of Rochefort, Dumanoir ran straight into the arms of a division of the Western Squadron under Rear-Admiral Sir Richard Strachan, which was in fact searching for the elusive Allemand. The luck in escaping his pursuers which that officer had enjoyed all through his long commerce-raiding cruise did not extend to his colleague. On 3 November, after a fight lasting two and a quarter hours, Dumanoir's entire squadron was captured. And that was the end of the Combined Fleet, the mighty instrument devised by Napoleon to be the agent of his conquest of England, but whose fate was to provide history with the classic example of British sea power.

British Casualties at Trafalgar

Ship	Killed	Wounded	Total
Lee Column			
Royal Sovereign (100)	47	94	141
Belleisle (74)	33	93	126
Mars (74)	29	69	98
Tonnant (80)	26	50	76
Bellerophon (74)	27	123	150
Colossus (74)	40	160	200
Achille (74)	13	59	72
Dreadnought (98)	7	26	33
Polyphemus (64)	2	4	6
Revenge (74)	28	51	79
Swiftsure (74)	9	8	17
Defiance (74)	17	53	70
Thunderer (74)	4	12	16
Defence (74)	7	29	36
Prince (98)	0	0	0
Weather Column			
†Victory (100)	57	102	159
Téméraire (98)	47	76	123
Neptune (98)	10	34	44
Leviathan (74)	4	22	26
Britannia (100)	10	42	52
Conqueror (74)	3	9	12
Africa (64)	18	44	62
Agamemnon (64)	2	8	10
Ajax (74)	2	9	11
Orion (74)	1	23	24
Minotaur (74)	3	22	25
Spartiate (74)	3	20	23
Total	449	1,241	1,690

'The mêlée was general . . .': a view of the battle drawing towards its end, with one of the British frigates on the left, and the schooner *Pickle* looking very trim on the right

Besides Lord Nelson, two captains were killed in the British fleet: Captain George Duff of the *Mars*, and Captain John Cooke of the *Bellerophon*.
The losses of the Combined Fleet will never be exactly known. Major-General J. F. C. Fuller makes this summary:

'The French and Spanish losses, given by Fraser,* are as follows: French, 3,373 killed and drowned and 1,155 wounded; Spanish, 1,022 killed, 1,383 wounded and between 3,000 and 4,000 prisoners. As the French loss in prisoners must, at least, have equalled the Spanish, the total allied losses probably amounted to some 14,000 officers and men.'

*Edward Fraser: *The Enemy at Trafalgar*
†It says much for the defensive strength of the three-deckers that, while so many were falling up above, on *Victory*'s lower deck only two men were hurt.
Number in brackets = number of guns.

Footnotes

Ch VI

1 Lord Keith's Downs squadron.

2

	Phoenix	Didon
Gun rating	36	40
Actual number of guns	42	46
Broadside weight	444 lbs	563 lbs
Crew	245	330
Tonnage	884	1,091

3 Nelson to Captain Fremantle, 16 August.
4 Lord Castlereagh, Secretary of State for War and Colonies.
5 The Prime Minister, William Pitt.
6 See p. 85.
7 See p. 85.
8 The boundary of the command would be extended to Cape St Vincent.
9 Nelson to Rear-Admiral Knight, 30 September.
10 The East India convoy from India and China, twenty-nine sail, besides cargoes worth £15 million, also carried Major-General Sir Arthur Wellesley, fresh from triumphs in the Mahratta Wars.
11 'I had been writing seven hours yesterday'; Nelson to Lady Hamilton, 1 October.
12 Nelson to Lord Castlereagh, 5 October.
13 See p. 131.
14 'We are one and I hope ever shall be', Nelson to Collingwood, 7 October.
15 Nelson to Lord Barham, 30 September.
16 See p. 165.
17 Keats, having made the long chase, would nevertheless miss the climax.
18 Nelson to Davison, 30 September.

19 See p. 86.

20 Napoleon to Villeneuve, 14 September.

21 Before leaving Toulon in March he had issued a piece of bombast containing the sentence: 'Every captain, who is not closely engaged, is not in his station; and a signal to recall him to his duty will be a stain on his character.' This was the prelude to five months' scrupulous avoidance of action.

22 This was quite correct; Nelson was planning to force the Combined Fleet out of harbour by an attack with bomb-vessels and rockets. The latter were Colonel Congreve's design, and he was expected to bring them out himself. They had a maximum range of 3,500 yards, but were very inaccurate. Congreve rockets saw some service in the Peninsular War, and there was a Rocket Troop at Waterloo.

23 See p. 29.

24 See p. 136.

25 Perhaps this may have been due to the unfortunate memory of the action against Sir Robert Calder, in which the Spanish squadron had had five out of six ships captured or severely damaged, the French loss being altogether incommensurate.

26 The authority for such statements as these must, of course, be the ships' logs, which in theory record all signals, movements and occurrences as they happen. The difficulties presented by these sources are pointed out on pp. 146 and 204–5, but it may be noted here that Signal No. 72 was logged by six ships with times varying from 5.40 a.m. to 6.09, while Signal No. 13 was logged by eight, with times varying from six o'clock to seven o'clock. These are early warnings that all

timings mentioned are approximate, arrived at by comparisons of likelihoods.

27 See *Witnesses*, p. 186.

28 There were three *Neptunes* present, French, Spanish and British, two *Achilles*, French and British, and two *Swiftsures*, French and British.

29 Admiral Gravina says eight o'clock; Dr Beatty in the *Victory* says 7.20; Mr James says 8.30; there are further variations.

30 See *Witnesses*, p. 199.

31 See *Witnesses*, p. 188.

32 See p. 48.

33 See p. 146.

34 See p. 146.

35 He also says that *Victory* and *Royal Sovereign* were 'about two miles' apart, which is incomprehensible.

36 See *Witnesses*, p. 188, for the reaction of Captain Lucas of the *Redoutable*.

37 See *Witnesses*, p. 195.

38 See *Witnesses*, p. 189.

39 Collingwood to Admiral Sir Peter Parker, 1 November 1805.

40 See p. 162.

41 A naval captain, of course, is the equivalent of an army colonel, while an army (or marine) captain is the equivalent of a naval lieutenant.

42 See p. 161.

43 See pp. 136–7.

44 See p. 162. The preponderance of dead to wounded in the beaten fleet is a characteristic of naval warfare; in a land battle, even a very severe one, these figures would probably have been reversed.

POSTSCRIPT

Nelson's previous fame, and the completeness of the victory at Trafalgar, gave the general public all it needed: a legend to counteract that of the all-conquering Napoleon. Praise for the departed hero and his crowning triumph was vociferous on all sides; it seemed not merely churlish but stupid to query it. Admiral Mahan, in the last paragraph of his biography of Nelson, expresses the prevailing nineteenth-century view in the nineteenth-century manner: 'The coincidence of his death with the moment of completed success has impressed upon that superb battle a stamp of finality, an immortality of fame, which even its own grandeur scarcely could have insured. He needed, and he left, no successor. To use again St. Vincent's words, "There is but one Nelson." ' This interpretation of the event and of the man was accepted by most; even professional naval opinion subscribed to it. The next edition of the signal book, in 1816, contained a new signal: 'cut the enemy's line in order of sailing in two columns' – the Trafalgar formation, justified by the Trafalgar experience. In 1811, Captain William Hoste of *Amphion*, one of Nelson's protégés and great admirers, commanding a squadron of frigates in the Adriatic, applied the Trafalgar method to an attack on a larger enemy squadron, and won a neat victory at Lissa – modern opinion would probably say, in spite of the method. But for a long time there were very few who questioned it.

As the twentieth century approached, however, it brought some doubts. Professor Edward Kirk Rawson, Superintendent of the United States Naval War Records, wrote in 1899: 'From the point of view of the professional student the battle was a terrible mêlée, planned with wise foresight by Nelson and carried through in confidence in the superior qualities of his fleet. His attack was a most daring exhibition of bravery and self-confidence. Its risks, however, were so great that it cannot be held up as an example to follow.'[y] This seems to be a very just estimate, confirmed by most modern writers. Thus Sir Julian Corbett, writing in 1910,[z] from time to time in his exhaustive analysis of Nelson's tactics, when faced with insuperable mysteries, falls back on the simple word 'genius' and disturbingly leaves it at that. Yet it is he who provides the clue to the mysteries, though he cannot bring himself to say that the famous man was mistaken. The same recognition of curiosities is present in Mr Oliver Warner's phrase 'the most unorthodox battle of the sailing era'.[aa]

There is no better illustration of the curiosity of Trafalgar than the case of two three-deckers (two out of the available seven, a high proportion of these important ships): *Téméraire* and *Prince*. *Téméraire* fought two French seventy-fours, ending with one locked to her on each side, completely masking her great broadsides, unable to move, and with 123 casualties aboard. *Prince* (which was said to sail 'like a haystack') was the last British ship engaged; the issue of the day was already fully decided when she entered the battle; she fired a few useful broadsides (one of them setting fire to the unfortunate *Achille*) and that was all; her casualties were nil. It is impossible to believe that this manner of using two powerful units was deliberate, and it cannot be admired in any way.

The only judgment that one can justifiably reach is the one suggested by Corbett, though in less precise terms: that Nelson jumped to conclusions about the fight ahead of him on 21 October. He believed that Villeneuve was fleeing into Cadiz, when in fact the French admiral was preparing to offer battle; so the British fleet remained in chase formation.[1] When at last Nelson realized, with some surprise, expressed in his repeated observation that they were putting a brave face on it, that the ships he had pursued from Toulon to Martinique and back again, and missed so often, were actually standing to await his attack, it was too late to do anything about it. The result was a mêlée; and, of course, a mêlée – a 'pell-mell Battle' – was just what Nelson wanted. But it did not have to be quite so badly arranged; that was where the mistake lay.

In the mêlée, the superiority of the British ships was evident. It lay chiefly in the quality of their gunnery, its speed and accuracy. Collingwood, for example, when he commanded *Dreadnought*, constantly practised his crew at the guns, telling them: '. . . if they could fire three well-directed broadsides in five minutes, no vessel could resist them; and from constant practice, they were enabled to do so in three minutes and a half.'

Pride in gunnery ran right through the British fleet, with the result that, once within effective range, the British generally fired at twice the rate of their opponents. This meant, of course, that once engaged each British ship had the destructive power of two, and this was the material factor which decided the day. There was also a moral factor, partly consisting in the eagerness for battle that every British crew displayed, partly in the zeal and ardour of their captains, now reflecting their highest professional polish after decades of war. Lord St Vincent may have thought 'There is but one Nelson'; Admiral Villeneuve thought otherwise. Later that year he was heard to say: 'To any other Nation the loss of a Nelson would have been irreparable, but in the British Fleet off Cadiz, every Captain was a Nelson.'[2]

As we have seen, the Battle of Trafalgar was a finale: the issue of the campaign itself was already decided when the Grand Army broke up its camps and began the march to the Rhine. Trafalgar did not save England; England was already saved. Nor did Trafalgar save the Third Coalition: Ulm was a hammer blow, followed by another in December – Napoleon's victory over the combined Austrian and Russian army at Austerlitz which caused Pitt to put aside a map of Europe with the words: 'Roll up that map; it will not be wanted these ten years.' Austria and Russia came to terms with Napoleon; Naples was overrun; in 1806 Prussia was decisively defeated: Europe was at the dictator's mercy. But England was safe, and henceforth unassailable. His only weapon against her was economic strangulation – the 'Continental System', which, of course, implied continental domination. But it was an attempt to enforce the Continental System that caused the Peninsular War, and, as General Fuller says, 'without the Peninsular War it is hard to believe that there would ever have been a Waterloo.' Following this chain of reasoning, he agrees that 'Trafalgar was the really decisive battle of the Napoleonic War'.

The long-term results were also important. Trafalgar placed British sea power on a pinnacle that was not seriously shaken until the Battle of Jutland in 1916. The intervening period contained the time of Britain's greatest prosperity and authority. Inevitably, also, an element of complacency developed. Lord Esher wrote in 1917: 'It is time that something was done at the Admiralty. There has been no critical or creative movement within its antique walls since the War began. That celebrated phrase of Mahan's about Nelson's ghostly, unseen, storm-tossed fleet, has been the Navy's undoing.'[3] Lord Esher was not only misquoting,[4] he was also exaggerating; but he had a point. The thunders of Trafalgar *had*, to some extent, become a lullaby, as though Britons were born to win such victories. The thunders of Jutland disabused them. Yet in the Battle of Jutland, and in the war that followed it, the example of Nelson continued to offer inspiration, and the result – if not the method – of Trafalgar recalled the true goal of professional endeavour.

Footnotes
  1 See p 140.
  2 Quoted by Mr Pole Carew in a letter to Lord Sidmouth, 3 December 1805.
  3 Lord Esher to Field-Marshal Haig, 6 May 1917.
  4 See p. 20.

WITNESSES OF TRAFALGAR

Eye-witness accounts compiled
by John Westwood

'The Royal Navy began to pay off its ships':
Rowlandson shows a lively scene at Portsmouth
Point

After the Peace of Amiens the Royal Navy began to
pay off its ships. Most ships reduced to skeleton crews
as soon as they reached their home port. One of them
was H.M.S. *Tromp*, a former Dutch ship which, like
most prizes, retained her old name when incorporated
in the British fleet:

'The old *Tromp* had hitherto been much infested with
rats, and now, since the provisions had been sent out
of her, and they had nothing to eat, they were like to
take possession of the ship from us by their fighting
and noise night and day; and our wooden-legged
cook killed many of them by throwing a broom-stick
at them when they got many together near the galley,
and he, with the boys, were almost continually at war
with them, and enjoyed the fun; so we reported the
rats to the master-attendant, and he sent off Hammond,
the rat-catcher, who soon poisoned them all except
one.

Mr. Oades, our carpenter . . . was a chubby little
fellow, and very fond of firing at the gulls, and when
he went below always left the musket ready and his
boy to call him when any gulls came near; and often
was the cry to Mr. Oades, and often he fired, but never
hit anything, because he said the powder was bad;
but the boatswain said the barrel was crooked, and
no wonder he could not hit anything; but this was
only quizzing him. At last there was a cry out for Mr.
Oades to make haste, for there was a large rat in the
dirt-tub, and down he came as quick as possible, crept
quietly along to the dirt tub, fired, and killed the rat,
the only one that was remaining, and which highly
delighted him; but the old boatswain said that he
almost touched it with the muzzle of the piece before
he fired. To conclude, little did poor Lewis Oades
think at this time that it would be his fate to be shot,
which actually happened three years after, on board
the *Téméraire* at the Battle of Trafalgar.'
(W. Richardson, *A Mariner of England* (1908), ed.
Spencer Childers, John Murray, London, pp. 197–8.)

The swift renewal of hostilities meant that crews on
many outlying stations never got home to enjoy the
liberation which they expected from the peace, and
some became mutinous:

'Napoleon's plans, by the wisdom and foresight of the
Ministry, were seen through, and orders arrived for
the detention of all the ships of the line (at all
serviceable) then in the Mediterranean, instead of
sending them to England. This created a partial
murmur amongst the different crews; but the firmness
and strict discipline of our captain and officers kept
our ship's company perfectly quiet. The crew of the
Gibraltar, however, broke out, and two of the

unfortunate men were hanged afterwards in Orestano
Bay, Sardinia.'
(W. S. Lovell, *Personal Narrative of Events from 1799
to 1815* (1879), W. Allen, London, p. 28.)

The re-mobilization of the fleet was soon retarded by
a shortage of men, both for repairing the ships and for
manning them. This shortage would persist for years;
few of the ships which fought at Trafalgar carried a
full complement despite the activities of the press
gangs. A ship's gunner of the time wrote:

'On March 8 of the following year (1803), after being
only six months in ordinary, a general press broke out
all over England, and the seamen and marines
belonging to the commissioned ships here landed, and
this day pressed three hundred men . . . soon after
our old ship was brought forward and put into the
dockyard basin, to be repaired . . . And in such a
hurry were they to get all these ships ready, that the
master carpenters of the ships in ordinary were
ordered to the dockyard to assist as working hands. A
party of them was set to work on our old ship, and
received extra wages for it, as well as being exempted
from attending duty on board their own ships.'
(W. Richardson, op. cit., pp. 197–200.)

The evils of impressment are not hard to discern in
the following account by an officer of the Impress
Service, whose zeal had evidently blunted his
sensibility:

'All my plans were suddenly thwarted by the Prime
Minister's celebrated message to the House of
Commons on the 8th of March, alluding to some
armaments in the ports of France. This threw the
whole country into a state of excitement which no
doubt you will remember; and we began to prepare
for war. I was walking the next day, very leisurely, up
Piccadilly when a naval acquaintance accosted me.
"You seem to be taking it very easily," he said. "You
are wanted at the Admiralty." I could scarcely believe
the assertion, but he repeated it with such positive
assurances that I hastened thither: and sure enough,
in the hall I saw a sheet of paper stuck up, and my
name on it – "Wanted, Lieut. D–" Upon inquiry, I
was ordered to proceed to Hull, upon the Impress
Service . . . Lord St. Vincent had changed the whole
system relating to the Impress Service by nominating
young and active officers to it instead of old ones . . .
The next day I left home for Hull, where I arrived in
due time. I had not been out of the stage one minute
when I met one of my shipmates of the *Crescent*, the
sailmaker. He hailed me with a cheerful countenance,
but when he heard the reason for my presence in that

town, he took to his heels and was out of sight in no time . . .

The Admiralty sent a vessel to receive such men as were pressed or that voluntarily entered for the Navy. When I had my doubts of the safety of any in my lock-up room, they were sent off to the vessel. But all my proceedings were under the inspection of my superior. There was also a surgeon appointed to inspect the men, as to their being in sound health, wind and limb. This examination took place in the apartments of my rendezvous every morning about 9 o'clock. On one occasion I had stopped a strong powerful man as he was coming to his labours in the dock (I have often wondered that he did not throw me into it). He replied to my questions that he was not a seaman but a carpenter, and took a ruler out of the slash pocket of his trousers to prove his assertion. "Carpenters," I observed, "are wanted in the Navy as well as seamen. Come along with me." When he resisted, I made the agreed signal to my men, who were watching my action. They instantly closed, and four of them took hold of the carpenter. In taking him to my place of security, they unluckily passed through the street where this man resided. He called out to his wife while passing under the window. She made her appearance and, when she saw him under the power of the press-gang, burst out in wild lamentations. Her screams brought a large number of persons to the spot, some of whom made an attempt to rescue her husband: but they failed . . . It appeared that he was a clever, useful man, much valued by his employers . . .

. . . On one occasion I was assaulted by a shower of brickbats: on another, a volley of either musket or pistol balls was fired into my room one evening as I was reading at my table. Fortunately I escaped any serious injury; but it became necessary for the Mayor to interfere, and some constables were directed to watch over the safety of my person. In my expeditions in quest of seamen I scarcely ever wore the same dress, and I managed to pick up men in greater numbers than expected . . . it soon became necessary to send a frigate to receive the seamen. When she arrived, a party of marines was landed to prevent any attempt at a rescue. This event caused considerable excitement. All the labourers at the various docks turned out, and at one time their shouts and threats gave reason to apprehend some serious disturbance. But the Mayor, assisted by all the Corporation, showed much spirit and determination, which kept all quiet. I had my share of abuse that day, but no one dared to lay hands on me.'
(W. H. Dillon, *Narrative of my Professional Adventures* (*1790–1839*), Navy Records Society (1953), Vol. 2, pp. 9–12.)

Apart from the Impress Service, pressing was undertaken at sea and in overseas ports by all Royal Navy ships. Nowhere in the world were merchant ships safe from its depredations. Even foreign ships could be victims. In 1800, Lieutenant Dillon had some experience of this work, which he later recounted with some pride:

'I told the Master that I should take away some of his men. This intention caused a terrible hubbub amongst the seamen: so I got up upon the quarter netting, hailed my schooner and demanded if the guns were loaded . . . Then I addressed the Master . . . "You see I am all ready, and if you do not deliver up some of your men, I shall order my men in the schooner to fire into you. I do not mind the consequences myself. I care not for my own life. But here I am, and will not quit you until I have at least 10 or 12 seamen out of this vessel."

The noise on board my schooner of moving the gun was heard: the lighted matches were seen: the muskets too were visible. A dead pause of some moments ensued: then I spoke to the Master again and asked what he would do. At last, one seaman was brought aft, and I questioned him. As he was a stout able-bodied man, I accepted him, and as soon as he brought up his bag he went into the little dinghy and was taken to the schooner. I now had the Muster Roll brought up, and called over the seamen by their names. I had to contend against every species of obstruction, the details of which I shall not enter into.

I remained on board *The Four Brothers* until 2 o'clock in the morning, and finally succeeded in taking from her 13 stout fellows; some capital seamen, one a Pilot of six feet. In fact most of them were not under 5 feet 10 inches. The Master requested me to give him a certificate of my having taken so many men, as it would, he hoped, prevent more being taken from him by other ships of war. I readily complied with that wish, and stated how courteously he had conducted himself towards me. I then left him. When I reached my own schooner, I found that my Padroon had placed all the pressed men in the hold. He had given them grog, then put them in irons, "as," he said, "I became alarmed at having such stout men about me on deck. I thought they might have taken the schooner from me, with my 12 lads." I was highly satisfied with the old tar's good management, and complimented him accordingly . . . I could not help feeling overjoyed at having performed one of those acts by which I had obtained some useful men to serve the Country, without any unpleasant result.'
(W. H. Dillon, op. cit., Vol. 1, pp. 391–2.)

'A general press broke out all over England';
Cruikshank's drawing displays the powerful
emotions aroused when patriotism received the
spur of forcible persuasion

Few of the men impressed in 1803 would return home
before 1814, if at all. And even those who escaped the
gangs found their lives disrupted. The social
implications of impressment are indicated by the
recollections of a Scottish sailor who, after twenty-five
years at sea and participation in the Battle of Cape
St Vincent, decided in 1801 to quit the seafaring life:

'For one year my prospects were as good as I could
have wished, and I was as happy as ever I had been
in my life. But in a few months after, the war broke
out again, and the press-gang came in quest of me. I
could no longer remain in Edinburgh and avoid them.
My wife was like a distracted woman, and gave me
no rest until I sold off my stock in trade and the
greater part of my furniture, and retired to the
country. Even until I got this accomplished I dared
not to sleep in my own house, as I had more than one
call from the gang.
I went to Cousland, nine miles from Edinburgh, in
the parish of Cranstown, and put up at one Robert
Moodie's, a small public house, not knowing what
was to be my next pursuit. I could obtain no
employment as a cooper, unless I lived in a large or
sea-port town, and there I could not remain . . . The
cultivation of the small garden attached to my cottage
occupied my mind for some time. I was becoming a
little more reconciled to my lot, when the press-gang
came out even to Cousland, and took away a neighbour
of the name of Murray. He had a large family, and,
through the interest of the minister and neighbouring
gentlemen, he got off. His impressment was a great
blow to my tranquillity for many months.'
(*The Life and Adventures of John Nicol* (1822),
W. Blackwood, Edinburgh, pp. 200–12.)

Many British people, including some of the victims,
regarded impressment as necessary, even though
they resented the way it was carried out. They seemed
to understand that anything was better than Bonaparte.
William Richardson, a former merchant seaman, was
several times impressed, and he still had bitter feelings
about the methods used many years later.

'People may talk of negro slavery and the whip, but
let them look nearer home, and see a poor sailor
arrived from a long voyage, exulting in the pleasure
of soon being among his dearest friends and relations.
Behold him just entering the door, when a press
gang seizes him like a felon, drags him away and puts
him into the tender's hold, and from thence he is sent
on board a man-of-war, perhaps ready to sail to some
foreign station, without seeing either his wife, friends,
or relations; if he complains he is likely to be seized
up and flogged with a cat, much more severe than the
negro driver's whip, and if he deserts he is flogged
round the fleet nearly to death. Surely they had better
shoot a man at once: it would be greater lenity!
It may be said that England cannot do without
pressing. Be it so; but then let it be done in a more
equitable manner, and let sailors arriving from long
voyages have liberty a month or more to spend their
money and enjoy themselves with their friends; then
I will be bound to say they will endure pressing with
more patience, be better satisfied, and not so ready to
desert.'
(W. Richardson, op. cit., pp. 292–3.)

Although in 1805 about half the Royal Navy's men
were pressed, many others were volunteers, attracted
to naval service at different ages and for different
reasons. One of England's seamen later wrote how,
as a small boy travelling through Oxfordshire, he
caught the sea fever:

'We had another source of relief in the antics of a
hairbrained sailor. From spinning yarns, which looked
amazingly like new inventions, he would take to
dancing on the roof of the coach; at the foot of a hill
he would leap off, and then spring up again with the
agility of a monkey, to the no small amusement of the
passengers. The more I saw of this reckless,
thoughtless tar, the more enamoured I became with
the idea of a sea life.'
(S. Leech, *Thirty Years from Home* (1844), John
Neale, London, p. 10.)

But the volunteers were soon disillusioned:

'. . . and in one of the vagaries of my youth, on the
9th May, 1805, I repaired to the rendezvous which

169

'The pleasantest part of the day': or of the week –
this drawing by George Cruikshank is entitled
'Saturday night at sea'

was opened on Tower-hill, and there offered my services to his Majesty. The regulating officer seeing me with an apron on, suspected that I was a runaway apprentice, but I soon undeceived him, and I was sent on board the receiving ship then laying off the Tower; to begin a career of life, which fancy had moulded into a variety of shapes, gilded by hope, with fortune, honour, and happiness, all in full view . . .

Whatever may be said about this boasted land of liberty, whenever a youth resorts to a receiving ship for shelter and hospitality, he, from that moment, must take leave of the liberty to *speak*, or to act; he may *think*, but he must confine his thoughts to the *hold* of his mind, and never suffer them to escape the *hatchway* of utterance. On being sent on board the receiving ship, it was for the first time I began to repent of the rash step I had taken, but it was of no avail, submission to the events of fate was my only alternative, murmuring or remonstrating, I soon found, would be folly. After having been examined by the doctor, and reported *sea-worthy*, I was ordered down to the hold, where I remained all night (9th May, 1805), with my companions in wretchedness, and the rats running over us in numbers. When

released, we were ordered into the admiral's tender, which was to convey us to the Nore. Here we were called over by name, nearly two hundred, including a number of the *Lord Mayor's Men*, a term given to those who enter to relieve themselves from public disgrace, and who are sent on board by any of the city magistrates, for a street frolic or night charge. These poor fellows have a sad time of it, as they are the derision of the old and more experienced and hardened sailors, who generally cut the tails from their coats, and otherwise abuse and ridicule them. Upon getting on board this vessel, we were ordered down in the hold, and the gratings put over us; as well as a guard of marines placed round the hatchway, with their muskets loaded and fixed bayonets, as though we had been culprits of the first degree, or capital convicts. In this place we spent the day and following night huddled together, for there was not room to sit or stand separate: indeed, we were in a pitiable plight, for numbers of them were sea-sick, some retching, others were smoking, whilst many were so overcome by the stench, they fainted for want of air.'
('J. Nastyface', *Nautical Economy* (1836), W. Robinson, London, x, pp. 1–3.)

One view of life on board comes from a recruit embarked in a line-of-battle ship of the Channel Fleet:

'. . . we began to feel discipline with all its horrors. Our crew were divided into two watches, starboard and larboard. When one was on deck the other was below: for instance, the starboard watch would come on at eight o'clock at night, which is called eight-bells; at half-past is called one bell, and so on; every half-hour is a bell, as the hour-glass is turned, and the messenger sent to strike the bell, which is generally affixed near the fore-hatchway. It now becomes the duty of the officer on deck to see that the log-line is run out, to ascertain how many knots the ship goes an hour, which is entered in the log-book, with any other occurrence which may take place during the watch. At twelve o'clock, or eight-bells in the first watch, the boatswain's mate calls out lustily, "*Larboard watch, a-hoy.*" This is called the middle watch, and when on deck, the other watch go below to their hammocks, till eight-bells, which is four o'clock in the morning. They then come on deck again, pull off their shoes and stockings, turn up their trowsers to above their knees, and commence *holy-stoning* the deck, as it is termed, (for Jack is sometimes a little impious in the way of his sayings.) – Here the men suffer from being obliged to kneel down on the wetted deck, and a gravelly sort of sand strewed over it. To perform this work they kneel with their bare knees, rubbing the deck with a stone and the sand, the grit of which is very injurious. In this manner the watch continues till about four-bells, or six o'clock; they then begin to wash and swab the decks till seven-bells, and at eight-bells the boatswain's mate pipes to breakfast. This meal consists of burgoo, made of coarse oatmeal and water; others will have Scotch coffee, which is burnt bread boiled in some water, and sweetened with sugar. This is generally cooked in a hook-pot in the galley, where there is a range. Nearly all the crew have one of these pots, a spoon, and a knife; for these are things indispensable: there are also basons, plates, &c. which are kept in each mess, which generally consists of eight persons, whose berth is between two of the guns on the lower deck, where there is a board placed, which swings with the rolling of the ship, and answers for a table. It sometimes happens that a lurch will dash all the crockery to pieces; they are then obliged to eat out of wooden or tin utensils, until they come into harbour, where they get another supply. At half-past eight o'clock, or one-bell in the forenoon watch, the larboard goes on deck, and the starboard remains below. Here again the *holy-stones* or *hand-bibles* as they are called by the crew, are used, and

sometimes iron scrapers. After the lower deck has been wetted with swabs, these scrapers are used to take the rough dirt off. Whilst this is going on, the cooks from each mess are employed in cleaning the utensils and preparing for dinner, at the same time the watch are working the ship, and doing what is wanting to be done on deck.

About eleven o'clock, or six-bells, when any of the men are in irons, or on the black list, the boatswain or mate are ordered to call all hands; the culprits are then brought forward by the master at arms, who is a warrant officer, and acts the part of John Ketch, when required: he likewise has the prisoners in his custody, until they are put in irons, under any charge. All hands being now mustered, the captain orders the man to strip; he is then seized to a grating by the wrists and knees; his crime is then mentioned, and the prisoner may plead, but, in nineteen cases out of twenty, he is flogged for the most trifling offence or neglect, such as not hearing the watch called at night, not doing any thing properly on deck or aloft, which he might happen to be sent to do, when, perhaps, he has been doing the best he could, and at the same time ignorant of having done wrong, until he is pounced on, and put in irons. So much for the legal process.

After punishment, the boatswain's mate pipes to dinner, it being eight-bells, or twelve o'clock; and this is the pleasantest part of the day, as at one-bell the fifer is called to play "*Nancy Dawson,*" or some other lively tune, a well-known signal that the grog is ready to be served out. It is the duty of the cook from each mess to fetch and serve it out to his messmates, of which every man and boy is allowed a pint, that is, one gill of rum and three of water, to which is added lemon acid, sweetened with sugar. Here I must remark, that the cook comes in for the perquisites of office, by reserving to himself an extra portion of grog, which is called the over-plus, and generally comes to the double of a man's allowance. Thus the cook can take upon himself to be the man of consequence, for he has the opportunity of inviting a friend to partake of a glass, or of paying any little debt he may have contracted. It may not be known to every one that it is grog which pays debts, and not money, in a man of war. Notwithstanding the cook's apparently pre-eminent situation, yet, on some occasions, he is subject to censure or punishment by his messmates, for not attending to the dinner properly, or for suffering the utensils of his department to be in a dirty condition. Justice, in these cases, is awarded by packing a jury of cooks from the different messes, for it falls to the lot of each man in a mess to act as cook in his turn. The mode or precept by which this jury is summoned is by hoisting a mess swab or beating a tin dish between decks forward, which serves as a proclamation to call the court together, when the case is fully heard and decided upon.

At two-bells in the afternoon, or one o'clock, the starboard watch goes on deck, and remains working the ship, pointing the ropes, or doing any duty that may be required until the eight-bells strike, when the boatswain's mate pipes to supper. This consists of half a pint of wine, or a pint of grog to each man, with biscuit and cheese, or butter . . .'
('J. Nastyface,' op. cit., pp. 5–11.)

New men, especially former merchant seamen, were struck by the speed with which orders were carried out:

'. . . "all hands make sail" followed, and instantly the shrouds on either side were filled with men like swarming bees. No voice was heard but his who gave command, and a noble voice it was; but his words were repeated in the outpoured shrillness of the silver calls of the boatswain and his mates; and when every man had set his foot in the rigging, with hands grasping the ratlines, "Away aloft!" – away the swarm rushed with an upward rapidity, as if the life of each depended on his being first. There was another pause: then "trice up! Lay (lie) out!" and the long, outstretched, naked limbs of the ship were everywhere upmingling in the blue of the sky, and down and out over the sea, alive with creeping things hurrying out to their extremities; between them and certain destruction was a curved swinging loose rope, on which they struck their feet; this was all that held them from plunging into the sea, or crushing to mummy on deck. Strange as it is, reader, there is not an atom of danger in this. I never saw an accidental fall from a ship's yards in my life.

I had seen sails set on board the Tender and other ships, but on a small scale; here and there a man dotted the shrouds and the yards; but on this occasion hundreds were rushing against each other, each only anxious to be first and to do his own work, at any expense of danger or life to others. All seemed riot, confusion, desperation; but all was silent, for all was in obedience to a sure design; it was order, precision, exactness, and familiarity with the action. "Let fall, sheet home, haul o'board, hoist away!" were the next orders, delivered in one breath and in an instant. It is vain that you will look, even in the most skilfully-manned merchant vessels, for anything which can glimpse a conception of a ship of war making sail from her anchorage. In a merchantman the sails are spread, and set stragglingly and partially, portions tumble

down, flap about, and slowly, creepingly spread at intervals, and from the several points; but with the words I have quoted, the instant flashing effect is magical and magnificent; the minute-ago naked masts, beams, and yards, the whole of the towering scaffolding and beautiful skeleton is clothed in fifteen thousand feet of graceful drapery, so perfectly fitted and so admirably put on; then out it swells, and curves in the wind: it is beauty itself. Not a word is spoken till "Belay;" then the rumbling of four or five hundred stamping feet, the rattling of blocks and pulleys, the whirring of ropes, and the grinding of the massive beams which are by these adjusted in their required positions, are all at once stopped. Still the immense and splendidly-compact machine lies motionless; the anchor has not yet quitted its mighty grip of the solid ground, ten fathoms beneath the surface of that glassy field on which she sits, but ready for her start. "Ship the capstern bars!" A few more turns, and the anchor is away. "Man the cat and fish!" (Odd things there are in a ship, reader, but I can't stop to explain) . . . Oh! how grand the ship did look when her sails were loosed, topsails sheeted home and hoisted, and she moved along at the pilot's word, leaving houses, town, ships, trees, and fields slipping backward! . . .'
(C. Pemberton, op. cit., pp. 100–1, 83.)

Amid the roughness and toughness of shipboard life, the misfortunes of an individual sometimes elicited an unexpected sympathy, sometimes a malicious satisfaction. Few sailors felt much sympathy towards midshipmen, those teenagers who all too often had not yet learned to temper power with sensibility. On board H.M.S. *Windsor Castle*, wrote a gunner,

'One of our midshipmen, a young sailor named Dalgleish, new rigged with uniform from top to toe, had been so seasick during the last night that he lay down on the deck between two of the guns, and when trying to get up in the morning could not; for the deck had been new caulked and the pitch not scraped off, and he stuck fast to it from head to foot. It was laughable to see how foolish he looked when extricated, and with a line of pitch sticking to his clothes from top to bottom.'
(W. Richardson, op. cit., p. 201.)

When the war restarted, Napoleon revived his plan of invading England. The Duc de Fezensac, who started his military service in the ranks at this time, later described this phase:

'The Emperor wished to attack the territory of England, to strike at her heart. He assembled on the coast three army corps, each of about 25,000 men, and a reserve of 40,000 . . . immense supplies were brought from all directions, all kinds of provisions to last three months. It was a question of transporting to England, in the presence of the enemy fleet, this very numerous army and its equipment. After many trials, it was decided to use long-boats armed with a gun, gunboats, and pinnaces. The latter were lighter and carried only infantry, while the others carried artillery, provisions, and some horses. Twelve or thirteen hundred of these boats were enough to transport 120,000 men, with field artillery, provisions and ammunition for several days. Another transport flotilla consisting of fishing and coastal boats, would convey horses, the siege artillery, and the remainder of the provisions and ammunition; nine hundred or a thousand boats would be sufficient for this. Later, the divisions assembled at Utrecht and Brest would be embarked by the French, Spanish and Dutch fleets.

But the difficulties facing the execution of this plan would have daunted the most adventurous and intrepid talent. The boats had to be built in all the ports of France, then despite the English cruisers they had to be assembled at Boulogne, Ambleteuse, and Étaples, which themselves had to be put in a state suitable to receive them. Trials had to be made of embarking and disembarking men and materials.

Storehouses had to be built on the coast for provisions and supplies . . .

Each company had four huts, built in two lines. Each hut held 16 men, making a total of 64. This was not much for battalions whose full strength was 800 men, or about 90 for each of their nine companies. But several men had permission to work in town, and others were absent for different reasons, so the number of places was sufficient . . . The base of the huts was one metre below the ground, which made them very damp. The sleeping place consisted of a big camp bed covered with straw, over which a woollen blanket was laid. Each man lay on this blanket, wrapped in his own linen sleeping bag with a haversack as pillow. Then another woollen blanket was laid on top. Thus the soldiers slept separately but together. Often the long winter nights were shortened by a soldier telling a story. To make sure he was being listened to, he would interrupt his story from time to time and exclaim *cric*, at which those who were still awake would reply *crac*; if everyone was silent, then the storyteller himself went to sleep . . .

The Boulogne camp, of which the Montreuil camp formed the left wing, has left strong traces in our contemporary history. All military men know the advantages of bringing troops together in camps. The

successes we won in subsequent campaigns are attributed to the Boulogne camp where, it is said, we were always busy with manoeuvres, military works, and all kinds of exercises. My readers will therefore be astonished to learn how little our leaders at Montreuil troubled themselves with our instruction, how little they profited from the precious time they had at their disposal. Marshal Ney led two big manoeuvres in autumn 1804, and again in 1805, in which I took part first as a private and then as an officer. It was a lot of trouble, and too tiring; we would leave before daybreak after having had some soup, and return at night, having nothing during the day apart from one distribution of brandy. General Malher, who replaced General Partouneaux, assembled the division barely three times and deployed it badly. There was no brigade manoeuvre at all, the general did not even come to the camp. Each colonel instructed his regiment according to his own fancy; a few theories were devised, some conscripts instructed, and each spring one recommenced the practical training of all the under-officers. General Malher even announced one day that he intended to issue the officers with muskets and drill them as a platoon. But happily, after complaints that the soldiers would make fun of them, this project was dropped . . .

At the beginning of March, each company was given a little garden to cultivate. This was a very good way of giving the soldiers something to do and at the same time provide them with free vegetables. But nevertheless they grumbled, for idleness has its attractions . . .

However, although the time spent in the camp was not properly exploited, the army did gain some advantages from its long stay there. Most important, it learned to live together, to learn to know one another. Firstly, camp life prepared us for marches and for encampments . . . Next, the generals, staff officers, superior officers of the different corps were together for a long period, got to know each other, and to appreciate each other. If in a brigade the colonels were mediocre, the general would note more attentively how his orders were carried out, while if the general was incompetent, then the colonels would get together and indicate to him, very respectfully, what should be done . . .'
(Général le Duc de Fezensac, *Souvenirs Militaires de 1804 à 1814*, J. Dumaine, Paris (1863), pp. 8–9, 13–15, 31–5. Trans. J. N. Westwood.)

While the French soldiers were tending their barrack-hut gardens along the Channel coast, the main British fleet was cruising off Brest, controlling thereby the vital western approaches. Smaller British squadrons

covered south-eastern England and watched French bases at Rochefort, Toulon and elsewhere. When Spain joined France this watch was extended to the Spanish ports. In August 1803 Admiral Collingwood, temporarily flying his flag in the *Venerable*, related to his father-in-law the conditions in which the British ships were operating off Brest:

'I am lying off the entrance of Brest harbour, to watch the motions of the French fleet. Our information respecting them is very vague, but we know they have four or five and twenty great ships, which makes it necessary to be alert, and keep our eyes open at all times. I therefore bid adieu to snug beds and comfortable naps at night, never lying down but in my clothes . . . with a westerly wind, it is impossible with one squadron to prevent ships getting into Brest harbour; for it has two entrances, very distant from each other, – one to the south of the Saints, but which, off Ushant, where we are, is entirely out of view. I take the utmost pains to prevent all access, and an anxious time I have of it, what with tides and rocks, which have more of danger in them than a battle once a week. I have not heard yet what ship I am to have; and indeed, as I am at sea already, neither the Admiralty nor myself seem to care much about it.'

Several months after this Collingwood returned to the subject of his flagship in another letter to his father-in-law:

'Now for my miseries, of which I have a good store just now. I came in from sea with orders from the Admiral to refresh my ship's company, and, poor creatures, they have been almost worked to death ever since. We began by discovering slight defects in the ship; and the farther we went in the examination, the more important they appeared, until at last she was discovered to be so completely rotten as to be unfit for sea. We have been sailing for the last six months with only a sheet of copper between us and eternity. I have written to Lord St. Vincent to ask him for a sounder ship . . .'
(G. L. N. Collingwood, *A Selection from the Public and Private Correspondence of Vice-Admiral Lord Collingwood* (1829), James Ridgeway, London, pp. 91–2, 95.)

The condition of the British ships, destined to cruise for month after month in stormy waters, varied. But while the monotonous struggle with wind and water strained the structures of the ships, it provided thorough training for the crews, a training which was denied the crews of the French and Spanish vessels as they lay snugly in harbour. From time to time ships whose condition seemed especially hazardous were allowed home for repairs. In June 1804 Captain Duff of H.M.S. *Mars* wrote to his wife:

'My old Mars is certainly a very fine ship; and if I could only persuade her to sail a little better, and could get a few good men, being now above *seventy* short of complement, I would not wish for a better ship. The ward-room officers seem to be pleasant good people, and I have no doubt we shall go on very well together. We have got a famous party of marines, and with them and the officers we can keep the Johnnies in very good order, if they should ever want it, which at present they do not.'

And three months later he could write, after a refit in a home dockyard:

'Since I wrote to you last, the Mars has got a great deal done to her. She is new coppered, has got a false keel, and everything I have asked is to be done; so that I am in great hopes I shall be able to show some of my friends how handsomely her stern is painted.' (*The Naval Chronicle*, Vol. XV, (1806), pp. 278–9.)

After her refit the *Mars* was ordered to join Collingwood, who by this time had been entrusted with the watch off Rochefort. Collingwood wrote another long letter to his father-in-law in November 1804. He was off Rochefort, flying his flag in the *Dreadnought*:

'I am really almost worn out with incessant fatigue and anxiety of mind. I am here watching the French squadron in Rochefort, but feel that it is not practicable to prevent their sailing, if it be their intention; and yet, if they should get past me, I should be exceedingly mortified. At this moment, and for two days past, it has blown a hard gale of easterly wind, and we are driven thirty leagues from the port. The only thing that can prevent their sailing is the apprehension that they may run amongst us, as they cannot exactly know where we are, to avoid us. The ship which I am now in is a very fine strong ship, but has been ill fitted out; for it was a part of Lord St. Vincent's economy to employ convicts to fit out the ships, instead of the men and officers who were to sail in them. The consequence is, that they are wanting in every kind of arrangement that skilful men would have made, and most of them have been obliged to be docked since their equipment, at a very great expense . . .' (G. L. N. Collingwood, op. cit., p. 97.)

One of the ships which had to be released for repair was H.M.S. *Kent* of the Mediterranean squadron:

'. . . we embarked a large supply of cattle and vegetables for our fleet off Toulon. On joining them, we found our ship very weak, and her timbers, from the looseness of several bolts, working very much, and causing her to make a good deal of water, – in fine weather from six to eight inches per hour, and in bad weather two feet, which kept increasing to nearly four, – until our arrival in England.' (W. S. Lovell, op. cit., pp. 36–7.)

Although the French navy stayed in port, Britain did not rule the waves absolutely. Throughout the wars against France, British shipping was liable to attacks by French privateers operating out of the lesser French ports. The master of one unlucky British ketch wrote from a French prison to his proprietors:

'I Ham sorry to Inform you of the Loss of the Ketch Endeavour Wich I suppose byfore this Time you to Well No of it. I Ham sorry that I Ever attempted to Sail from Lyme with a fowle Wind but I Done as i thought for the Best but it Did not prove to be so. I went out Into Lyme Road Sunday morning the weather being fine, as soon as I got the Rudder Replaised but in the Evning I Did Not like the wind it freshend up to the E S E and I went into the Cob again and the Tuesday morning the sky lookd finer I venturd out again. . . . I got Under Way about 7 O Clock in the Evning and at 8 the Next Morning I was taken about 2 Leagues to the Westard of Portland by the Quinieoliea Cutter Privatier Mounting 10 – 8 Pounders 4 Swivels and 68 men with Small Arms etc. We was chasd into a Place called Breiea Bettwen Some Rocks under a Battry by 2 English frigates wich Put me in Hopes the Ketch is Retaken again.

They strip Her Cabbin of all the stores they could find, Guns and shot and all our Cloathes and then stove the boat and turned Her adrift and She Sunk.

Their is Now in this Prison Near 13 Hundred Prisoners and 11 Hundred of them taken in Coasting Vessels by Privateers. The Living is verry bad consisting of only 1 Pound of Bread 3 ounces of Beef gave to us in the Morning and in the afternoon a few Horse Beans Boiled in a Little Water and a little Straw to Lye on. We are all going to be Marchd to Paris, Near 4 H. and 80 Miles as Bonnapartiea is Coming Here with His army to get ready to Envade England and wants this Prison for Barracks . . .' (From a letter in Bucklers Hard Maritime Museum.)

During these years, officers were reluctant to allow their men shore leave, largely because they feared a high desertion rate. In any case, apart from the regular trips to take on fresh water, and perhaps vegetables, most ships stayed on station. Some fortunate crews were granted shore leave at Gibraltar, perhaps because desertion there was considered more difficult:

'. . . on such days parties of the crew were permitted
to go on shore on "liberty," which "liberty" was to
hasten to the first tavern and drink themselves into a
state of helpless infirmity; which not to do would be
symptomatic of cowardly lubberliness, or worse: and
no further harm comes of "liberty" than a head-ache
occasionally, or a fit of fever and death. For though
drunkeness at sea is obnoxious to severe punishment,
in harbour it is not a failing considered, nor even a
sign of progress to degradation: that degradation,
however, is nothing; it is not even a note of coming
inattention to duty.'
(*The Life and Literary Remains of C. R. Pemberton*
(1843), Charles Fox, London, p. 122.)

Nelson never quite understood why he lost sailors
through desertion. After all, he did more for his men
than he need have done, and they knew it. But he
never realized that men torn from their homes and
placed in what were virtually floating prisons wanted
something more than the fresh vegetables which he
took such pride in supplying to them. In 1804 he
issued a memorandum to be read to the men of all his
Mediterranean squadron. His reference to deserters
abandoning their wives and families must have been
heard with some cynicism by his crews, of whom
about half were pressed men:

'When British seamen and marines so far degrade
themselves in time of war, as to desert from the
service of their own country, and enter into that of
Spain; when they leave 1s per day, and plenty of the
very best provisions, with every comfort that can be
thought of for them – for 2d a day, black bread, horse
beans, and stinking oil for their food; – when British
seamen or marines turn Spanish soldiers, I blush for
them: they forfeit, in their own opinion, I am sure,
that character of love for their own country, which
foreigners are taught to admire. A Briton to put
himself under the lash of a Frenchman or Spaniard
must be more degrading to any man of spirit than any
punishment I could inflict on their bodies. I shall leave
the punishment to their own feelings, which, if they
have any, and are still Englishmen, must be very
great.
    But, as they thought proper to abandon voluntarily,
their wives, fathers, mothers, and every endearing
tie, and also, all prospect of returning to their native
country, I shall make them remain out of that
country, which they do not wish to see, and allow
others, who love their country, and are attached to
their families, to return in their stead. And as they
have also thought proper to resign all their pay, I shall
take care that it is not returned to them . . .'

Evidently this memorandum did not obtain the
expected result, for another soon followed, in which
there was no more reference to the enjoyable menus
and daily comforts of the British sailor:

'Lord Nelson is very sorry to find that notwithstanding
his forgiveness of the men who deserted in Spain, it
has failed to have its proper effect, and that there are
still men who so far forget their duty to their King
and Country, as to desert the service, at a time when
every man in England is in arms to defend it against
the French. Therefore Lord Nelson desires that it
may be perfectly understood, that if any man be so
infamous as to desert from the service in future, he
will not only be brought to a Court Martial, but that
if the sentence should be *death*, it will be most
assuredly carried into execution.'
(T. J. Pettigrew, *Memoirs of the Life of Vice Admiral
Lord Viscount Nelson, K.B.* (1849), T. W. Boone,
London, Vol. 2, pp. 355–6.)

For the British squadron in the Mediterranean, there
was little chance of prize money and, it seemed, a
diminishing chance of action. The entry of Spain into
the war, however, seemed to promise more excitement.
A midshipman later wrote of that uneasy period
when Spain had almost, but not quite, become a
belligerent:

'. . . we proceeded to Gibraltar, and from thence to
Cadiz, where we took on board a million and sixty
thousand dollars. We anchored near a handsome
French seventy-four and a frigate; the former, called
L'Aigle, the name of the other I forget. Whenever we
passed near them, some of their crew would abuse
us; we told them to come outside, and see how soon
we would take the change out of them . . .'

The British Admiralty, however, had already issued
instructions which assumed, or assured, Spanish
hostility.[1] The same midshipman continues:

'At this period four of our frigates, under Sir Graham
Moore, were cruising off Cape St. Vincent to intercept
the four Spanish frigates, loaded with treasure,
expected home. We spoke our ships off there, and a
few days afterwards they fell in with the Spaniards,
took three, and the unfortunate fourth blew up in the
action with all her crew.
    I always did think, and my opinion has never changed,
that it was a cruel thing to send only four frigates to
detain four others, when by increasing the force to
two or three line-of-battle ships, this might have been
effected without loss of blood, or honour to the
Spaniards. If it was necessary to detain these vessels

and treasure from political motives, in order to make the king of Spain declare his equivocal conduct, it would have been humane to have sent such a force as would have put resistance out of the question; for what man, who was not a traitor, could yield without fighting (and with such a valuable cargo on board), to a force, in all appearance, not greater than his own . . .'
(W. S. Lovell, op. cit., pp. 37–8.)

Lord Nelson had arrived off Toulon in 1803 to take command of the Mediterranean squadron. A midshipman of his squadron later published some memories of those months spent off Toulon:

'Whilst off Naples official notice reached us of the declaration of war against France, and we proceeded immediately off Toulon, where, in the course of a short time, Lord Nelson arrived in a frigate, and took the command of the fleet in the Mediterranean. His lordship's flagship (the *Victory*) joined us in a few weeks, having on her passage out captured a French frigate, and some merchant vessels. We continued to cruise in the Gulf of Lyons from June, 1803, until the 24th of July, 1804, without ever going into any port to refit. It is true that occasionally the whole fleet ran from the heavy gales of the Gulf of Lyons, and took shelter in various outlandish places in Sardinia, where we could get wood and water, such as at Agincourt sound – amongst the Magdalen islands . . . There was a small village seven or eight miles off, at one of the Magdalen islands, where some few got their linen washed, but most of us in the fleet were put to our shifts to get that necessary comfort (clean linen) accomplished.

These long cruises used to put our wits sadly to the test for an appearance of a bit of white linen above our black cravats, particularly when we had to answer the signal for a midshipman on board the flagship.

Soap was almost – indeed, I might say, quite – as scarce an article as clean shirts and stockings. It was a common thing in those days of real hard service to turn shirts and stockings inside out, and make them do a little more duty . . .

. . . Our noble and gallant chief used to manage to get us fresh beef twice a week – that is to say, so many live bullocks were embarked on board each ship, and we killed them as we wanted them – by which means, with the assistance of oranges that were procured occasionally, a few cases of scurvy occurred in the fleet, notwithstanding our long stay at sea. But as for articles of luxury – tea, potatoes, soap, and other sea stores for our messes – we had none.

The inhabitants of Sardinia were as wild as their

country; the mountaineers and lowlanders generally were engaged in a kind of petty war with each other. Both parties always went armed, and murders frequently took place. At one of the anchorages in the straits, another mid and myself were attending a watering party – one of these fellows rode down with a bag of cheese, made of goat's or sheep's milk, for sale; he was armed with a long gun and pistols, and we had no firearms with us. Some dispute in the bargaining, for want of understanding each other's language, arose; the Sard very coolly mounted his horse, and taking up his cheeses, rode off a short distance, and fired at us; the ball passed through the sleeve of the mate's coat, and near my head . . .

Our long Cruise of near fourteen months off Toulon, amidst nothing but gales of wind, and heavy storms of most terrific thunder and lightning, met with no reward in the shape of prize-money.'
(W. S. Lovell, op. cit., pp. 30–33.)

Nelson continued to watch Toulon until 1805. Among the powerful French squadron lying there was the line-of-battle ship *Intrépide*. A 19-year-old officer of this vessel later gave his view of 1803–4. Writing some time after Trafalgar, he followed the fashion of blaming Villeneuve for the French lack of success. The French were always reluctant to question Napoleon's judgment, but it is interesting to note that whereas Napoleon regarded Villeneuve's escape from the Battle of the Nile as admirable, and evidence of his fitness for high command, the writer of this

the affairs of the navy prevented the accomplishment of these great aims; the Admiral's health, worn down by bad climates, deteriorated daily, and we had the pain of losing this leader who incarnated so many hopes. He died the 18 August, 1804, during a sortie, on board his vessel *Bucentaure*. His squadron buried him at the top of Cape Sepet, his habitual observation point, and erected a monument in the form of a pyramid, which future generations of sailors will contemplate with respect.

In my career I had already seen many officers, but never met a real leader who could give, like the leader we had just lost, an impression of superior will capable of transforming men and dominating events. Nothing less than a leader of this stamp would have been enough to confront the English squadron, which had been brought to a high degree of perfection by continuous practice at sea and a long sequence of successes. The famous Nelson who commanded it is in my opinion one of the most accomplished seamen who ever lived; a man of rare intelligence, valiant, of indomitable energy, and in addition an implacable enemy of our nation. He made war on us less from duty than from hatred, and drew from this feeling an ardour and an energy which he knew how to share with each of his sailors.

Napoleon chose Admiral Villeneuve to fight such an enemy. He was an officer of merit, well-educated, and with distinguished manners, but one of the least suited for such a hard task. Reserved and hesitant by nature he found it difficult to live down in the navy the memory of the Battle of Aboukir, where his conduct remained unjustifiable in the minds of all stout-hearted men; although his personal courage was never doubted, he lacked that type of courage which is needed to tempt fortune and to master it. He never believed in the success of the plan in which he had to participate, and his lack of faith soon infected those under his command. Enthusiasm cooled down again, activity diminished. It seemed that in a few weeks all chance of winning had been lost, and that the sole aim henceforth was to avoid meeting the enemy for as long as possible.'
(*Revue des Deux Mondes*, July 1905, pp. 410–12, trans. J. N. Westwood.)

Meanwhile the monotonous existence of the squadron watching Rochefort was broken by Napoleon's first plan to assemble his ships in the West Indies.[2] Captain Duff of the *Mars* wrote to his wife in December 1804:

'We have still our good easterly wind, which I hope may continue for these six weeks, or till I be relieved; as we have fine smooth water, and now and then we

account, like other officers, has chosen to regard it as rather discreditable:

'. . . the *Intrépide* joined the squadron which Napoleon had placed under the orders of Admiral Latouche-Tréville, and which was intended to assist in his projects against England. If this great sailor had not died, it is possible that events would have taken a different course. The role which Napoleon had allotted to his fleet was only for the stout-hearted. It was a question of keeping the English squadrons busy for a few hours, so that the crossing of the Channel would be unrestricted: the Grand Army would invade England, followed perhaps by the turning upside-down of the world.

After his arrival at Toulon, de Latouche had infected his squadron with his own ardour. We were moored in the outer roads, and two of our vessels in turn were ceaselessly on watch at the entrance of the channel, in order to reply to the insults of the English. As soon as the latter approached, as they were wont to do without suffering any damage, the scouts slipped their cables and within eight minutes were under sail and chasing the enemy. If the latter were supported, additional vessels of ours went to sea. It was continual manoeuvres, followed by engagements which trained our crews and commanders. The Admiral, established on the top of Cape Sepet, dominating the Toulon approaches, observed everything both inside and outside, preparing for Nelson worthy adversaries. Unfortunately the bad luck which at that time dogged

get a little fish, with our trowl: we have as yet tried it only once, and that for a short time; when I got a very good turbot for my share.

We have had two very good sermons from our Chaplain, last Sunday and to-day, and he reads the prayers very well.'

But in late January Captain Duff had more important things to write about:

'We fell in with the Colossus this morning, and have now bore up with a fair wind for Ushant, where I suppose we shall meet Admiral Cornwallis to-morrow. The Rochfort squadron has of course got out, and it is supposed to have gone to Brest. I think it the best thing that could happen, as we shall have only one port instead of two to watch. It was quite a farce to say, that our squadron was blockading the ships in Rochfort; we were only running great risk with our own: for I was always convinced that the French might have got out any day they pleased, without our ever seeing them. They must however have passed very near us in the night, from the situation we were in, and the place where they were seen; and had we met, I think we should have given a good account of them.'
(*The Naval Chronicle*, Vol. XV, p. 282.)

This, of course, was Missiessy's abortive escape from Rochefort on 11 January. On 2 March Napoleon issued the orders for his new plan of concentration in the West Indies for the attack on the Channel.[3]

On 27 March, Captain Duff told his wife of how Napoleon's plan had been executed at Brest:

'The French fleet have got out of Brest Harbour, and are anchored in Berthaume Bay. We were within four or five miles of them, our inshore ships just out of gun-shot. We are all clear for action, but it depends entirely upon them to come to it, or not. If they do, I trust we shall be victorious, and have a lasting peace. They are at present four sail of the line more than us; but if we do our duty, I think we shall give a very good account of them. Should I unfortunately fall, I hope that our friends will take care of you and our dear little ones. I have done all, my dearest Sophia, to make you and them comfortable, that our small funds would allow; but I am sorry to say, they are very small indeed. I regret much you never would allow me to speak of making a settlement, nor would look at the one I had made.'
(*The Naval Chronicle*, Vol. XV, p. 283.)

Ganteaume's escape attempt failed ignominiously.[4] Villeneuve was more successful, although by the time

he reached Martinique the Rochefort squadron had gone home. Sub-lieutenant des Touches of the *Intrépide* later described this phase of the Toulon squadron's activity:

'. . . we left on March 29 for the West Indies, thereby beginning that interminable voyage in which, badly commanded, held back by the slower ships, we crossed the seas, haunted by the spectre of Nelson, and ended up six months later at the disaster of Trafalgar.

However, fortune at first seemed to favour us. Nelson, learning that the French squadron had left Toulon, hurried into pursuit. Misled by certain signs, and by skilfully-managed rumours, he went as far as Egypt in search of it. Meanwhile we quietly effected our union with the Spanish squadron at Cadiz on 8 April. We then made sail directly for Martinique, where we arrived on 12 May . . .

The boredom of this crossing and the hesitations of the command had led to a certain lassitude, one consequence of which was that my brother Oliver, then a midshipman on the *Fougueux*, resigned on arrival at Martinique. I tried to dissuade him, but he said he was tired of that idle life, and would fight the English on his own account and in his own way. He had made the acquaintance of some Saint Malo sailors who with their privateers were waging ceaseless war against the English in the Gulf of Mexico, ravaging the coasts and taking merchant ships . . .

During our stay in the West Indies we recaptured Diamond Rock, which commands the entry into the roadstead of Fort Royal, and we made several demonstrations against the Windward Islands. We were awaiting the squadron . . . which was supposed to reinforce us. As it did not come, we set our course back to Europe. This was not very good, because unfortunately we had wasted time in the West Indies without gaining the advantage of that reinforcement, and it was unlikely that we would meet it while crossing the Atlantic. Despite hesitation and delays, we were still ahead of Nelson, and with our course set for the Channel approaches we could hope that Admiral Villeneuve would decide to break through and at any cost carry out the programme placed before him by the Emperor. But he heard about an English squadron cruising in the approaches, and instead of resolutely accepting combat he changed course to Ferrol, which was senseless.'
(*Revue des Deux Mondes*, 1905, pp. 412–13.)

However, Villeneuve did not succeed in reaching port unscathed. Des Touches later described the action between Villeneuve and Admiral Calder's squadron.

'After having evaded off Brest the squadron of Admiral Cornwallis, which we could have fought to our advantage, we encountered off Cape Finisterre another English squadron, commanded by Admiral Calder and consisting of 15 ships, of which four were three-deckers. On July 22, in mist, we came upon this squadron about 20 leagues from Ferrol. Neither admiral seemed in a hurry to get to grips, but a fight was inevitable, although it had no decisive result. The persistent mist was a great hindrance. I was at my action station on the forecastle, from which I transmitted to the senior officers such indications as might help them manoeuvre the ship. We supported with our gunfire as long as possible two Spanish ships, the *Firme* and the *San Rafael*, which, having been dismasted, drifted into the English squadron and were taken. Our mizzen mast threatened to fall, and we had to leave the battlefield so as not to share the same fate. Admiral Villeneuve did nothing to rescue the imperilled ships and this uncertain battle, known as the Battle off Cape Finisterre, turned to our disadvantage, because in spite of our enormous numerical superiority we caused no damage to the English . . .

Admiral Calder made no attempt to exploit the timidity of his opponent, and we were able to enter Vigo Bay on July 27. There we landed the sick. Later Admiral Villeneuve set sail on July 30 with 15 ships, including two Spanish. He had finally made the decision which he should have made long ago, to leave behind the three Spanish ships, whose slow speed made them incapable of taking part in our operations.'
(*Revue des Deux Mondes*, 1905, p. 415.)

Nelson, depressed by his fruitless chase across the Atlantic and back, disembarked from the *Victory* at Portsmouth. Villeneuve, with an entirely justified lack of confidence in Napoleon's genius as a naval strategist and in his own squadron's ability to beat the British, went to Cadiz. Among French naval officers, who in their relations with each other and with their commander did not at all resemble a band of brothers, Villeneuve's decision was widely condemned. The opinion of des Touches is quite representative:

'As the dénouement came closer, so did the worries of the Admiral seem to increase. Hardly appreciating the grandeur of his role, or rather crushed by the importance of a mission whose achievement he felt was beyond his ability, he lived in perpetual uncertainty, oscillating between equally reasonable choices and ending most often by making a choice which was not reasonable. So as not to bump into the

English forces awaiting him in the Channel approaches, and perhaps in the hope of luring them into pursuit, he went first to the north-west, then south, and then in desperation ended up by entering Cadiz on August 21. It was at that time that Napoleon was waiting with the Grand Army at Boulogne for the moment to strike at England, with his eyes looking seaward.

At Cadiz we found ourselves one of a combined fleet of 33 French and Spanish vessels. It was an imposing fleet, but for many reasons there were sources of weakness concealed behind the outward appearance. We could judge the others by what we knew of our *Intrépide*, which was a former Spanish ship. Although she was rated as 80 guns, her scantling was so weak that she could only carry 24- and 18-pounders instead of 36- and 24-pounders in her batteries. She did not sail well, and was inferior to a 74-gun ship in good condition. She was even more inferior to an 80-gun ship, the best type of ship which had ever been built. Our crew was small, but at least it was of good quality, which is more than could be said of the Spanish crews, who had been obliged by the British cruising ships to rot in port for years.

We received at this time a new commander to replace de Peronne. He was a Provencal called Infernet. A man of colossal height and heroic courage, who won imperishable renown at Trafalgar. He spoke very little French and preferred to express himself in his dialect. But to satisfy our needs we needed many captains of this temper.

About this time there was a rumour that the Emperor, tired of the hesitations of Admiral Villeneuve, had decided to replace him. In fact Admiral Rosily, destined to take his place, had taken the coach at Paris to go to Cadiz. This news made Villeneuve at last take action. Like an animal at bay who no longer cares how many enemies are facing him, he decided to give battle, after having wasted so many good chances, and after having given Nelson the time to catch up with him off Cadiz.'
(*Revue des Deux Mondes*, 1905, pp. 415-16.)

This unfair appreciation of Villeneuve's conduct was, of course, written some years after Trafalgar, and reflects not so much its writer's prejudice as the success with which Napoleon's régime diverted the blame onto its chosen scapegoat. Meanwhile, Napoleon in August 1805 was abandoning his cross-Channel enterprise.[5] One of his officers, encamped near Boulogne, wrote later:

'It only needed forty-eight hours to take our flotilla out of its ports and move it across the Channel. In summer the Channel is subject to long calms, during which the English cruising ships would not have been able to operate. So the boats which were propelled by oars as well as by sails could have made the crossing even in the presence of the English squadron. Fogs during the winter offered the same chance. In these two cases an invasion could have been risked without the help of our own fleet. But with our fleet, the risk could have been taken in any season . . .

. . . A naval battle took place off Ferrol, which was indecisive. Villeneuve's pessimism grew. Nobody can doubt the personal courage of this unfortunate admiral, but his indecisive and anxious character always made him exaggerate difficulties and dangers . . .

At this time Napoleon, at Boulogne, was preparing the despatch of the army. All the equipment was embarked and there had been several trials of embarking the men. Each regiment, each company, knew its place and we could have left without any delay. At the same time, new huts were being built and there were growing rumours of a continental war. Would we go to England, or Germany, or would we be condemned to spend another winter in this wretched camp? This last possibility was the only one which frightened us . . .

Luckily the new European coalition enabled Napoleon to replace this expedition, so often and so fruitlessly advertised, by a great European war . . .'
(De Fezensac, op. cit., pp. 42–5.)

After a short stay in England, Nelson rejoined the *Victory* at Portsmouth. One of the last persons to speak to him in London was a retired officer friend who later, writing in the third person, described this encounter:

'. . . his Lordship called on him two days before he left town, in 1805, and expressing himself happy to find he was so comfortably situated, asked him to walk with him down the Strand, as far as Salter's shop, which he was proud to do. The crowd, which waited outside of Somerset House till the noble viscount came out, was very great. He was then very ill, and neither in look nor dress betokened the naval hero, having on a pair of drab-green breeches, and high black gaiters, a yellow waistcoat, and a plain blue coat, with a cocked hat, quite square, a large green shade over the eye, and a gold headed stick in his hand, yet the crowd ran before him and said, as he looked down, that he was then thinking of burning a fleet, &c. They gave his lordship repeated and hearty cheers; indeed the two pedestrians could hardly get to Salter's shop, so dense was the crowd . . . Lord Nelson said during the conversation . . . "I have still the coffin which that good fellow Hallowell made for me, on board your

ship"; adding, "I always keep it in my cabin." '
(*Memoirs of the Life and Services of Sir J. Theophilus Lee* (1836), self-published, London, p. 175.)

The *Victory* soon joined the British ships already cruising in force off Cadiz. An officer of the *Bellerophon* described this phase:

'The Bellerophon, and three more sail of the line, which were up the Straits, joined Admiral Collingwood on the 23rd, and Sir R. Calder's squadron on the 31st. Our fleet then consisted of twenty-six sail of the line, and we immediately resumed the blockade of Cadiz with the greatest severity, till Lord Nelson joined and took the command on the 29th of September. His plan being to give the enemy an opportunity of coming out, he only left a squadron of frigates cruising off the harbour, whilst the fleet continued cruising to the N.W., frequently out of sight of land. As we knew the enemy, who were now reinforced by five sail of the line in Cadiz, had positive orders to put to sea, and retrieve their character, after their action with Sir R. Calder, we were in momentary expectation of their coming out, and every ship that was perceived coming from the in-shore squadron was expected to convey the welcome intelligence. Every one was in the highest spirits; and so confident were our people of success, that on the very morning of the action, when we were bearing down on a superior fleet, they were employed in fixing the number of their prizes, and pitching upon that which should fall to the lot of each of our ships . . .'
(*The Naval Chronicle*, Vol. XV, p. 204.)

Villeneuve's first move came on 18 October:

'On 26 Vendémiaire, Year XIV (October 18) at 5 o'clock in the evening, Admiral Villeneuve, commanding the Combined Fleet, gave the signal to cast off and to successively hoist the boats, prepare to make sail, and to send an officer for orders. The wind at the time was from the west. The *Fougueux* was moored between the forts of Puerto Real and Puntalés and was therefore too far up the bay to make sail easily . . .

During the following day seven or eight ships and some frigates tacked out. The *Fougueux* asked permission to proceed, lowered her boats, and warped out to a position opposite Cadiz.

On the 28th (October 20) at dawn the Admiral signalled the fleet to get moving as soon as possible, the wind being southwesterly, very fresh, veering to west-south-west. At 8 a.m. all except the *Rayo* were under sail. During the day the wind varied from S.W.

to W.N.W., with squalls and heavy rain. Several signals were made; in particular, there was a signal to form three columns . . .'
(From the report of Commander Bazin of the *Fougueux* to the Ministry of Marine, first published in E. Desbrière, *La Campagne Maritime de 1805 : Trafalgar* (1907), Etat-Major-Section Historique, p. 216, trans. J. N. Westwood.)

The Spanish Rear-Admiral Don Antonio de Escaño, Chief of Staff to Admiral Gravina, on board the *Principe de Asturias*, described the Combined Fleet's movements on 19 and 20 October:

'I know that by the last mail General Gravina sent an account, dated October 18, in which he informed your Excellency that Admiral Villeneuve had made it clear that he had decided to sail the next day and that he had wished to know if the Spanish fleet was able to fulfil its role. Your Excellency is not unaware of the General's reply which, in short, was that his squadron was ready, assembled, and would follow the movements of the French, this being in accordance with the successive orders which your Excellency had communicated. With this understanding the French Admiral went back to his ship and then signalled to weigh anchor and haul in boats. These signals were immediately acknowledged by this ship and were followed by the issue of most strict and urgent orders to recall pickets and to embark those artillerymen and sailors who for various reasons were on shore. In the morning of the 19th several Spanish and French ships went to sea in accordance with Admiral Villeneuve's signal, but our own ship was unable to do this because the wind had backed to the S.W. But during the morning of the 20th, with the wind in the E.S.E., we got out in succession.
  Hardly was the Combined Fleet at the harbour mouth when the wind backed to the S.S.W., so strongly and threateningly that one of the first signals hoisted by the *Bucentaure*, flying the flag of Admiral Villeneuve, ordered the double-reefing of topsails. This change of wind inevitably led to much straggling until 2 p.m. when, happily, the wind shifted to the S.W. The horizon being clearly visible, signals were made to form five columns and to close up. An advanced frigate indicated by signal that eighteen enemy ships were in sight and, in consequence of this warning, we sailed with our decks cleared for action. At three o'clock we wore together and made for the Straits, maintaining the same five-column formation. Soon afterwards we sighted four enemy frigates, which on Admiral Villeneuve's orders were chased by ours while the *Achille*, *Algésiras*, and *San Juan*, forming part of the

Observation Squadron, were ordered by our own ship to support them, with orders to rejoin the main force before sunset. At 7.30 p.m. a French ship informed us that the *Achille* had sighted eighteen enemy sail of the line in line of battle. Then we began to see coloured lights quite close, which could only be from enemy frigates located between the two fleets. At 9 p.m. the enemy fired signal guns and by the length of time between the flash and the sound – eight seconds – they must have been two miles distant.'
(From *Parte dado por el Mayor D. Antonio de Escaño al Principe de la Paz*, an official report first published in E. Desbrière, op. cit., pp. 145–6. Trans. J. N. Westwood.)

An officer of H.M.S. *Bellerophon* described the British movements from the time that Captain Duff's *Mars*, of the Advance Squadron, fired her warning gun, to the night before the battle:

'We were not long kept in that state of anxiety and suspense, which you will naturally suppose every one in our situation must have felt, for about nine o'clock in the morning of the 19th of October, the Mars was observed firing guns and making signals for the enemy's fleet being getting under weigh. The Admiral immediately made signal for a general chase, and to clear for action, which was obeyed with the greatest alacrity, and in ten minutes the whole fleet was under sail, steering for the Straits, which was supposed to be the enemy's destination, for the purpose of forming a junction with the Carthagena and Toulon squadrons. The Bellerophon, Belleisle, Leviathan, Orion, and Polyphemus, soon showed their superiority of sailing, and got far a-head of the rest of the fleet: at day-light in the morning we were in sight of the Rock of Gibraltar, but, on a frigate's making signal for the enemy's fleet bearing N.E., wore, and again formed the order of sailing: the day was unfavourable and the weather squally, so that we did not get sight of the enemy, though our small vessels formed a chain betwixt them and us. In the following night we got so close to them as to perceive plainly their signals, and every one was in the most anxious state of suspense, till day-light the next morning (21st), when the enemy was plainly discerned about seven miles to leeward of us, and about five leagues from Cape Trafalgar.'
(*The Naval Chronicle*, Vol. XV, pp. 204–5.)

Midshipman Badcock, writing some years later, adds colour to this description, and continues the story to the morning of 21 October:

'. . . on the 19th the enemy came out of port. The wind

'The enemy was bearing down on us under full sail': A Spanish impression of the English approach to the Combined Fleet, much less tidy than text-book diagrams

was light and the day rather hazy, so that the body of our fleet never perceived them. Sunday we had a fresh breeze, when some of the headmost ships saw the enemy in shore, but they were too close under the land to be attacked. All hearts towards evening beat with joyful anxiety for the next day, which we hoped would crown our anxious blockade labours with a successful battle. When night closed in, the rockets and blue lights, with signal guns, informed us the inshore squadron still kept sight of our foes, and, like good and watchful dogs, our ships continued to send forth occasionally a growling cannon to keep us on the alert, and to cheer us with the hope of a glorious day on the morrow.

And the morrow came; and with it the sun rose, which, as it ascended from its bed of ocean, looked hazy and watery, as if it smiled in tears on many brave hearts which fate had decreed should never see it set. It was my morning watch; I was midshipman of the forecastle, and at the first dawn of day a forest of strange masts was seen to leeward. I ran aft and informed the officer of the watch. The captain was on deck in a moment, and ere it was well light, the signals were flying through the fleet to bear up and form the order of sailing in two columns.

The wind had moderated considerably in the night, but still our fleet, which consisted of twenty-seven sail of the line, four frigates, a schooner, and cutter, was much scattered. Our ship had been previously prepared for battle, so that with the exception of stowing hammocks, slinging the lower yards, stoppering the topsail-sheets, and other minor matters, little remained to be done. All sail was set, and the different ships tried to form line in two divisions, but the lightness of the wind, and the distance of the sternmost from the van, prevented anything like speed in the manoeuvre; in short, the line never was properly formed, for the brave and gallant chiefs of each division were too eager to get into battle to wait for this.'
(W. S. Lovell, op. cit., p. 44.)

One of the officers in Rear-Admiral Louis's squadron at Gibraltar was Francis Austen of the *Canopus*, brother of the novelist Jane Austen. He was a man of a certain originality of mind: one of his suggestions to the Admiralty was that in tropical climates ships' cheeses should be whitewashed. On the 21st, while Nelson's ships were in action, he was writing home:

'We have just said adieu to the convoy, without attending them quite as far as was originally intended, having this day received intelligence, by a vessel despatched in pursuit of us, that on Saturday, 19th,

the enemy's fleet was actually under way, and coming out of Cadiz.

Our situation is peculiarly unpleasant and distressing, for if they escape Lord Nelson's vigilance and get into the Mediterranean, which is not very likely, we shall be obliged, with our small force, to keep out of their way; and on the other hand, should an action take place, it must be decided long before we could possibly get down even were the wind fair, which at present it is not. As I have no doubt but the event would be highly honourable to our arms, and be at the same time productive of good prizes, I shall have to lament our absence on such an occasion on a double account, the loss of pecuniary advantage as well as of professional credit. And after having been so many months in a state of constant and unremitting fag, to be at last cut out by a parcel of folk just come from their homes, where some of them were sitting at their ease the greater part of last year, and the whole of this, till just now, is particularly hard and annoying ...

I do not profess to like fighting for its own sake, but if there have been an action with the combined fleets I shall ever consider the day on which I sailed from the squadron as the most inauspicious one of my life.'

A week later Francis Austen's 'most inauspicious' day had indeed come to pass:

Combate Naval sostenido en las aguas del

'Alas! my dearest Mary, all my fears are but too fully justified. The fleets have met, and, after a very severe contest, a most decisive victory has been granted . . . I cannot help feeling how very unfortunate we have been to be away at such a moment, and, by a fatal combination of unfortunate though unavoidable events, to lose all share in the glory of a day which surpasses all which ever went before, is what I cannot think of with any degree of patience.'
(From J. H. Hubback, *Jane Austen's Sailor Brothers* 1905, pp. 154–6.)

The manoeuvres of the morning of 21 October, as the British columns prepared their attack, are described in the log of the 74-gun Spanish *Montanez*, which was twenty-ninth in Villeneuve's line:

'As it grew lighter, we sighted the enemy squadron to windward, at about two leagues' distance and in two lines, with all sail set bearing eastwards; that is, it was directed towards us . . . at 6.30 the General made the signal to form order of battle on the starboard tack. A little later came the signal that the enemy squadron was smaller than ours and could be attacked. The enemy was bearing down on us under full sail, his deployment indicating the intention of attacking our rearguard and centre. At 6.45 our General made the signal to close the distance between ships to a cable's length. We distributed to our men, whose spirit was gay and who were very keen that action should commence, a portion of bread, cheese, and wine. The squadron tried to form the line but was not helped by the weak wind. At 8 o'clock the General hoisted the signal to wear together, which the squadron carried out. At 10 o'clock there was an order for the Reserve to get into proper order and at 10.30 another which ordered the ships at the head of the line to keep a cable's length interval. At this time we also tried to reduce the interval astern of the *Algésiras*, hailing the *Bahama*, which let her main topsail aback to let us pass, and in this way we moved up to place ourselves a cable's length astern of the *Algésiras*. At 11 o'clock a French ship signalled that the line of battle formed by the squadron stretched out too much in the rear. A little later the *Santa Ana* signalled that the ship at the head was hauling to the wind and that the others were following her. A little later a frigate made the signal for the Reserve Squadron to get into proper order. The squadron was carrying only topsails, the wind was feeble, and we were all tacking and moving away in order to get into formation, but had not succeeded in forming the line. The enemy squadron was still in two open columns to larboard, with a full press of sail

falgar el día 21 de Octubre de 1805 entre la escuadra combinada de Francia y España y la Inglesa al mando del
Vice-Almirante Nelson
Primera posición al empezar el combate

and bearing down on our rearguard and centre, the ships at the heads of his columns being three-deckers. At 11.30, being within cannon-shot range, the General made the signal to open fire, which we obeyed, directing our fire at the leading ship of the right column. All our centre and rearguard also opened fire, and so did the enemy, the fire on both sides being very lively.'
(E. Desbrière, op. cit., pp. 375–6.)

Closer to the head of Villeneuve's crescent-shaped column, the thirteenth ship was the *Redoutable* of Captain Lucas, part of whose official report follows. In the main this confirms the previous account, although the times given for certain events do not coincide. This discrepancy of times is noticeable in the reports and logs of both fleets, and reflects the difficulty of keeping meticulous records during the battle. But its overstatement of the *Victory*'s and *Téméraire*'s armaments was merely the result of a natural desire to exaggerate the strength of former enemies:

'At 9 o'clock, the enemy deployed in two groups and, with all sails, including studding sails, set, bore down on our fleet with a light breeze from the W.S.W. The Admiral, now estimating that the enemy was going to concentrate on our rear, wore the fleet together to face the other direction. In the new order the *Redoutable* was to be the third ship astern of the flagship *Bucentaure*. I therefore hurried to place myself astern of this ship, leaving the necessary space for the two ships which were to take their places between her and my ship. One of these was not very far from her proper station, but the other was not making the slightest manoeuvre to get into her position and was far to leeward of the line which was commencing to form ahead of the Admiral. Towards 11 a.m. the two divisions of the enemy fleet were approaching our fleet. One, led by the three-decker *Royal Sovereign*, flying the flag of Admiral Collingwood, was directed towards the rear ships of our new deployment while the other, led by the 110-gun ship *Victory* flying the flag of Lord Nelson, and by the 110-gun *Téméraire*, was manoeuvring to attack our main body. At 11.15 our rearward ships opened fire on the *Royal Sovereign*, which fired some shots at us at long range, to which I did not deign to reply. I was still in the wake of the flagship but there was a gap between her and myself which had not been closed by the two ships which should have been ahead of me; one was too far to leeward to be able to come and take up her position while the other, as I already stated, had not been very far from her place, but had moved a long way from it

when she went to fire at the *Royal Sovereign*, which was more than a half-gunshot distant. The division led by Lord Nelson was advancing towards our main body, its two leading three-deckers ostensibly manoeuvring to envelop the French flagship; one of them was trying to pass across her poop. As soon as I recognised this intention, and moreover being certain that the ships which were supposed to be ahead of me would not be able to take their places, I put the bowsprit of the *Redoutable* on the poop of the *Bucentaure*, with the full intention of sacrificing my ship in the defence of the Admiral's flag . . .'
(E. Desbrière, op. cit., pp. 198–9.)

Sub-lieutenant des Touches of the *Intrépide* summarized this preliminary stage of the battle:

'At dawn on the 21st the two squadrons became aware of each other, and battle seemed inevitable. The Admiral signalled to us to get into order of battle in a single line, on the larboard tack, in order to give the most damaged ships the chance to return to Cadiz. We therefore turned about and set course towards the north. The *Intrépide* was part of the vanguard commanded by Rear-Admiral Dumanoir; the *Bucentaure* and the *Santissima Trinidad*, flying the flags of vice-admirals Villeneuve and Gravina, were in the middle of the line of battle. The rearguard extended in the distance under the command of Rear-Admiral Magon in the *Algésiras*. Instead of ordering the vanguard to get into wind so that the line-ahead formation could be properly formed, the Admiral constantly signalled to sail closer to the wind, so that the line lost its shape more and more, with vessels moving off in all directions leaving wide gaps which the English were bound to exploit.

The English moreover appeared to have no other object than to prevent our escape. Their squadron, divided into two columns, came on us from the windward side, propelled by a westerly breeze, and led by vice-admirals Nelson and Collingwood, flying their flags at the head of each column in the three-deckers *Victory* and *Royal Sovereign*.

This manner of engaging was contrary to the most simple prudence, since the English ships came at us one by one, at a very low speed, and should have succumbed in turn to the superior force which faced them, but Nelson knew his own squadron, and ours. He contented himself with signalling to his captains these simple words: 'England expects that every man will do his duty,' and, sure that each ship would take the shortest path to action, he had the *Victory* directed into the most important part of our line, where the French and Spanish three-deckers seemed to form

an invincible barrier. It is there that he found death amidst that magnificent triumph, so much desired and so long prepared.'
(*Revue des Deux Mondes*, 1905, pp. 417–18.)

From the British side, perhaps the best description was written by Midshipman Badcock of the *Neptune*. The *Neptune* was a powerful 98-gun ship which, with the 98-gun *Téméraire*, followed close behind the 100-gun *Victory*. Nelson was evidently determined to lead his column into battle, even though the *Victory* could be outpaced by the *Neptune*. The 'double line' of the enemy which this eyewitness mentions did not really exist, but was the impression given by the disarray of the Combined Fleet's single line:

'The old *Neptune*, which never was a good sailor, took it into her head to sail better that morning than I ever remember to have seen her do before. About ten o'clock we got close to the *Victory*, and Captain Fremantle had intended to pass her and break the enemy's line, but poor Lord Nelson himself hailed us from the stern-walk of the *Victory*, and said, "*Neptune*, take in your studding-sails and drop astern; I shall break the line myself." A signal was then made for the *Téméraire* (98) to take her station between us and the *Victory*, which consequently made us the third ship in the van of his lordship's column.

At this period the enemy were forming their double line in the shape of a crescent. It was a beautiful sight when their line was completed: their broadsides turned towards us, showing their iron teeth and now and then trying the range of a shot to ascertain the distance, that they might, the moment we came within point blank (about six hundred yards), open their fire upon our van ships – no doubt with the hope of dismantling some of our leading vessels before they could close and break their line. Some of them were painted like ourselves – with double yellow sides; some with a broad single red or yellow streak; others all black; and the noble *Santissima Trinidada* (138), with four distinct lines of red, with a white ribbon between them, made her seem to be a superb man-of-war, which indeed she was. Her appearance was imposing; her head splendidly ornamented with a colossal group of figures, painted white, representing the Holy Trinity, from which she took her name. This magnificent ship was destined to be our opponent. She was lying-to under topsails, top-gallant sails, royals, jib, and spanker; her courses were hauled up; and her lofty towering sails looked beautiful, peering through the smoke, as she awaited the onset. The flags of France and Spain, both handsome, chequered the line, waving defiance to that of Britain.

Then, in our fleet, union-jacks and ensigns were made fast to the fore and fore-topmast-stays, as well as to the mizen rigging, besides one at the peak, in order that we might not mistake each other in the smoke, and to show the enemy of our determination to conquer. Towards eleven, our two lines were better formed, but still there existed long gaps in Vice-Admiral Collingwood's division. Lord Nelson's van was strong; three three-deckers (*Victory*, *Téméraire*, and *Neptune*), and four seventy-fours; their jib-booms nearly over the others' taffrails, the bands playing "God save the King," "Rule Brittania," and "Britons strike home;" the crews stationed on the forecastle of the different ships, cheering the ship ahead of them when the enemy began to fire, sent those feelings to our hearts that ensured us victory. About ten minutes before twelve, our antagonists opened their fire upon the *Royal Sovereign* (110), Vice-Admiral Collingwood, who most nobly, and unsupported for at least ten minutes, led his division into action, steering for the *Santa Ana* (112), which was painted all black, bearing the flag of Admiral Gravina, during which time all the enemy's line that could possibly bring a gun to bear were firing at her. She was the admiration of the whole fleet.'
(W. S. Lovell, op. cit., pp. 44–6.)

On the gun decks of ships of this period there was a particular air of expectancy, almost of anti-climax, once the preparations for battle had been made:

'Everything was now in order, fires extinguished, fearnaught screens round the hatchways for passing powder from the magazines; shot racks drawn from under their peaceable coverings, and arranged ready for their work; guns cast loose, crowbars for pointing the guns lying at hand on the deck; tompions out all ready for a game of thunder . . . my friend the goat sent down to the cable tier – the captain's ducks and geese left in the coops, to cackle and quake and take their chance – the doctor's saws and knives and probes and bandages and tourniquets, all laid in order in the cockpit; and I devoutly hoping, as tempted by curiosity I looked at them, that I might be blown away all together, rather than that he should exercise his skill on my limbs or carcass. And every man and boy was mute as he stood at his station. Here and there might be seen one drawing the knot of his handkerchief, girt around his loins, or that of his head bandages; all grim in lip and glistening in eye . . . But don't you imagine, reader, that I was not frightened in all this. Faith, there was something in the orderly stillness of lying there for half an hour with all this preparation for destruction and death that made me think there

might be worse places than the counting house after all. There was no noise, no laugh, no show of hilarity; yet was there some interjectorial jesting bandied about which called up grim smiles, but no laugh. Men, shirtless, with handkerchiefs bandaged tightly round their loins and heads, stood with naked brawny arms folded on their hairy and heaving chests, looking pale and stern, but still hushed; or glancing with a hot eye through ports . . . I felt a difficulty in swallowing. Now, if we had gone at it at once, without this chilling prelude, why I dare say I should have known very little about that thing which we call fear. "Stand to your guns!" at last came in a peal through the stillness from the captain's speaking trumpet; it swept fore and aft with such clear force, as though it had been spoken within a foot of the ear, and seemed to dash down into the holds, and penetrate to the very keel. The instant change this produced was magical. "Take good aim! Ready the first *platoon*!" Ready? Aye, every one *was* ready; stern, fixed, rigid, in soul – pliant, elastic in body. "Captains of the guns, watch the falling of the first shot, and point accordingly." Not a word was replied; even the everlasting "ay, ay, sir," was refused now.'
(C. R. Pemberton, op. cit., pp. 111–13, 117.)

As the British ships crept closer to the Franco-Spanish line, there was time for the officers to encourage their crews. An officer of the *Victory* described this tense interval:

'Previously to the commencement of the battle of Trafalgar, Lord Nelson went over the different decks of the *Victory*, saw and spoke to the different classes of seamen, encouraged them with his usual affability, and was much pleased at the manner in which the seamen had barricaded the hawse holes of the ship. All was perfect death-like silence, till just before the action began. Three cheers were given his Lordship as he ascended the quarter-deck ladder. He had been particular in recommending cool, steady firing, in preference to a hurrying fire, without aim or precision, and the event justified his Lordship's advice.'
(*The Naval Chronicle*, Vol. XV, pp. 13–14.)

Meanwhile, in the *Redoutable*, which was destined to take the force of the *Victory*'s onslaught, Captain Lucas was making his rounds:

'Preceded by the drums and fifes which I had on board, I went, at the head of my officers, around all the decks. Everywhere I found brave men burning with impatience to begin the battle. Many of them said to me, "Commander, don't forget about boarding!"

At 11.30 the Combined Fleet hoisted their flags. That of the *Redoutable* was raised in an imposing manner: the drums were beating by the flags, the musketeers presented arms, and there were seven "Vive l'Empereur!" cheers from the officers and men.
At 11.45 the enemy group which was heading for our main body was within range, and the *Bucentaure* and her consort ahead began to fire on the *Victory*. I had a large number of gun-captains brought on to the upper deck to point out to them how badly our ships were firing: all the shots were too low and fell into the water. I persuaded them to aim well and with the intention of dismasting the target.'
(E. Desbrière, op. cit., p. 199.)

Captain Lucas's opinion that the French guns were aimed too low conflicts with the general run of opinion after the battle, which was that the tendency of the Combined Fleet to shoot at the rigging of the British ships was a mistake. The British, aiming lower, caused hundreds of casualties, and it was the carnage caused by their cannon balls which induced so many French and Spanish ships to strike their colours. An additional factor in the British success was their ability to fire their guns at least twice as fast as their less experienced enemy. It was this known superiority of British gunnery which, in the opinion of many, justified Nelson's tactics at Trafalgar, tactics which placed the *Victory*, and even more the *Royal Sovereign*, under the fire of several enemy ships for an extended period. Des Touches later commented:

'The audacity with which Admiral Nelson had attacked us, and which had so completely succeeded, arose from the complete scorn which, not without reason, he professed for the effects of our gunfire. At that time our principle was to aim at the masts and, in order to produce any real damage, we wasted masses of projectiles which, if they had been aimed at the hulls, would have felled a proportion of the crews. Thus our losses were always incomparably higher than those of the English, who fired horizontally and hit our wooden sides, letting fly splinters which were more murderous than the cannon ball itself. We were still using the linstock match to fire our guns, which despatched the ball with an excruciating delay, so that if the ship was rolling, as it was on October 21, complete broadsides flew over the enemy's mastheads without causing the slightest damage. The English had flintlocks, rather crude, but very superior to our linstocks . . . they used . . . a horizontal fire thanks to which, if they did not score a direct hit, they at least scored a useful hit by ricochet. It was only towards the end of the war that one or two of our captains freed themselves from this absurd principle of firing at the rigging, a legacy of the solemn battles of the Seven Years War and which was still recommended in 1833, when my eldest son was in a training ship.' (*Revue des Deux Mondes*, p. 424.)

The log of the *Bellerophon*, the fifth ship in Collingwood's division, tersely summarizes the opening phase of the battle, and also chronicles the *Bellerophon*'s own fight against heavy odds as she reached the enemy line:

'12.10 Royal Sovereign opened fire on the enemy's centre. – 12.13 answered 16 general.[6] – 12.20 Royal Sovereign, at the head of the larboard division, broke the enemy's line astern of a Spanish three-decker, and engaged her to leeward, being followed by the Mars, Belleisle, and Tonnant, who engaged their respective oponents. – 12.25 opened our fire on the enemy. – 12.28 Victory, at the head of the starboard division, opened her fire on the enemy. – 12.30 engaging both sides in passing through the enemy's line, astern of a Spanish two-decker (El Monarca.) – 12.35 fell on board the French two-deck ship l'Aigle, whilst hauling to the wind, our fore-yard locking with her main one, kept up a brisk fire both on her, on our starboard bow, and a Spanish two-decker (El Monarca) on the larboard bow, at the same time receiving and returning fire with a Spanish two-decker (Bahama) on the larboard quarter, and receiving the fire of a Spanish two-decker (St. Juan Nepomuceno) athwart our stern, and a French two-decker (la Swiftsure) on the starboard quarter: the action soon after became general. At one the main and mizen-top-masts fell over the starboard side, main-top-sail and top-gallant-sail caught fire. – 1.5 the Master, and 1.11 the Captain fell, still foul of l'Aigle, and keeping up a brisk fire from the main and lower decks; quarter-deck, poop, and forecastle being nearly cleared by the enemy's musketry, chiefly from troops on board l'Aigle. – 1.20 the jib-boom was shot away. – 1.40 l'Aigle dropt astern under a raking fire from us as she fell off, our ship at this time quite unmanageable from braces, bowlines, &c. shot away.' (*The Naval Chronicle*, Vol. XV, p. 206.)

According to an officer on board the *Bellerophon*, the engagement with the *Aigle* was intense though brief:

'. . . l'Aigle twice attempted to board us, and hove several grenades into our lower deck, which burst and wounded several of our people most dreadfully, she likewise set fire to our fore chains; our fire was so hot, that we soon drove them from the lower deck, after which our people took the coins out, and elevated their guns, so as to tear her decks and sides to pieces:

when she got clear of us, she did not return a single shot whilst we raked her, her starboard quarter was entirely beaten in, and, as we afterwards learnt, 400 men *hors de combat*, so that she was an easy conquest for the Defiance, a fresh ship: we were well matched, she being the best manned ship in the Combined, and we in the British fleet. Unfortunately situated as we were, I have no doubt she would have struck, had we been able to follow and engage her for a quarter of an hour longer; but had we been fairly alongside her, half an hour would have decided the contest; for I must say I was astonished at the coolness and undaunted bravery displayed by our gallant and veteran crew, when surrounded by five enemy's ships, and for a length of time unassisted by any of ours. Our loss, as might be expected, was considerable, and fell chiefly on our prime seamen, who were foremost in distinguishing themselves; twenty-eight, including the Captain, Master, and a Midshipman, were killed outright; and 127, including the Captain of Marines, who had eight balls in his body, and his right arm shot off, before he quitted the deck; Boatswain, and five Midshipmen, were badly wounded, and about forty more slightly, so as not to be incapable of duty; nineteen of the wounded had already died before we left Gibraltar. I consider myself as very fortunate in having escaped unhurt, as our class suffered so severely.' (*The Naval Chronicle*, Vol. XV, p. 207.)

On the battery decks, men who were in action for the first time soon habituated themselves to the noise, smoke, and carnage. The following account of how a battle appeared on the gun decks in this period is by a sailor who later became a well-known dramatist:

'Two minutes since all was so death-like quiet – now such yelling, hurraing, leaping, tugging, clattering of ropes, and grumbling of blocks, as if all the tenants of the lower regions, black from the smoke, had broken loose and gone mad. Now the rookery on our starboard side gives a second edition, embellished with bar, grape, and canister. But it falls harmless; nobody is hurt by it, except the tough oak; two-thirds of the intended pelting either goes over us or falls short. The fellows point their guns badly; there is a little wabbling sea which, though it does not shake our steadiness, causes them to roll and reel to it; let but the breeze continue only half an hour, and we shall make fishes' meat of most of them, if they will stay so long. I cannot resist the invitation of curiosity, but poke my head through an idle port . . . Bursting forth from the many black iron mouths, and whirling rapidly in thick rings, till it swells into hills and

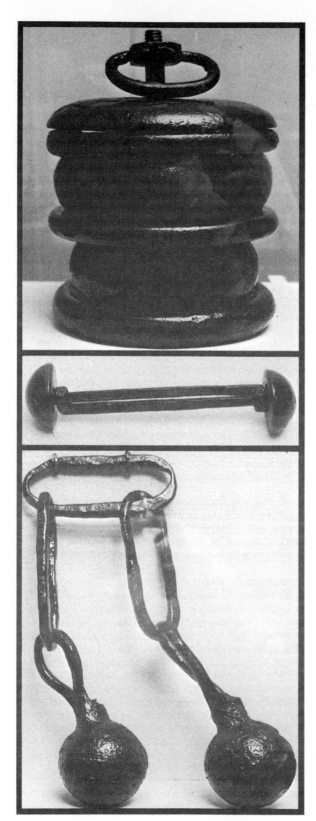

'The shots were playing their pranks pretty freely'. Top left: grape shot; centre, bar shot and (below) chain shot, both effective for cutting up rigging or slicing off heads or limbs; top right: a sponge; bottom: worm

mountains, through which the sharp red tongue of death darts flash after flash, and mingling fire, the smoke slowly rolls upward like a curtain, in awful beauty, and exhibits the glistening water and the hulls of the combatants beneath; while the lofty mastheads and points of yard arms, seem as if cut away from the bodies to which they belong, and sustained, or resting on the ridges of the dense and messy vapours alone. The ensigns are partially enveloped in the clouds; so much of them as is visible shivering in the multiplied concussions, as though they fluttered in anticipation of victory, or trembled in the expectation of defeat. And ever and anon, amid the breaks of the cannon's peal, the shrieks and cries of the wounded mingled with the deep roar of the outpoured and constantly-reiterated "hurra! hurra! hurra!" A chorus of cataracts sweep over the rippled smiles of the patient, passionless, and unconscious sea. Sulphur and fire, agony, death and horror, are riding and revelling on its bosom; yet how gently, brightly-playful is its face! To see and hear this! what a maddening of the brain it causes! yet it is a delirium of joy, a very fury of delight!'
(C. R. Pemberton, op. cit., p. 119.)

The eighth ship of Collingwood's division was the *Revenge*, which got into action at about 1.30. As she broke through the enemy line she became entangled with the French *Aigle* and fired two broadsides into the latter before getting clear. But she then received a terrific cannonading from the Spanish three-decker *Principe de Asturias* and three other ships. She was soon helped by the *Dreadnought* and the *Thunderer*, but not before she had been holed nine times beneath the waterline and had had her masts weakened by cannon shots. Probably she was lucky to lose only twenty-eight killed and fifty-one injured during the entire battle. One of her seamen later published his impressions:

'We were now unable to work the ship, our yards, sails, and masts being disabled, and the braces completely shot away. In this condition we lay by the side of the enemy, firing away, and now and then we received a good raking from them, passing under our stern. This was a busy time with us, for we had not only to endeavour to repair our damage, but to keep to our duty. Often during the battle we could not see for the smoke, whether we were firing at a foe or friend, and as to hearing, the noise of the guns had so completely made us deaf, that we were obliged to look only to the motions that were made . . .

. . . As we were closely engaged throughout the battle, and the shots were playing their pranks pretty

freely, grape as well as canister, with single and double
headed thunderers all joining in the frolic; what was
termed a *slaughtering one*, came in at one of the lower
deck ports, which killed and wounded nearly all at the
gun, and amongst them, a very merry little fellow,
who was the very life of the ship's company, for he
was ever the mirth of his mess, and on whatever duty
he might be ordered, his spirits made light the labour.
He was the ship's cobbler, and withall a very good
dancer; so that when any of his messmates would
sarve us out a tune, he was sure to trip it on light
fantastic toe, and find a step to it. He happened to be
stationed at the gun where this messenger of death and
destruction entered, and the poor fellow was so
completely stunned by the head of another man being
knocked against his, that no one doubted but that he
was dead. As it is customary to throw overboard those,
who, in an engagement are killed outright, the poor
cobbler, amongst the rest, was taken to the port-hole
to be committed to the deep, without any other
ceremony than shoving him through the port: but,
just as they were about to let him slip from their hands
into the water, the blood began to circulate, and he
commenced kicking. Upon this sign of returning life,
his shipmates soon hauled the poor snob in again, and,
though wonderful to relate, he recovered so speedily,
that he actually fought the battle out; and, when he
was afterwards joked about it, he would say, "it was
well that I learned to dance: for if I had not shown
you some of my steps, when you were about to throw
me overboard, I should not be here now . . ."

. . . We had a midshipman on board our ship of a
wickedly mischievous disposition, whose sole delight
was to insult the feelings of the seamen, and furnish
pretexts to get them punished. His conduct made
every man's life miserable that happened to be under
his orders. He was a youth not more than twelve or
thirteen years of age; but I have often seen him get
on the carriage of a gun, call a man to him and kick
him about the thighs and body, and with his fist would
beat him about the head; and these, although prime
seamen, at the same time dared not murmur. It was
ordained however, by Providence, that his reign of
terror and severity should not last; for during the
engagement, he was killed on the quarter-deck by a
grape-shot, his body greatly mutilated, his entrails
being driven and scattered against the larboard side;
nor were there any lamentations for his fate! – No!
for when it was known that he was killed, the general
exclamation was, "*Thank God, we are rid of the young
tyrant!*" '
('J. Nastyface', op. cit., pp. 20, 25–8.)

Even when a ship was completely dismasted it could still fight on. The *Royal Sovereign* found one way of bringing her broadside to bear, according to an officer of Captain Blackwood's frigate *Euryalus*:

'After the Royal Sovereign, Admiral Collingwood's Ship, was dismasted, the Euryalus was sent to assist her. Such was the spirit of the men, even at this time, that they hailed her with, "My little Ship, heave our head round that our broadsides may bear, and we shall soon be at the sally-port." The Euryalus then hove her head round, and she gave her opponent, the Santa Anna, a broadside that crushed her side in. After Captain Blackwood had performed this service, Admiral Collingwood sent him down to the Victory, to inquire the state of Lord Nelson's health. Captain Blackwood went in his own boat, which was rowed down the whole fleet. It is an honourable agreement between two contending fleets, that they never fire on the Frigates, nor on any cutter or boat, unless they make a part of the opposing force. Captain Blackwood got on board the Victory through one of the ports, while she was engaging the Santissima Trinidada'. (*The Naval Chronicle*, Vol. XIV, p. 469.)

On board the frigate *Euryalus*, hovering watchfully between the two British divisions, the officers had a grandstand view of the battle:

'It was Lord Nelson's intention to have begun the action by passing ahead of the Bucentaure (Villeneuve's Ship), that the Victory might be ahead of her, and astern of the Santissima Trinidada. But the Bucentaure fired four broadsides at the Victory before his Lordship

ordered the ports to be opened, when the whole broadside, which was double shotted, was fired into her, and the discharge made such a tremendous crash, that the Bucentaure was seen to heel. A short time after this, Admiral Villeneuve sent below, to inquire the number of her then killed and wounded, which proved to be the amazing number of 365 killed and 219 wounded.'

(*The Naval Chronicle*, Vol. XIV, pp. 468–9.)

Captain Lucas of the *Redoutable*, one of the few French captains subsequently praised by Napoleon, reported the heroic fight of his ship, which was in the thick of the battle for the crucial first two hours. Evidently he believed that when the *Victory* temporarily ceased fire it was because she could no longer continue, whereas British accounts assert that these short intervals occurred whenever the *Victory*'s officers thought that the *Redoutable* was trying to surrender. Some other discrepancies of detail may be ascribed to the familiar shortcomings of human perception and memory; Lucas was writing his report in captivity at Reading, and had little chance of checking his details:

'. . . the *Victory* . . . ran alongside us, overlapping our stern so that our poop was opposite her quarter-deck. In this position the grapnels were thrown aboard her. The after ones were cut, but the forward ones held. Our broadsides were fired with the guns' muzzles touching, resulting in horrible carnage. We continued cannonading each other for some time. We were able to load several guns with the help of rope-handled sponges. Several guns were fired with the breeching tackle fully paid out because we could not get the barrels through the ports owing to the block caused by the side of the *Victory*. By means of the firearms located in our batteries we so much hindered the enemy loading his guns that he stopped firing at us . . . I had the trumpet sounded, the accepted signal in our training exercises for calling the boarding parties. They came up in such good order, with the officers and midshipmen at the head of their respective companies, that one would have said it was only a practice. In less than a minute our upper decks were covered with armed men who threw themselves on to the poop, the nettings, and the shrouds. It was impossible for me to distinguish who was the bravest. Then there began a lively musketry exchange . . . our fire became so superior that in less than fifteen minutes we had silenced that of the *Victory*. More than two hundred grenades were thrown aboard her, with the greatest success, her upper decks were littered with dead and wounded, and Admiral Nelson was killed by our musket fire. Almost immediately the upper decks of the enemy were evacuated and the *Victory*

completely ceased fighting us. But it was difficult to get on board her because of the movement of the two ships and because with her third battery deck she was higher than us. I ordered the cutting-away of the slings of the main yard, and to place the latter to serve as a bridge. Midshipman Yon and four sailors managed to get on board the *Victory* via the anchor and told us there was nobody in the battery decks, but just as our brave men were about to jump over to join them, the three-decker *Téméraire*, which no doubt had seen that the *Victory* had stopped fighting and would inevitably be taken, came alongside to starboard and riddled us at point blank range with all her guns. It would be difficult to describe the horrible carnage produced by the murderous broadside of this ship. More than 200 of our brave men were killed or wounded. I was wounded at the same time, but not badly enough to warrant my leaving my post. Being unable to undertake anything on the side where the *Victory* lay, I ordered the rest of the crew to go promptly to the battery decks and to fire at the *Téméraire* with those starboard guns which had not been dismounted by the collision with the latter ship. This order was carried out, but we were so weakened and there were so few serviceable guns that the *Téméraire* riposted with great advantage. Soon afterwards, a third two-decker, whose rating I do not know precisely, approached and placed herself at the poop of the *Redoutable* and fired at us at pistol-shot range. In less than half an hour our ship was so riddled that it was little more than a pile of débris . . . An 18-pounder on the main deck and a 36-pounder carronade on the forecastle had burst, killing and wounding many of our men. Both sides of the ship, with the covers and the bars of the gun-ports, were mangled. Four of our six pumps were smashed; so in general were all our ladders, which badly hampered communication between the battery decks and the upper decks. All the decks were covered with the dead and buried beneath wreckage and fragments from various parts of the ship. Very many wounded had been killed on the orlop deck. Of the ship's complement of 643, 522 were out of action, including 300 killed and 222 wounded. The latter included almost all the officers. Of the 121 remaining, a large part were employed in powder supply on the orlop deck and near the bilges, so that the upper decks and the battery decks were completely deserted; thus we could no longer offer any resistance. Anyone who has not seen the *Redoutable* in this state can have no idea of the disaster which befell her. I know of nothing on board which had not been cut up by shot, and among all this horrible carnage the brave men who had not yet succumbed, together with the wounded who were

crowding the orlop deck, were still shouting "Vive l'Empereur." . . . I only waited until I knew for certain that the inflow of water into the ship was large enough to ensure her early sinking; as soon as I had this assurance I gave the order to lower the flag . . . It was then about 2.30 in the afternoon. Soon afterwards the *Victory*, *Redoutable* and *Téméraire*, still attached by each other's fallen rigging and, moreover, all deprived of the use of their rudders, formed a group which drifted according to the wind and was involuntarily driven down on the *Fougueux* . . .'
(E. Desbrière, op. cit., pp. 200–2.)

In popular imagination the death of Nelson would be the climax of Trafalgar. The death of a hero inevitably inspires the myth-makers, and the circumstances of Nelson's death are well embellished with invention. It does seem established that on going into action

Nelson was advised to cover his decorations, which seemed likely to attract sharpshooters. That he refused to take this advice was quite unexceptional. Other officers behaved similarly, as a matter of officerly principle. Captain Rotheram of the *Royal Sovereign*, for example, went into battle wearing a cocked hat so oversized and over-decorated that even his admirers admitted it looked ridiculous. But on being advised to take it off, the captain replied, 'I have always fought in a cocked hat, and I always will.' And he did.

It is also well established that one of the musketeers in the mizen-top of the *Redoutable* must have been Nelson's assailant; whether in fact he was aiming at Nelson is another question. The range was certainly short, twenty yards perhaps, or less, but muskets were not accurate weapons. At the time some satisfaction was expressed by the British that all the marksmen in the *Redoutable*'s mizen-top were soon killed by

counter-fire, but as late as 1863 the circumstances of this 'revenge' were being discussed in *The Times*. At first a Midshipman Collingwood was named as the man who had avenged Nelson, but then a retired naval officer, John Pollard, wrote from Greenwich Royal Naval Hospital:

'Having seen several letters in *The Times* lately with reference to my name, I feel at length called on to come forward to state a few particulars, which differ materially from your correspondent's statements of yesterday.

It is true my old shipmate Collingwood, who has now been dead some years, did come in the poop for a short time. I had discovered the men crowding in the tops of the Redoutable, and pointed them out to him, when he took up a musket and fired once; he then left the poop, I conclude, to return to his station on the quarter-deck.

I remained firing till there was not a man to be seen in the top; the last one I saw coming down the mizen rigging, and he fell from my fire also.

King, the quartermaster, was killed while in the act of handing me a parcel of ballcartridge, long after Collingwood had left the poop. I remained there till some time after the action was concluded, assisting in rigging the jurymast; then I was ushered into the ward-room, where Sir Thomas Hardy and other officers were assembled, and complimented by them as the person who avenged Lord Nelson's death, which fact was afterwards gazetted.'
(*The Times*, 13 May 1863.)

The surgeon of the *Victory*, Dr Beatty, later wrote his *Authentic Narrative of the Death of Lord Nelson* (1807), which attracted a wide public and was the basis on which subsequent accounts, reliable and unreliable, were assembled. Closer to the event, he had drawn up his official surgeon's report, which he sent in when the *Victory* reached England in December 1805:

'About the middle of the action with the combined fleets, on the 21st of October last, the late illustrious Commander in Chief, Lord Nelson, was mortally wounded in the left breast by a musket ball, supposed to be fired from the mizen-top of the Redoutable, French ship of the line, which the Victory fell on board of early in the battle. His Lordship was in the act of turning on the quarter-deck, with his face towards the enemy, when he received his wound; he instantly fell, and was carried to the cockpit, where he lay about two hours. On his being brought below, he complained of acute pain about the sixth or seventh dorsal vertebra; of privation of sense, and motion of the body, and inferior extremities; his respiration short and difficult; pulse weak, small, and irregular. He frequently declared his back was shot through; that he felt every instant a gush of blood within his breast; and that he had sensations which indicated to him the approach of death. In the course of an hour, his pulse became indistinct, and was gradually lost in the arm; his extremities and forehead became soon afterwards cold: he retained his wonted energy of mind, and exercise of his faculties, until the latest moment of his existence; and when victory, as signal as decisive, was announced to him, he expressed his pious acknowledgments thereof, and heartfelt satisfaction at the glorious event, in the most emphatic language. He then delivered his last orders with his usual precision; and in a few minutes afterwards expired without a struggle.

COURSE AND SITE OF THE BALL, ASCERTAINED SINCE DEATH.

The ball struck the fore part of his Lordship's epaulette, and entered the left shoulder immediately before the processus acromium scapulae, which it slightly fractured; it then descended obliquely into the thorax, fracturing the second and third ribs; and after penetrating the left lobe of the lungs, and dividing in its passage a large branch of the pulmonary artery, it entered the left side of the spine, between the sixth and seventh dorsal vertebra; fractured the left transverse process of the sixth vertebra, wounded the medula spinalis, and fracturing the right transverse process of the seventh vertebra, it made its way from the right side of the spine, directing its course through the muscles of the back, and lodged therein about two inches below the inferior angle of the eighth scapula.

On removing the ball, a portion of the gold lace, and pad of the epaulette, with a small piece of his Lordship's coat, was found firmly attached to it.'
(*The Naval Chronicle*, Vol. XV, pp. 39–40.)

Also in 1805 Dr Beatty, with the *Victory*'s purser (Bourke), published a joint statement describing the last hours of Nelson. Many other variations have been played on this theme, and it is perhaps worth remembering the remark of W. James in his *Naval History of Great Britain* (1837), that 'well would it have been for Lord Nelson's memory, had the listeners around his dying couch possessed discernment enough to distinguish, and friendship enough (as writers) to separate, the irrelevant utterings of a mind in a paroxysm of delirium, from the patriotic effusions of the same mind, when lit up, for a moment or so, by a ray of returning reason'.

However accurate or inaccurate may be the following

account by Bourke and Beatty, its acceptance by the British public in itself makes it worthy of quotation:

'A few minutes before Lord Nelson was wounded, Mr. Bourke was near him. He looked stedfastly at him, and said, "Bourke, I expect every man to be upon his station!" Mr. Bourke took the hint, and went to his proper station in the cockpit.

At this time his Lordship's Secretary, Mr. Scott, who was not, as has been represented, either receiving directions from him, or standing by him, but was communicating some orders to an officer at a distant part of the quarter-deck, was cut almost in two by a cannon-shot. He expired on the instant, and was thrown overboard. Lord Nelson observed the act of throwing his Secretary overboard, and said, as if doubtful, to a Midshipman who was near him, "Was that Scott?" The Midshipman replied, he believed it was. He exclaimed, "Poor fellow!"

He was now walking the quarter-deck, and about three yards from the stern, the space he generally walked before he turned back. His Lordship was in the *act of turning* on the quarter-deck, with his face towards the enemy, when he was mortally wounded in the left breast by a musket-ball, supposed to have been fired from the mizen top of the Redoutable, French ship of the line, which the Victory had attacked early in the battle.

He instantly fell. He was not, as has been related, picked up by Captain Hardy. In the hurry of the battle, which was then raging in its greatest violence, even the fall of their beloved Commander did not interrupt the business of the quarter-deck. Two sailors, however, who were near his Lordship, raised him in their arms, and carried him to the cockpit. He was immediately laid upon a bed, and the following is the substance of the conversation which *really* took place in the cockpit, between his Lordship, Captain Hardy, Mr. Bourke, and Mr. Beatty: –

Upon seeing him brought down, Mr. Bourke immediately ran to him. "I fear," he said, "your Lordship is wounded!" – "Mortally! mortally!" – "I hope not, my dear Lord; let Mr. Beatty examine your wounds." – "It is of no use," exclaimed the dying Nelson; "he had better attend to others."

Mr. Beatty now approached to examine the wound. His Lordship was raised up; and Beatty, whose attention was anxiously fixed upon the eyes of his patient, as an indication the most certain when a wound is mortal, after a few moments glanced his eye on Bourke, and expressed his opinion in his countenance. Lord Nelson now turned to Bourke, and said, "Tell Hardy to come to me." Bourke left the cockpit. Beatty now said, "Suffer me, my Lord, to

probe the wound with my finger; I will give you no pain." Lord Nelson permitted him, and, passing his left hand round his waist, he probed it with the fore-finger of his right.

When Bourke returned into the cockpit with Captain Hardy, Lord Nelson told the latter to come near him. "Kiss me, Hardy!" he exclaimed. – Captain Hardy kissed his cheek. – "I hope your Lordship," he said, "will still live to enjoy your triumph." – "Never, Hardy!" he exclaimed; "I am dying – I am a dead man all over – Beatty will tell you so – bring the fleet to an anchor – you have all done your duty – God bless you!" Captain Hardy now said, "I suppose Collingwood, my dear Lord, is to command the fleet?" – "Never," exclaimed he, "whilst I live;" – meaning, doubtless, that, so long as his gallant spirit survived, he would never desert his duty.

What passed after this was merely casual: his Lordship's last words were to Mr. Beatty, whilst he was expiring in his arms, "I could have wished to have lived to enjoy this; but God's will be done!" – "My Lord," exclaimed Hardy, "you die in the midst of triumph!" – "Do I, Hardy?" – He smiled faintly – "God be praised!" These were his last words before he expired.'
(*The Naval Chronicle*, Vol. XV, pp. 38–9.)

For the ordinary seamen, surgery was on a first-come, first-served basis. The dead and the apparently dead were thrown overboard so as not to encumber the decks, while the wounded were taken below. A surgeon wrote from Gibraltar:

'Mr. Chivers, Surgeon of the Tonnant, told me a man who was working one of the quarter-deck guns was shot through the great toe; he looked at his toe, which hung by a fragment of skin, and then at his gun, and then at his toe again; at last he took out his pocket knife, gave it to his comrade – "Jack, cut that bit of skin through for me." – "No," says the other, "go down to the Doctor, man." – "D—n it, I'm ashamed of going down to him for this trifle, just whip it off for me, its only a bit of skin." In this way they were going on, when the carronade near him took a cant accidentally, from a roll of the Ship, and crushed the whole of that part of his foot; he was then obliged to leave the deck, but is now on board, and doing well.'
(*The Naval Chronicle*, Vol. XIV, p. 494.)

Another anecdote came from the captain of the *Leviathan*. Like many others of the wounded, including the Spanish Admiral Gravina, the sailor described in this letter later died from gangrene:

'We had passed through the line, and had assisted in

disabling and silencing the French Admiral's ship, and the four-decker, Santissima Trinidada; we were much galled by a distant cannonade from a separated few of the enemy's ships; at last, the Saint Augustin, of 74 guns, bearing the pendant of Commodore Cagigal, gave us an opportunity of closing with him, which was immediately embraced, and he was soon taken. While this was doing, a shot took off the arm of Thomas Main, when at his gun on the forecastle; his messmates kindly offered to assist him in going to the Surgeon; but he bluntly said, "*I thank you, stay where you are; you will do more good there:*" he then went down by himself to the cockpit. The Surgeon (who respected him) would willingly have attended him, in preference to others, whose wounds were less alarming; but Main would not admit of it, saying, "*Avast, not until it comes to my turn, if you please.*" The Surgeon soon after amputated the shattered part of the arm, near the shoulder; during which, with great composure, smiling, and with a steady clear voice, he sang the whole of "Rule Britannia". The cheerfulness of this rough son of Neptune has been of infinite use in keeping up the spirits of his wounded shipmates, and I hope this recital may be of service to him.

In a postscript dated Plymouth, 1 December, Captain Bayntun added, "I am sorry to inform you, that the above-mentioned fine fellow died since writing the above, at Gibraltar Hospital, of a fever he caught, when the stump of his arm was nearly well." '
(*The Naval Chronicle*, Vol. XV, pp. 16–17.)

Even when the wounded were taken below they were not safe from further injury, as the following account makes clear. The writer of this letter was an army officer serving aboard the French ship *Pluton*:

'A cannonball, penetrating the main gun deck, killed two men and wounded several others, including myself. I fell, bathed in the blood of myself and of the dead. I was unconscious for some time. When I came to, I recognised the voice of one of my soldiers, whom I asked to take me to the Surgeon's post. He told me that he would already have done so, but had thought I was dead. I was wounded in three places. In the left eye, which I thought I had lost but which has been open for four days now. In the left hand, which will be the longest to heal. And the one which has caused me the greatest pain was the blow I received on my weak chest, near the collar bone and from one shoulder to the other. It was swollen by four or five inches for five days.

After this, when I was stretched out on a mattress, I was again wounded in two places on my head by

splinters thrown by a cannonball which passed through the orlop deck and which killed a surgeon – this shows the poor quality of our ship, even though it is new. What made things worse was that at first I could not see, and later a dozen wounded fell on to my body, making me suffer considerably. They had to dress my wounds again.'
(W. H. Dillon, Vol. 2, pp. 57–8, trans. J. N. Westwood.)

The *Intrépide* was the last French ship to strike her colours; her forlorn advance into action was later described by des Touches:

'Finally, after several attempts, and with the assistance of the only available boat, we managed to turn, and the commander shouted in a stirring voice, "to the *Bucentaure*!" That was where the battle was hottest.

Amid the smoke and the confusion of battle one could hardly make out the group formed by the flagship, surrounded by enemies and having close to her only the *Redoutable*; the latter was a small 74-gunner, crushed by the mass of the *Victory* but resisting with such valour that she almost took Nelson's ship by boarding. Everywhere the English had numerical superiority. None of them stayed inactive. Having the wind, they were able to go anywhere where they were most needed, taking no notice of the leeward ships which were too far away to take part and which were destined to succumb one by one in useless combats. Moreover, the superiority of our adversaries' gunnery meant that our crews were rapidly decimated while their own only had trifling losses.

When we got close to the *Bucentaure* and *Redoutable*, they were dismasted and their guns were almost silent. Only the heroism of their defenders permitted the continuation of the hopeless and unequal fight against almost undamaged ships firing broadside after broadside. It was to the most intense part of this battle that Captain Infernet was leading us. He wanted, he said, to relieve the Admiral, take him on board, and rally around us the ships which could still fight. The attempt was mad and he could not have believed in it himself; it was a pretext that he made for continuing the battle, and so that it would not be said that the *Intrépide* had left the battlefield while she still had a gun and a sail intact. A noble folly which cost us much, but which we committed with joy and which others should have imitated!

We had the honour of attracting numerous opponents: the *Leviathan, Africa, Agamemnon, Orion,* and *Téméraire* of 100 guns threw themselves at us and when, after five o'clock in the evening, we lowered our flag, the only one still flying, the *Intrépide* was dismasted, had lost two thirds of her crew and, riddled with cannonballs, the port covers ripped away, she was making water everywhere. But at least honour had been saved, the task accomplished, duty fulfilled to the very end.

I passed the entire battle on the forecastle, where I was in charge of manoeuvring and musketry. It was from here, too, that I was to lead my boarding company; this was my most ardent wish but I was unfortunately unable to fulfil it. One of my concerns was to stop the masts falling, and I was able to preserve the mizen mast long enough for us to manoeuvre a bit. At the height of the action, the British *Orion* passed ahead of us in order to rake us. I arranged my men in order to board her and, showing a midshipman the *Orion*'s movements, sent him to the Captain to ask him to manoeuvre into a boarding position. I looked after the rest and, seeing the ardour of my sailors, I already imagined myself master of the English ship and returning with her to Cadiz, with our colours hoisted above hers. I waited anxiously, but the *Intrépide* made no move. I rushed to the poop and on my way discovered my midshipman lying flat, terrified by the sight of the *Téméraire* which was moving alongside at pistol-shot range, thundering at us with her upper guns. I gave my messenger what he deserved, a hearty kick in the backside, and went myself to explain my plan to the Captain. But it was too late . . .'
(*Revue des Deux Mondes*, pp. 418–20.)

Dumanoir's four escaping ships were not as unscathed as his critics later claimed and when, on 3 November, he was intercepted by a British squadron under Admiral Strachan, the issue was not in doubt. However, the French, weary and outnumbered, fought for almost a day before surrendering. In common with other French officers, Dumanoir was interned at Tiverton in Devon. Here, in late 1805, he read in *The Times* a criticism of his withdrawal from the Battle of Trafalgar, and immediately persuaded that paper to publish his rejoinder:

'This disposition, and the disabled state of the ships under my command, made me adopt the only proper conduct that remained, which was to keep the wind, that I might have it in my power to repair during the night, and to wait the chances of the following day. This is, what the Editor of the article concerning me calls, "precipitately taking to flight." It was then three-quarters past five, and the combat had ceased. The *Formidable* had had 65 men killed or wounded; her masts severely damaged; all her tackling, and the greater part of her shrouds, cut to pieces; her sails

entirely crippled. She made besides four feet water in an hour, by reason of the shots she had received below water-mark. The three other vessels were nearly in the same state, and were indebted only to a smooth sea for the preservation of their masts. This is probably what the same Editor calls being a mere spectator of the combat. Next morning, seeing on the scene of action only the English and their captured vessels, I judged that our fleet had re-entered Cadiz, and I took the tack for open sea.'
(*The Times*, 2 January 1806.)

H.M.S. *Prince* (98) should have been one of the leaders, but was in fact the last British ship to get into action, only opening fire three hours after the beginning of the battle:

'We were unfortunately a very dull sailer, and in consequence, being unable to keep our station, were put out of the line, and when at daylight the combined fleet was discovered to leeward, and our fleet bore up in chase, we were astern of the whole fleet, and were totally unable to gain our place, though second to Collingwood on the leeline. It was poor satisfaction that we had a magnificent sight of the battle, but at length we passed through the disabled ships on both sides and perceived a French 90 gunship (the "Achille") making all sail for Cadiz, with only her mizen topmast gone. We stood towards her and should have had no chance of coming up with her, but pouring in our broadside brought down her foremast, and she took fire. With the hope of disabling us in masts, she only fired at our rigging, and only having four shots in the hull, we had but six men wounded, and fortunately, although much cut about, not a stick was disabled . . .

It came on to blow, and we had to look out for ourselves on a lee shore, with rigging and masts damaged, though all standing.

The sight in the morning was most deplorable, most of the prizes had been sunk, four only had gone to Gibraltar, whither we also shaped our course, leaving a few of our own fleet riding out the gale at anchor.'
(From the diary of Henry Mason, by courtesy of the National Maritime Museum.)

During the battle no British ship had struck her colours, nor received mortal injury, but several ships afterwards lay helpless, holed and dismasted. The *Colossus* had suffered the most casualties (200, of which forty were killed), followed by the *Bellerophon* (150), *Royal Sovereign* (141) and *Victory* (132). On board the *Revenge*, which had seventy-nine casualties, tidying up began as soon as the last shot had been fired:

'We were now called to clear the decks, and here might be witnessed an awful and interesting scene, for as each officer and seaman would meet, (oh! what an opportunity for the Christian and man of feeling to meditate on the casualty of fate in this life,) they were inquiring for their messmates. Orders were now given to fetch the dead bodies from the after cock-pit, and throw them over-board; these were the bodies of men who were taken down to the doctor during the battle, badly wounded, and who by the time the engagement was ended were dead. Some of these, perhaps, could not have recovered, while others might, had timely assistance been rendered, which was impossible; for the rule is, as order is requisite, that every person shall be dressed in rotation as they are brought down wounded, and in many instances some have bled to death.

The next call was, "all hands to splice the main brace," which is the giving out a gill of rum to each man, and indeed they much needed it, for they had not ate or drank from breakfast time: we now had a good night's work before us; all our yards, masts, and sails were sadly cut, indeed the whole of the sails were obliged to be unbent, being rendered completely useless, and by the next morning we were partly jury-rigged: we now began to look for our prizes, as it was coming on to blow hard on the land, and Admiral Collingwood made signals for each ship that was able, to take a prize in tow, to prevent them drifting into their own harbour, as they were complete wrecks and unmanageable.'
('J. Nastyface', op. cit., pp. 21–2.)

The captain of J. Nastyface's ship, the *Revenge*, described the battle in a series of letters to his father, of which the one that follows was written in December, after his ship had reached Spithead. His description of the British order of battle is probably closer to the truth than many subsequent and superficially more precise accounts:

'. . . the *Victory* I see is now coming in, with Lord Nelson's Flag half mast down – I have seen several plans of the action but none to answer my idea of it – indeed scarce any plan can be given; it was irregular & the ships got down as fast as they could & into any space where they found the Enemy without attending to their place in the line – A regular plan was laid down by Lord Nelson some time before the Action, but not acted upon; his great anxiety seemed to be to get to leeward of them, lest they should make off for Cadiz before he could get near – I must tell you an anecdote of a French woman – the Pickle schooner sent to me about Fifty people saved from the Achille which was burnt and blew up, amongst them was a young French woman about five and twenty & the wife of one of the Main Topsmen – when the Achille was burning she got out of the gun room Port & sat on the Rudder chains till some melted lead ran down upon her, & forced her to strip and leap off; she swam to a spar where several men were, but one of them bit and kicked her till she was obliged to quit & get to another, which supported her till she was taken up by the Pickle & sent on board the Revenge. Amongst the men she was lucky enough to find her Husband – We were not wanting in civility to the lady; I ordered her two Pursers shirts to make a petticoat.'
(From a letter of Captain Moorsom, 4 December 1805, by courtesy of the National Maritime Museum.)

Immediately the battle was over those British ships which could do so busied themselves with setting sail; according to eye-witnesses they worked as though they had not just emerged from a wearying battle.

While coping with their own difficulties the British crews were also responsible for the safety of their prizes. Going on board these, they were often surprised by the carnage wrought by the British guns. Sixteen-year-old Midshipman Badcock wrote to his father in London:

'I was on board our prize the Trinidada getting the prisoners out of her, she had between 3 and 400 killed and wounded, her Beams where coverd with Blood, Brains, and peices of Flesh, and the after part of her Decks with wounded, some without Legs and some without an Arm; what calamities War brings on, and what a number of Lives where put an end too on the 21st; several of our ships have suffered very much; and we have lost the pride of the English Navy, the Brave Admiral Nelson, who fell by a Musket Ball in this memorable Action. We have still a very brave Adml to command Collingwood, who in this last Action fought like a Tyger . . . at dusk Mr Frenchman thought he had got enough and so made off. The Prisoners we have on board say they expected to give us a good licking, they heard we had only 21 ships of the Line and they had 33, their officers told them now the English would pay for all . . . This Action is a famous thing for me it will get me a Commission without Interest, as I have a claim on the Service, and my country.'
(*English Historical Review*, 1890, p. 769.)

Sixty-four years later Midshipman Badcock had become one of Queen Victoria's rear-admirals, had changed his name to Lovell, learned to put i before e except after c, and had just published his recollections. In these he wrote rather more than he had written to his father:

'During the time we were going into action, and being raked by the enemy, the whole of the crew, with the exception of the officers, were made to lie flat on the deck, to secure them from the raking shots, some of which came in at the bows and went out at the stern. Had it not been for the above precaution, many lives must have been sacrificed. My quarters were the five midship-guns on each side of the maindeck. I was sent on board the *Santissima Trinidada*, a few days after the action, to assist in getting out the wounded men, previous to destroying her. She was a magnificent ship, and ought now to be in Portsmouth harbour. Her top-sides, it is true, were perfectly riddled by our beautiful firing, and she had, if I recollect right, 550 killed and wounded; but from the lower part of the sills of the lower-deck ports to the water's edge, few shot of consequence had hurt her between wind and water, and those were all plugged up. She was built of cedar, and would have lasted for ages, a glorious trophy of the battle; but "sink, burn, and destroy," was the order of the day, and after a great deal of trouble, scuttling her in many places, hauling up her lower-deck ports, – that when she rolled the heavy sea might fill her decks, – she did at last go unwillingly to the bottom.

. . . Of all our hard-earned prizes, only four got safe to Gibraltar.'

(W. S. Lovell, op. cit., p. 50.)

Among the prizes lost during the storms was des Touches's *Intrépide*:

'. . . in the half-darkness, while the tempest was still gathering its forces, we had to pass through a leeward gunport more than eighty wounded who were incapable of movement. With infinite trouble we did it, by means of a bed-frame and capstan bars. We were then taken in tow by an English frigate, which we followed, rolling from side to side and making water everywhere. At a certain point I noticed that the work of the pumps was slowing down, and I was told that the door of the storeroom had been forced and that everybody, French and English, had rushed there to get drunk. When I got to these men, reduced to the state of brutes, a keg of brandy had just been broken and the liquor was running along the deck and was lapping the base of a candle which had been stuck there. I only just had time to stamp out the flame, and in the darkness threatening voices were raised against me . . . With kicks and punches I made them get out of the storeroom, I barricaded the door, and reached an understanding with the English officer to avert the danger which seemed imminent.

. . . I wished to stay on the *Intrépide* up to the last

agonised minute of one of my friends, who had been judged too badly injured to be transferred. He was a sub-lieutenant called Poullain, with whom I was closely connected, and who had begged me not to leave him in the anguish of his last hour . . .

When I had heard the last sigh of my poor comrade, there were just three of us alive on the *Intrépide*: an artillery captain and a midshipman who had not wished to leave me . . . our situation grew worse every minute. Among these bodies and spilt blood, the silence was disturbed only by the sound of the sea, and a dull murmur made by the water in the hold as it rose and spread in the vessel. Night began to close in, and the vessel settled deeper in the water, making it easy to calculate that it would have disappeared before daybreak. Having nothing more to do, I let myself fall asleep but the artillery officer, become nervous, heaped wooden débris up on the deck and wanted to set fire to it, as he preferred a quick death to the slow agony which was being prepared for us. I saw his intention in time to oppose it absolutely. We found a lantern, which was fixed to the end of a rod, which I advised him to wave. By a lucky chance, the *Orion* passed within hailing distance. We hailed her, and a boat took us off. Soon afterwards, the *Intrépide* disappeared beneath the waves.'

(*Revue des Deux Mondes*, pp. 421–3.)

Another of the lost prizes was the Spanish *Monarca*, whose prize crew struggled for several days to save her:

'Our second Lieutenant, myself, and eight men, formed the party that took possession of the Monarca: we remained till the morning without further assistance, or we should most probably have saved her, though she had suffered much more than ourselves; we kept possession of her however for four days, in the most dreadful weather, when having rolled away all our masts, and being in danger of immediately sinking or running on shore, we were fortunately saved by the Leviathan, with all but about 150 prisoners, who were afraid of getting into the boats. I can assure you I felt not the least fear of death during the action, which I attribute to the general confidence of victory which I saw all around me; but in the prize, when I was in danger of, and had time to reflect upon the approach of death, either from the rising of the Spaniards upon so small a number as we were composed of, or what latterly appeared inevitable from the violence of the storm, I was most certainly afraid; and at one time, when the ship made three feet water in ten minutes, when our people were almost all lying drunk upon deck, when the Spaniards, completely worn out with fatigue, would no longer work at the only chain pump left serviceable; when I saw the fear of death so strongly depicted on the countenances of all around me, I wrapped myself up in a union jack, and lay down upon deck for a short time quietly awaiting the approach of death; but the love of life soon after again roused me, and after great exertions on the part of the British and Spanish officers, who had joined together for the mutual preservation of their lives, we got the Ship before the wind, determined to run her on shore: this was at midnight, but at daylight in the morning, the weather being more moderate, and having again gained upon the water, we hauled our wind, perceiving a three-decker (El Rayo) dismasted, but with Spanish colours up, close to leeward of us: the Leviathan, the first British ship we had seen for the last thirty hours, seeing this, bore down, and firing a shot a-head of us, the Rayo struck without returning a gun.' (*The Naval Chronicle*, Vol. XV, pp. 207–8.)

Unluckiest of all were the prizes driven ashore. When the *Indomptable*, carrying survivors from the foundered *Bucentaure*, met this fate, over 1,000 men were drowned. Commander Bazin of the *Fougueux* later reported how his ship had met a similar end:

'At 8 p.m. the *Fougueux* lost her mizenmast and at 10 p.m. requested assistance from the vessel which was towing her, saying that she was sinking, and from 11 p.m. to 6 a.m. they were evacuating the ship. At 6 a.m. the *Fougueux* was abandoned by her enemies, who had taken off in the night about 40 Frenchmen, including several wounded, but were not able to save everybody. I have been able to question several of those who escaped from the wreck. From their report it would appear that the pumps were insufficient, that the abandoned ship was thrown ashore twenty-eight hours after she was captured and that only about 30 men got safely on shore who, added to those on board the English ship, could bring to 110–120 the number of men surviving from the crew of 682 on the day of departure.

I must tell you of their position, at least of those who are at present in enemy hands. Several are wounded, and all are in the most frightful distress because they were almost entirely naked when they were rescued. *There was sixteen months' pay due to the crew of the Fougueux.*' (E. Desbrière, op. cit., p. 218.)

The gales which began on 21 October continued, with intermissions, for some weeks, and not the least of the British achievements was the safe return of the damaged vessels and the maintenance, with the seaworthy ships, of the watch on Cadiz and other ports. In November a small detachment of British ships, including the Trafalgar veteran *Orion*, entered the Mediterranean. An officer on board the frigate *Melpomène* later described the state of the weather:

'The whole fleet was now in a very perilous situation': an artist's impression of the great storm

'... the morning of the 15th, about nine o'clock, a most tremendous squall came on, accompanied with thunder, lightning, rain, and sleet, which obliged us to clew up all our sails; shortly afterwards the main-mast was struck by lightning, the fluid exploded by the pumps, and knocked myself and a seaman down; the sensation I felt was that of a severe electric shock, shaking every bone in my body, but, thank God! it did me no further injury; the seaman, poor fellow! was a good deal burnt, but he afterwards recovered. On examining the main-mast we found it splintered in many places . . .

The next day we stood towards Barcelona . . . but between nine and ten in the morning of the 17th, the sea rose all round us, angry, black, threatening clouds, accompanied with water-spouts, and heavy flashes of lightning, gave us warning that a tempest of no common kind was approaching; several land birds of various descriptions, blown from land not in sight, settled on the deck and rigging, in hopes of shelter from the pitiless storm . . . but when the first burst of the tempest came on, they were blown to leeward, and probably perished. In the midst of all this we had to fire guns at the water-spouts to break them, furl the sails, and prepare for another gale. At eleven a heavy sea pooped us, stove in the dead lights, and filled the captain's cabin with water; the wind increased to a perfect hurricane, and at one, the lightning again struck the ship and hurt the main-topmast and the main-mast. At two the storm stay-sails were blown

to atoms, and the ship became entirely unmanageable; whole seas, at times, rolled over her, one of which, breaking on the quarter, struck the rudder, and the rudder-head gave way, it was immediately chocked, and the ship was then steered by the rudder pennants. Between three and four, the main topmast was blown over the side, the rudder-chains gave way, and we found the main-mast sprung a few feet above the quarter-deck. The whole of the night, the rudder, having nothing to confine it, thumped about a great deal, and made us fear it would shake the stern-post. In the morning of the 18th, the ship fortunately took a heavy plunge, and the rudder unshipped itself from the stern and sank. The sea at this period was most heavy and breaking; it stove the quarter boats, and caused the ship to strain so much that it was necessary to keep the pumps constantly going . . . On the morning of the 20th the weather became moderate, and towards evening, having completed our jury-rudder, we succeeded in shipping it, and found to our great joy it answered with a little care very well. The 21st we had a steady breeze from the S.W., which enabled us to shape our course for Malta . . . the ship was strained all to pieces.'

(W. S. Lovell, op. cit., pp. 57–60.)

The news of Trafalgar was brought to England by the armed schooner *Pickle*, whose captain landed at Falmouth and rushed by coach to London. He arrived in the night, but his news was regarded as important enough to warrant the awakening of Lord Barham and, later, Pitt. From London the news spread rapidly, many newspapers reproducing Collingwood's despatch in full.

At Portsmouth there was a squadron of Britain's ally, Russia, on its way to the Mediterranean. Its commander, Admiral Seniavin, described how the news affected Portsmouth people:

'. . . the news was received at Portsmouth of the fight off Trafalgar. I cannot describe the joy about the victory and the sadness about the death of Nelson! Only someone who had seen the delight of the English in similar circumstances could describe it on this occasion. From early morning the broadsheets were carried along the streets, describing the battle and the death of Nelson; sadness and joy mingled on the face of every one, and everywhere could be heard the exclamation: Immortal Nelson! The ships and the fortress were firing their guns all day, and at night the town was wonderfully illuminated. The better houses were decorated with transparent pictures. One showed Nelson at the moment when the shot penetrated his chest and he had fallen into the arms of those surrounding him. Another portrayed Brittania with sorrowful face accepting the crown of victory. At night the streets were crowded. The garrison stood to arms and the regimental bandsmen played the National Anthem: *Brittania, Rule the Waves!*'

(V. Bronevskii, *Zapiski morskogo ofitsera* (1836), Russian Imperial Academy, St Petersburg, Part 1, p. 60, trans. J. N. Westwood.)

Footnotes
1 See p. 46.
2 See p. 45.
3 See p. 61.
4 See pp. 62–3.
5 See p. 118.
6 This refers to Signal 16, 'Engage the enemy more closely'.

APPENDICES

A. Nelson to Lord Melville, 14 February 1805; contd. (See also p.59)

'. . . Therefore I shall now state my reasons, after seeing that Sardinia, Naples, and Sicily were safe, for believing that Egypt was the destination of the French fleet, and at this moment of sorrow I still feel that I have acted right.

1. The wind had blown from NE to SE for fourteen days before they sailed; therefore they might without difficulty have gone to the westward. 2. They came out with gentle breezes at NW and NNW. Had they been bound to Naples, the most natural thing for them to have done would have been to run along their own shore to the eastward, where they would have had ports every twenty leagues of coast to take shelter in. 3. They bore away in the evening of the 18th, with a strong gale at NW or NNW, steering S or S by W. It blew so hard that the Seahorse went more than thirteen knots an hour to get out of their way. Desirable as Sardinia is for them, they could get it without risking their fleet, although certainly not so quickly as by attacking Cagliari. . . . However, I left nothing to chance in that respect, and therefore went off Cagliari.

. . . Having afterwards gone to Sicily, both to Palermo and Messina, and thereby given encouragement for a defence, and knowing all was safe at Naples, I had only the Morea and Egypt to look to: for although I knew one of the French ships was crippled, yet I considered the character of Bonaparte, and that the orders given by him on the banks of the Seine would not take into consideration winds or weather; nor indeed could the accident of even three or four ships alter, in my opinion, a destination of importance: therefore such an accident did not weigh in my mind, and I went first to the Morea and then to Egypt. The result of my inquiries at Coron and Alexandria confirms me in my former opinion, and therefore, my Lord, if my obstinacy or ignorance is so gross, I should be the first to recommend your superseding me; but on the contrary, if, as I flatter myself, it should be found that my ideas of the probable destination of the French fleet were well founded, in the opinion of his Majesty's ministers, then I shall hope for the consolation of having my conduct approved by his Majesty, who will, I am sure, weigh my whole proceedings in the scale of justice.

I am &c.

NELSON AND BRONTE.'

B. Comments on the Problem of Logs (See also p. 146)

General

Every allowance has to be made for the stress of the occasion upon the log-keeping officers. Once battle was joined, allowance has to be made also for the smoke which would have veiled the whole scene. Further allowance has to be made for cramped conditions and short-handedness in small vessels like *Pickle* and *Entreprenante*. With this said, it is fair to award the palm for the worst line-of-battle-ship log to *Swiftsure*, and for the best of all to the frigate *Euryalus* – another mark of the professionalism of her captain, Henry Blackwood.

Royal Sovereign

As the first British ship to be fired upon and to open fire, she would be particularly noted in ideal (smoke-free) conditions. One would expect the highest degree of agreement about her early action, and, indeed, one obtains it, but not without some startling discrepancies. The time-span between the earliest log entry concerning *Royal Sovereign* and the latest is 1 hour and 8 minutes. *Africa* records receiving Signals 63 and 8 at 11.32, and adds: 'same time Admiral Collingwood . . . commenced the Action.' *Dreadnought*, the tail-end ship of Collingwood's line, and standing to windward of him, records him cutting the enemy line at 12.40. *Orion*, near the tail of Nelson's line, also a good point of vision, corroborates with 12.35. But *Belleisle*, next in line to *Royal Sovereign*, and so most intimately concerned, says 12.04 – a discrepancy of 36 minutes with the *Dreadnought*, 31 minutes with *Orion*!

Mr James says *Royal Sovereign* passed under the stern of *Santa-Ana* at 12.10, and that for 'upwards of 15 minutes' she was 'the only British ship in close action'. But *Belleisle* says that she cut the enemy's line only 9 minutes after her flagship, and *Bellerophon*, the sixth ship in Collingwood's line, logs his cutting of the line at 12.20, and her own at 12.30.

The most we can safely say is that Collingwood started firing some time between 11.55 and 12.15, and cut the line some time between 12.05 and 12.20, probably nearer to the latter.

Victory

It is difficult to know what to make of *Victory*'s log; to say the least, it is unhelpful. In her case the extent of discrepancy in the time of engaging is 55 minutes, between her own 12.04, and *Spartiate*'s 12.59. *Spartiate* was the tail-end ship of Nelson's line, also to windward, in a good observation position. Her log is by far the most meticulous of any line-of-battle-ship's, and is quite specific that *Victory* 'commenced firing' at 12.59. She is supported by *Dreadnought*, which 'observed the *Victory* commence action' at 12.55, and to some extent by *Conqueror* (fifth of Nelson's line) which says 12.45. *Téméraire*, however, Nelson's second, says she passed through the enemy at almost exactly the same time as the *Victory*: 12.25. *Neptune*, immediately behind *Téméraire*, says: 'At noon the *Victory* opened her fire upon the Enemy.'

Mr James gives the time of firing *Victory*'s larboard forecastle carronade – the first of her broadside – as 1 o'clock; the only safe statement is that she passed through the enemy some time between 12.25 and 12.59.

Self
It will be no surprise that similar discrepancies apply to ships' accounts of themselves. Thus *Neptune* logs firing a broadside into *Bucentaure* at 12.10 – 15 minutes before *Téméraire*, the ship in front of her! *Mars* – a very poor log – records herself passing through the enemy with *Belleisle* and *Tonnant* at the same time as *Royal Sovereign*. We can only suppose that this log was a subsequent compilation. *Achille*, seventh in Collingwood's line, records herself in action at '¼ past noon' – i.e., just about the time the flagship, well ahead, was cutting through! *Britannia* records herself as opening fire over two hours before she cuts the line – and so on.

Cease Fire
The maximum discrepancy is 1¾ hours: 4.30 to 6.15. The consensus would suggest between 5 and 5.30, probably nearer the latter.

The Battle of Trafalgar ended on a suitably dramatic note: the blowing-up of the French *Achille*. Having been engaged at different times with her British namesake, *Belleisle*, *Swiftsure* and *Polyphemus*, she caught fire in her fore-top, probably due to the flashes of her musketry and swivel guns. The only way to deal with the fire was to cut away the mast, but while she was engaged in doing this, the three-decker *Prince* gave her a broadside which brought the mast down; the flaming fore-top fell on the boats in the waist of the ship and set the decks on fire. *Prince* at once stopped firing, and sent her boats to save *Achille*'s crew; *Swiftsure* did the same, while the schooner *Pickle* and cutter *Entreprenante* also tried to help. It was difficult work, made more dangerous by *Achille*'s guns going off in the heat. Sad to relate, when she finally exploded, her commanding officer, Enseigne de Vaisseau Cauchard, and a large number of her crew

were still aboard. It must have been a heart-stopping moment: a dreadful sound, and an even more dreadful sight. One might expect that in this case, at least, the logs might display some accuracy and agreement; on the contrary, their discrepancies stretch to 2½ hours!

Ship	Time of explosion logged
Royal Sovereign	—
Belleisle	5.10
Mars	—
Tonnant	5.40
Spartiate	5.54
Bellerophon	sunset
Colossus	—
Achille	—
Victory	—
Polyphemus	7.00
Téméraire	—
Leviathan	noted, but no timing
Neptune	'shortly' after 4.30
Conqueror	—
Africa	—
Prince	5.50
Ajax	observed burning, no timing
Agamemnon	5.30
Britannia	'soon after' 5.30
Minotaur	—
Dreadnought	5.45
Swiftsure	—
Revenge	6.15
Defence	—
Thunderer	noted, but no timing
Defiance	—
Euryalus	5.20
Sirius	5.40
Phoebe	observed burning at 4 o'clock
Naiad	5.10
Pickle	noted, but no timing
Entreprenante	5.30

Mr James says 5.45, which seems to be a reasonable average of probabilities.

INDEX

Sources

a Sir Charles Grant Robertson, *England under the Hanoverians*, Methuen, 1934.

b Wheeler and Broadley, *Napoleon and the Invasion of England*, Bodley Head, 1907.

c William James, *The Naval History of Great Britain*, R. Bentley & Son, London, 1886, Vol. iii.

d David Chandler, *The Campaigns of Napoleon*, Weidenfeld & Nicolson, 1967.

e A. T. Mahan, *The Influence of Sea Power upon the French Revolution and Empire 1793–1812*, Sampson Low, Marston, London 1892.

f R. W. Thompson, *The Price of Victory*, Constable, 1960.

g Julian Corbett, *The Campaign of Trafalgar*, Longmans, 1910.

h A. T. Mahan, *The Life of Nelson*, Sampson Low, Marston, 1899.

i Ibid.

j Piers Mackesy, *The War in the Mediterranean, 1803–10*, Longmans, 1957.

k Major-General J. F. C. Fuller, *Decisive Battles of the Western World*, Vol. ii, Eyre & Spottiswoode, 1955.

l Robert Chaussois, *Les Grandes Batailles Navales De L'Histoire*, in *Historama*, special edition no. 7.

m A. T. Mahan, *The Life of Nelson*, quoting Phillimore, *The Last of Nelson's Captains*.

n Oliver Warner, 'Wellington meets Nelson', in *History Today*, February 1968.

o Thiers, *History of the Consulate and Empire*, v., p. 159, H. Colburn, London, 1845–62, trans. D. F. Campbell.

p E. Desbrière, *Projets et Tentatives de débarquement aux Iles Britanniques*, Army – Etat Major – Section Historique, 1793–1805.

q E. Desbrière, *La Campagne Maritime de 1805: Trafalgar*, (1907), trans. and ed. Constance Eastwick, Clarendon Press, Oxford 1933.

r Clarke and McArthur, *Life of Nelson*, Cadell & Davies, London 1809.

s Sir N. H. Nicolas, *The Dispatches and Letters of Vice-Admiral Lord Viscount Nelson*, Colburn, London 1844, vi, p. 457.

t William James, *The Naval History of Great Britain*, R. Bentley & Son, London 1886, Vol. iii, p. 316.

u E. Desbrière, *Projets et Tentatives de débarquement aux Iles Britanniques*, Army – Etat Major – Section Historique, 1793–1805.

v Alfred de Vigny, *Servitude et Grandeur Militaire* (*The Military Necessity*), trans. Humphrey Hare, Cresset Press, 1953.

w Claude Manceron, *Austerlitz*, Allen & Unwin, 1963.

x This and other eyewitness accounts from *L'Epopée Impériale, racontée par la Grande Armée*, présentée par Théo Fleischman (Librairie Académique Perrin, 1964), trans. J. A. Terraine.

y *Twenty Famous Naval Battles: Salamis to Santiago*, Isbister, London 1900.

z *The Campaign of Trafalgar*, Longmans.

aa *Great Sea Battles*, Weidenfeld & Nicolson (Warner, Oliver) 1969.